NURTURE THE
WOW

ALSO BY DANYA RUTTENBERG

*Surprised by God: How I Learned to Stop
Worrying and Love Religion*

EDITED BY DANYA RUTTENBERG

The Passionate Torah: Sex and Judiasm
Yentel's Revenge: The Next Wave of Jewish Feminism
Jewish Choices, Jewish Voices: War and National Security
Jewish Choices, Jewish Voices: Social Justice
Jewish Choices, Jewish Voices: Sex and Intimacy

NURTURE THE
WOW

*Finding Spirituality in the Frustration,
Boredom, Tears, Poop, Desperation, Wonder,
and Radical Amazement of Parenting*

Danya Ruttenberg

FLATIRON
BOOKS

NURTURE THE WOW. Copyright © 2016 by Danya Ruttenberg. All rights reserved. Printed in the United States of America. For information, address Flatiron Books, 175 Fifth Avenue, New York, N.Y. 10010.

www.flatironbooks.com

Designed by Steven Seighman

The Library of Congress Cataloging-in-Publication Data is available upon request.

ISBN 978-1-250-06494-3 (hardcover)
ISBN 978-1-250-05387-9 (e-book)

Our books may be purchased in bulk for promotional, educational, or business use. Please contact your local bookseller or the Macmillan Corporate and Premium Sales Department at (800) 221-7945, extension 5442, or by e-mail at MacmillanSpecialMarkets @macmillan.com.

First Edition: April 2016

10 9 8 7 6 5 4 3 2 1

For Yonatan, Shir, and Nomi—
my light.

Author's Note

This is a work of nonfiction; all the stories are true. In a few cases, however, I have changed the name and identifying characteristics of the parents and/or children who shared their experiences with me in order to protect their privacy, upon their request.

Contents

———◆———

NURTURE THE
WOW

Introduction

———◆———

*"Despair, bliss, despair, bliss. And it's only
Tuesday. It's only 11 in the morning. Despair
again. Bliss again."*

—Merle Feld[1]

Everything is terrible. Nothing can possibly ever be right. I
gave my son Yonatan more tomatoes, but his brother Shir
wants more tomatoes, too! Even though he has tomatoes on
his plate! Shir is howling, hysterical: He *needs* more tomatoes! He doesn't want these! Oh no! He wants those! He
wants cottage cheese, but wait, actually, no, he doesn't!

I'm exasperated, I'm annoyed, I'm irritated. Just an hour
ago Shir had been so sweet and charming during his annual
physical. He was delighted to tell his doctor that he had just
turned three, that he could jump up and down, that he was
wearing big-boy underpants now. He gamely weathered the
eye exam, was brave about the otoscope even though it hurt
his ear and even braver when the doc needed to check the
health of his testes, even though he really didn't like *that*.

Regardless, he obediently did all the things asked of him, was gleeful in picking out his Mickey Mouse sticker, cheerful and patient when we had to wait on the nurse for something.

Now it's dinnertime, and I'm holding what is ostensibly the same child, but he's beside himself, crying, screaming, demon-possessed. He makes a move to throw his plate on the ground, and when I manage to intercept him, he gets even more frenzied. Oh, come *on,* I think to myself, where did that adorable, engaging, puppy-like kid go? Why won't you just . . . chill out? But then I realize that he's probably so upset now precisely *because* he was so calm earlier. It was hard to get poked and prodded, and though he had held it together there, maybe he needs to fall apart now.

As soon as this thought hits me, I am flooded by that feeling—the same one I've been experiencing on a regular basis for six years, since Yonatan was born. It's a thick compassion, a sense of being stretched to my limit and finding, against all odds, more love available. It's the feeling that keeps me going through the exhausting nights and willful disregard for our rules and basic respect; it's the feeling that helps me interpret the pouncing on my head and toppling me backward as joyful and fun; it's the feeling that allows me to read *Captain Underpants* or *Moo Baa La La La* another time, and another time, and another time after that. It's the feeling that enables me to see my kids as the fragile, vulnerable, resilient, exquisite little creatures that they are. It's a feeling that doesn't come from within me as much as flows through me, from someplace else.

Part of me wants Shir to just *stop* and calm down and let

me eat my dinner like the civilized human being I used to be (before kids). But this little boy of mine is unnerved by a hard afternoon and wants some comfort as he expresses this. And at that moment, the most important thing for me is to get that feeling—the sweetness, the grace—to him. To be the conduit that lets it pour onto him, into him, through him.

So I hold him, and I pet him, and I whisper into his ear that it's going to be OK, and that he can cry until he doesn't need to anymore. And once I'm able to offer him tenderness—after first rediscovering the well of love in myself—it doesn't take him very long to calm down. Not very long at all.

My mother always said that she never believed in God until she had kids. Something about my brother and I coming into being—from sex into clumpy cells, and then somehow into little creatures that emerged from within her with noses, ear canals, and personality quirks—changed everything about how she understood the world to work. She never told me, really, what had happened for her, but if I had to guess, I'd imagine words like *miracle, impossibility,* and *soul* would be involved.

Obviously, not everybody has the same experience, but it does seem to be the case for a lot of us that becoming a parent tends to rearrange our perception of the world and ourselves in ways that are both easy to articulate and impossible to name.

Some of that transformation is physical, of course, with fatigue and perhaps stretch marks and how we think about living in bodies and human reproduction and what it means that there's now a whole new person here who has skin and hair that grows and who poops and all the rest of it. Some of it's logistical—life as we once knew it is now inexorably different, and that has implications for how we think about our time, our relationships, our careers, our pocketbooks, and all the identity questions that go with these things. Much of it is emotional, from a powerful, often overwhelming new understanding of love, to extreme tests of our patience, our compassion, and our ability to really see another person and their needs.

For many of us, becoming a parent can reboot our experiences of spirituality—or show us, for the first time, where our spirituality is installed. Certainly that was true for my mother, and it was true for me as well, though in a different way. When Yonatan was born, I was a thirty-four-year-old rabbi who had spent a lot of time chasing, and sometimes finding, transcendent experiences. And even so, my son threw my understanding of God, prayer, and practice utterly against the wall. Things look very different over here, on the other side of three children and so many long hours of care.

It's been a long, strange road. I didn't grow up religiously observant, or particularly interested in my tradition, faith, or any of that stuff. My family went to services a couple of times a year and held Passover seders, but that was about it; my bat mitzvah was much more of a social event than a holy coming-of-age ritual. I became interested in philosophy in high school, which led, somehow, to a college major in comparative religion, with a focus on early Christianity. I was drawn to the big questions, the meaning of life stuff—though I was pretty sure there weren't any easy answers.

When my mother died of cancer my junior year, we observed Jewish practices for grief and mourning for the same reasons that so many people turn to their tradition at major life events. I wouldn't say it was a deliberate or thoughtful choice; it was more like, this is just how you do a funeral, of course you invite people into the house of mourning afterward, it's just what you *do*. As part of that, I decided to go to synagogue once a week to say the Mourner's Kaddish—it's customary for a child to say the Kaddish for a parent three times a day for almost a year, but going once a week was about my limit. Little by little, though, over a year of services, things started to shift. I started to *enjoy* attending services, singing the prayers. I wasn't quite sure why, but I began to look forward to Friday evenings.

I realized that my academic study of religious ritual and thought actually gave me a whole new set of tools with which to understand the Jewish prayerbook—to see how the liturgy was designed to carry people on a certain kind of journey, with peak and less peak moments and a means of opening and closing the experience.

At the same time, in grief, I was torn open, more open than I'd ever been. Weird stuff started happening—things that might be best described as "mystical experiences," not that I called them that at the time. I'd have moments, usually when I was alone, when I'd find my mind quiet, feeling suddenly both focused and open, and like the lines between me and everything else maybe weren't as defined as they had been. Or I'd feel a powerful energy around me, pouring through me, suffusing me. They were strange encounters that I didn't know how to make sense of, so I went looking for language to help me understand them. For the first time, I was willing to consider the possibility that all of my academic, philosophical questioning might, in fact, be awfully personal.

After college I moved to San Francisco, and eventually found myself in a synagogue where the rabbi—Alan Lew was his name—said startling, eye-opening things, things that made a lot of sense to me. He talked about how the stories in the Torah were actually metaphors that could illuminate the messy, fragile gorgeousness of our humanity. He claimed that Judaism was a series of intentional gestures aimed at pushing us to become softer, kinder, more gentle, more aware of the sacred, more in tune with the divine and ourselves. I learned that this faith tradition could enable us to grow into people who lived out empathy and service. I was hooked.

After a few years of intensive study with Rabbi Lew, the still, small voice of my intuition—which, these days, I consider the voice of the divine—started making noise about rabbinical school. The prospect was preposterous, but the little voice got louder and louder until I finally gave in to it and packed myself off for five years of study, mostly in Los Angeles.

Part of rabbinical school involves a year in Jerusalem, though, so we can make our Hebrew less embarrassing and learn some good Torah. During that year I found a dance party that I really liked, called the Boogie. It's a funky, unpretentious affair, with eclectic world music and a down-to-earth hippie vibe. People dance like they're alone in their living rooms. It's joyous. One night in January, a cute boy with a shaggy beard and a great smile made eye contact with me. We danced next to each other for a bit, and then he introduced himself. His name was Nir, he was a graduate student. Unlike a lot of secular Israelis, he didn't find the fact that I was studying to be a rabbi off-putting or bizarre, despite the fact that lady rabbis are not very common in Israel, where ultra-Orthodox ideas about Judaism dominate the public discourse. Nir just wanted my number.

That was ten years, three-ish weddings, and three kids ago. (Between the civil elopement for visa purposes, the party in Israel with his family, and the California wedding that bound us according to Jewish law, we have nuptials pretty well covered.) Now we live in the Chicago area with our kids; Yonatan, at the time of this writing, is a sweetheart of a kindergartner missing a couple of teeth, frequently lost in the rich folds of his imagination. Shir was almost two years old when I started this book and just three when I finished; he's an exuberant, effusive little trickster, a wayward forest gnome. Nomi was born after this manuscript went into production, too late to be included in any of its stories, barely on time for a mention here but already lighting up our home. I can't believe my good luck, that these people are part of my life, that I get to love all of them as my family, and to learn from all of them as the greatest teachers that I have in my life—when I'm able to actually hear what they're telling me. This, too, is so much of the work.

Somewhere in my first year or two of parenthood, it dawned on me—through the haze of fatigue, laundry, diapers, and tantrums (Yonatan's and mine both)—that I actually had access to a treasure trove of wisdom that could help me do the exhausting, frustrating, challenging work of loving and raising my kid. It took me a while to realize it, though, because how I was changing as a mom seemed to be taking me away from my tradition's ideas about what spiritual practice is supposed to be. It had been panic-inducing for some time there, honestly, feeling like I was on a boat that was drifting, slowly, from the island on which I'd made my home for almost fifteen years.

And yet, when I looked more closely, I realized that the treasures that had sustained me for so long could nourish me through this new, hard, bewildering thing. In fact, the Jewish tradition (as well as other religious traditions that I'd studied, even if I didn't live as intimately with them) can actually illiminate the work of parenting—the love, the drudgery, the exasperation, all of it.

This fact isn't necessarily intuitive, though, because, let's face it, for thousands of years, books on Jewish law and lore were written by men, mostly talking to other men. These guys were, by and large, not engaged in the intimate care of small children. Somewhere else, far from the house of study, other people—women, mothers—were wrangling tantrumy toddlers and explaining to six-year-olds that they really did have to eat what was on their plate. At least, I assume that was what was happening—again, for most of history, the people who were raising children weren't writing books, so we don't totally know.

This means a few things. This means that a lot of the dazzling ideas found in our sacred texts about how to be a person—how to fully experience awe and wonder; how to navigate hard, painful feelings; how service to others fits into the larger, transcendent picture—was never really explicitly connected to the work of parenting. It just didn't occur to the guys building, say, entire theological worldviews around love and relationships to extend their ideas to the *kinder*— probably because the work of raising children just wasn't on their radar screen.

For example, the Babylonian Talmud is the Jewish tradition's great compendium of rabbinic culture. It contains legal debates, legends, wise words, deep theology, and stories from and jokes about the lives of the ancient rabbis. It's a huge work; if you study one double-sided page every single day, you'll get through the whole thing in seven years. It's comprised of thirty-seven tractates and covers the comprehensive, and sometimes outrageous, hypothetical gamut— from the status of an egg that's laid during a certain part of a holiday[2] and instructions about what to do if a snake attempts to drink your wine while you're on a boat,[3] to the number of alcoholic drinks one must consume in order to repel demons.[4] An entire order—a seven-tractate set— deals with issues related to women, addressing things like marriage, divorce, and suspected adultery.

But you know what isn't in there? There's no *Masechet*

Yeladim, no tractate dedicated to children and the process of raising them. Kids come up, sure, as asides in inheritance law, in trying to figure out who is obligated to pay for a wet-nurse (if she can be afforded), in sorting out some of the logistics of the Passover seder. But you don't hear the rabbis swapping stories about the funny thing their seven-year-olds said the other night or what to do if the toddler tries to climb up to where the Sabbath lamp is burning, let alone what to call the heart-melting experience of chubby little arms wrapping themselves around your neck or how to deal with despair when a kid is suffering in a way that can't be fixed. Children just didn't enter many of the discussions of the talmudic rabbis—even though most of them were fathers.

A few years ago, the Dalai Lama gave a lecture in Boulder, Colorado, to an audience of about eight hundred people. He talked about the importance of kindness, the role it can play in people's lives, and how it fits in Buddhist thinking. After he finished his remarks, it was time for questions. A man in the front row jumped up and began speaking at length about his three children, ages two, three, and five—about how he wants to raise them to be good Buddhists but the reality on the ground with such little kids is just so challenging. What advice did the Dalai Lama have to offer him amidst the chaos of life with small children?

The Dalai Lama's interpeter began to translate his question, but the Dalai Lama interrupted him with his famous, infectous giggle.

"Tee hee hee! Why you ask me? I'm a monk. Next question!"[5]

Even though centuries' worth of thinking and writing about what spirituality is and how to access it were developed by men who were, by and large, oblivious to one of the most transformative experiences a human can have (parenting), there are still a ton of great resources, concepts, frameworks, and lenses already sitting in the metaphysical warehouse, in the theological library of the ages. There are ideas in there—about relationships, about drudgery, about pain—that can have a dramatic impact on our experience of the good, the crazymaking, the confounding work of raising kids. Ideas that can help make the hard parts easier and the magical stuff even more so. What do ancient sources of wisdom—Judaism in particular—have to offer parents? In this book I will make some of those connections explicitly, hauling some important concepts out of religious storage that might have a big impact on how we regard the work of parenting.

But it's not a one-way street. If our sacred texts can shine a light on the experience of parenting, those engaged in the work of raising children also have something to offer our constantly evolving thinking about what religion and spirituality are and can be. What would the Babylonian Talmud look like if we were writing it today? How are our experiences of power and powerlessness, of frustration, awe, humility, and those breathtaking moments of connection part of a larger story? How can the insights gleaned through the work of raising kids offer new perspectives on what the holy even is, and how a person might experience it?

My biggest question, though, is this: What if parenting were considered a spiritual practice in its own right? There are a lot of things we think of as spiritual work these days—such as prayer, meditation, painting, writing, yoga, hiking, running, and more. But what if engaging in the intimate care of our children was understood as a legitimate path to understanding the universe, the transcendent, and our place in it? My suspicion is that some mothers throughout history have experienced the work of parenting in deep ways—not necessarily because people of one gender are inherently more or less or differently spiritual than people of other genders, but because the work of caring for kids can be chock-full of powerful moments.[6] And even if those mothers didn't experience something special, that doesn't mean we can't.

Raising kids forces us into a lot of different emotions, processes, skills, encounters with the world and ourselves—to say nothing of the variety of ways in which we relate to the tiny little people in front of us. When we care for our children, we can go so far down into love that we might find infinity on the other side; we can use the boring and the hard moments to pop us open; we can find new means of experiencing our bodies; we can open the doors of perception in immersive play; and even find within the depth and intensity of these bonds something akin to the mystic. We experience transcendent love in a million decidedly nontranscendent moments every single day. What if we engaged our parenting as a serious spiritual practice—that is, as an ongoing, repeated activity that, performed with intentionality, can transform how we understand ourselves, others, the world around us, and our place in it? If we go deep enough into our parenting, it can take us everywhere.

So this book is about that. It's written as a series of meditations on various themes, dancing around these three questions: *What can religious and spiritual traditions teach parents? What can parents teach religious and spiritual traditions? How is parenting a spiritual practice in its own right?*

It's anchored in the Jewish tradition because that's what I know best, what I practice every day, what gives my own life shape and meaning and heft. I believe, though, that the things Judaism brings to this conversation might be informative, useful, and illuminating to parents of any background. And every once in a while, a voice from another religious tradition (whether that voice be from a dead theologian or an actual I-talked-to-them-yesterday friend) says it best, so I lean on that wisdom, too. This book is primarily illustrated by stories of babies, toddlers, and elementary school kids because that's the world I live in now, but parents of teenagers and adults have told me that most of these ideas have relevance long after the kids have gone through puberty.

This book is not a guide to raising spiritual children—or any kind of children, for that matter. Like so many parents, I'm muddling along, trying to figure out how best to care for the specific human beings I have been issued, and I'm not always sure if I'm making the right decisions. (I mean, I think we're doing OK, but we should probably set up a therapy fund just in case.) I'm certainly not going to tell anyone else whether they should co-sleep, cry-it-out, attach, or free-range their kids. This is not a parenting book; it is a parenthood book. It's about the adult's experience of parenting—about what it so often is, and what it can be. The details of raising children will have to be sorted out elsewhere, family by family.

Sometimes, in this book, I talk about mothers. And sometimes I talk about parents. Obviously, these days, people of all genders are getting up in the middle of the night and attemping to enforce nap time and rearranging their work schedules when another virus comes to town. But childcare has been women's work for most of history, and as such, some of the parenting baggage that affects people's experiences today—as well as some of the parenting context of Judaism and other religious traditions—is gendered. So my use of language is inconsistient; I haven't found a single elegant way to encompass both our historical legacy and the shifting-under-our-feet contemporary reality in one easy pronoun.

Needless to say, parents, and parenting, look like a lot of things these days, with all sorts of family configurations, gender identities, and biological and nonbiological connections in play. A person is a parent if they parent. Love is what makes this kid *your* kid. We're all in this together, one big, chaotic village of people trying to figure out where that other tiny shoe went, kissing a knee that just got scraped, taking a deep breath when the screaming starts, and hoping to remember to pick up milk on the way home. These acts of care are our work, our offering. They are our holy office, a liturgy of love.

CHAPTER ONE

So Much Is Different Now

Parental Love as a Portal to Infinity

———◆———

There had been so much pain, and then there was pushing, with more pain. Then, suddenly, here was the nurse, gingerly placing my son in my arms.

"Oh," I said.

There he was.

In one moment, so much abstraction became real. Embodied. This was my son. I hadn't been aware that I had been missing anybody in my life until, suddenly, he had arrived.

The day and a half in the hospital was surreal, blurry. A haze of sleep, sleeplessness, and baby. It seemed immediately clear that his name would be Yonatan—which, in its English spelling, Jonathan, shares its first letter with my mother's name, Janie. From the moment we uttered his name, we knew it was right. This was who he came into the world as. He wasn't some generic baby. He was himself. Already.

We all went home midday on a Thursday. Nir urged me

to go outside and get some fresh air, just to walk around the block. Reluctantly, I left our newborn with his father and ventured out into the February afternoon.

Everything was surreal, off. The cars were driving very fast. The noises of the birds and the Green Line train were disorientingly loud. Colors seemed brighter. Everything was pulled up into a sort of supercharged three-dimensionality: extra solid, but also extra strange. I had never experienced the wind on my face so powerfully. As I walked, I wept. I was overwhelmed. Out by myself for the first time after Yonatan's birth, I began to understand how radical a change had just taken place. I was returning to the world, but I wasn't the same.

Later that day, I wrote in my journal, "All the doors in my heart have been blown open and now I'm standing in this great overwhelming light."

Blinking in the glare, I began to try to understand what this love pouring through me was all about. It's not that I hadn't loved before, both Nir and in other relationships, family and friends, lots of people in a lot of different ways. But something about what I was feeling for Yonatan was unlike anything I'd ever experienced.

How do we make sense of this parental love? What are we supposed to do with it?

Among other things, this love makes us do stuff. Sure, oxytocin courses through our veins when we snuggle up to our kids. But oxytocin only has a half-life of about three minutes[1] and, as I would soon see, it takes more than that for us to be willing to get up a zillion times in the middle of the night, to let someone vomit in our laps, to decide not to leave a colicky baby out in the snow. This aching, pulsing love is what pushes us to offer up who we are, and can be, to these insane little creatures that have, somehow, almost inexplicably, come into our care.

Our culture has long been invested in the notion of a mother's love being untainted, virtuous—a redemptive light that shines with maximum sentimentality. Victorians referred to mothers as the angels of the house. The mother was selfless; she embodied morality and unceaseless giving. As Virginia Woolf described it, the mother

> . . . was intensely sympathetic . . . utterly unselfish. She excelled in the difficult arts of family life. She sacrificed daily. If there was a chicken, she took the leg; if there was a draught she sat in it. . . . Above all, she was pure.[2]

She was pure, and her love was pure. (She was also white and wealthy, but that is, perhaps, a whole other conversation.)[3] This Victorian ideal of uncomplicated selflessness became, on so many levels, the defining standard against which mothers were judged into, through, and beyond the twentieth century.

In fact, the myth of mommy's perfect love persists today: A perusal of any online greeting card site will offer cards that say "Mothers are angels" and "Moms know love by heart." "What can I wish you on Mother's Day? You're already so rich in all the things that really count . . . a loving heart, a joyous spirit." "Moms have a special magic."[4]

The idea that maternal love is full of this unsullied magic doesn't leave a lot of room for moms to be angry, resentful, frustrated, exhausted, at the end of their ropes, and hiding in the bathroom while the toddler rages outside because she just needs one . . . second . . . alone. And how is a woman who radiates a saintly, selfless mother's love supposed to also be a savvy negotiator, a cunning businessperson, a driven intellectual doggedly pursuing her research? This stereotype of mothers' love both sets us up for unattainable standards and complicates our ability to move through the world.

This myth of mom's perfect love also belies a lot of people's lived experience. Plenty of people have suffered tremendously at the hands of mothers who were capricious or cruel, who discounted their child's needs, who were withdrawn or abusive—or all of these things.

Do all mothers love their children well? Of course not. Is parental love somehow better, more pure, more moral, more redeemed than the love siblings feel for one another? Than that of lovers? Friends? Are nonparents simply never capable of reaching the depths of emotion that parents experience?

No no no, nope, I'm not saying that. But I am saying that I have experienced my love for my own children as metamorphic, with implications I couldn't have anticipated. This love has broken me open and has changed me, utterly, surprisingly. For a lot of parents—of whatever gender—the experience seems to be similar.

This love, it's big. It changes us. It's messy and it's complicated and it swirls around all the exhaustion and frustration and irritation and ambivalence and desperate desire for grown-up conversation. Parenting isn't one long extended frolic in a sunny meadow as unicorns and butterflies cavort nearby. It's gross and it's gooey and it's crazymaking and it's hard as *hell*. But inside all of it, there is this feral, fierce love for our children that drives us and changes us and takes us to the brink of insanity, and back from it, again and again and again.

What is love, anyway? And what does it mean to love?

The story we're told by our culture is that, when the protagonists of the romcom finally, after eighty-eight minutes of complications and reversals, get together and share that first kiss at the airport gate before she gets on the plane, the relationship itself will be straightforward and easy. Once love is in the picture, it all snaps into place.

Which, as anyone who has loved, or tried to love, can attest, is a joke. Love is hard. Love is a painful mirror for our imperfections. And, most importantly maybe, love isn't a single, fixed state. It's an action, or a series of actions. The feminist theorist bell hooks cites author M. Scott Peck's definition of love, based on the work of the philosopher Erich Fromm. Love is, she claims, the "will to extend one's self for the purpose of nurturing one's own or another's spiritual growth."[5] "The will to extend yourself": to push past your comfort level; to, you know, work really hard. That means doing things you never thought you'd do, and may not particularly want to. But you do them. You stretch and extend, because someone needs you to, so that they can grow.

That kind of extending of the self looks like all sorts of things. In my marriage, for example, it's meant that during a conflict I've had to sit uncomfortably—holding my peace despite *really* wanting to process things verbally—because my husband needs some solitude and emotional space before moving toward a resolution. I think about the times I've had to battle my boredom at the sandbox so that I can actually engage with my kids, who really want me to talk about fire trucks with them. Extending the self is about the moment when the tantrum is going down right as you need to be getting somewhere and you realize you have to slow down and pull, from underneath your annoyance and your desire to just physically force the child out the door, some compassion to help dial down her out-of-control feeling. It's about the willingness to get out of bed at two a.m. to be with the child who's totally shaken by a nightmare. According to hooks, love is in the nurturing of our own or another's spiritual growth; we do that all the time. It's about enabling our beloveds to feel secure, enabling them to be able to do the work they need to do. It's about enabling them to feel the warm rays of our attention on their skin, even when we kind of actually want to just zone out and play Candy Crush on our phone. Sometimes it means taking care of their physical needs even if we're not home emotionally—keeping them fed and safe and warm counts for an awful lot when you just want to hide under the bed or catch the next flight to Tijuana. So, OK, let's add Candy Crush back to that list, too.

Fred Rogers, the Presbyterian minister behind the TV show *Mr. Rogers' Neighborhood*, said once that "to love someone is to strive to accept that person exactly the way he or she is, right here and now."[6] Here and now. Screaming his head off because you won't let him play with your glasses. Nastily grabbing a toy out of another child's hand. Miraculously unable to hear your repeated call to stop playing *now* and wash hands for dinner. Absolutely determined to leave the grocery store with some ridiculous, disgusting food item you have no intention of buying.

That moment when we say, I accept you—even though being with you is awfully hard right now—that's love. It doesn't mean there aren't consequences—we don't have to accept terrible behavior. But part of how we love our children is in choosing, again and again, to take the whole child, including the demonic parts that might be in charge after hearing "no" at the grocery checkout. And as Rogers notes, loving is about a *striving* to accept, not the completed act of acceptance itself. This striving is also kind of an extending of the self. And the choice to accept someone, no matter who and how they are—well, there's nothing more conducive to their spiritual growth than that.

"Look at me!" Most parents hear this about 28,805,348 times a day. God knows I do. Look, Mommy, I'm jumping on the couch! Look, Mommy! I found a stick! Look, Mommy, I climbed up on the chair myself! Look, Mommy! I'm wearing your shoes! As psychologist Becky Bailey notes, "Children want and need to be seen."[7] I mean, we all do, right? There's nothing I want more, some days, than for Nir to pat me on the head and say, simply, "You've worked hard." Or, "You were really brave." Or even, "I see that you're sad." I want, I think we all want, desperately, to be seen for who we are. I, for one, feel most loved when I feel accepted as myself, warts and all. So, too, with our kids.

Philosopher Sara Ruddick also talks about this work of loving our children as the attempt to see them. She writes that a parent

> learns to ask *"What are you going through?"* and to wait to hear the answer rather than giving it. She learns to ask again and keep listening even if she cannot make sense of what she hears or can barely tolerate the child she has understood. Attention is akin to the capacity for empathy, the ability to suffer or celebrate with another as if in the other's experience you know and find yourself.[8]

Part of the work of loving our children is about being able to ask them "What are you going through?" and to listen to what they tell us—through words or some other means of communication. To hear their answer even on the days we most want to throw in the parenting towel or (proverbially) wring their sweet little necks with our bare hands. To try to find our children where they really are, and to suffer or celebrate with them "as if in the other's experience you know and find yourself." Part of love is about extending ourselves in empathy in order to understand the other and having, as Ruddick puts it, "faith that love will not be destroyed by

knowledge, that to the loving eye the lovable will be re-
vealed."[9] Love is about seeing the other exactly as they are.
And seeing that person more clearly, even through the flaws
or imperfections or pain, is a chance to more thoroughly
encounter the beloved.

Last week I heard Shir calling for me at two a.m. I stumbled down the hall to him, still mostly asleep. He was hot to
the touch and asking for milk. I shook myself awake-er and
took him into the kitchen, filled a sippy for him, took off the
sweater blanket his grandmother had knitted for him, and
checked his temp: 103.9. Ugh.

I gave him some Children's Tylenol, changed his diaper,
held him while he sucked down his milk. He burrowed into
me, a little boy who didn't feel well. I stroked his hair. Kissed
his sweaty little forehead. When he seemed to be slowing
down, I whispered to him, "Do you want to go back to your
bed now?" He whispered back, "No!"

So while I was sitting there, exhausted, on the floor of
the kitchen, with this fevery child in my arms, watching him
try to insert his forehead into the hollow of my neck, I asked,
wordlessly, "What are you going through?" And even though
the answer I would have liked to hear was, "Now that I have
medicine and milk I'm ready to go back to bed like I normally do," what I got from him, through his body language
and his tiny little whimpers, was, "I don't want to be alone."

Being able to see him in this moment helped me to love
him, and helped me be able to respond to him in love. This
time, anyway, his emotional need was one that I was able to
meet. So I took him over to the futon in the guest bedroom

and we lay down together. He coughed in my face. He tossed and turned and fidgeted and generally had a hard time getting comfortable. He didn't feel good, and he wanted his mama. He slung his little arm around my shoulder, he wriggled into that little spot in the crook of my arm that is both utterly sweet and absolutely not comfortable for me. I was tired. I was cranky. He fell asleep diagonally, snoring like a trucker through his stuffy nose.

I wanted to push him away, to send him back to his bed or at least get him solidly on the other pillow to ensure some—any—possibility of getting some damn sleep. But this was something I could do for him. It's not a particularly heroic example—I don't think I deserve special cookies for taking care of my sick kid. But most of the time, our acts of nurturing, these little moments of being willing to hear our children's stories and to let those stories matter, are pretty mundane.

The next morning Shir, fortified by sleep and fever meds, was playing with the just-emptied laundry basket. I was trying to convince him to bring it into his bedroom so we could put the dirty clothes in it, like you're supposed to. (I'm not sure if you're *supposed* to let the clean laundry sit in the basket for five or six days and pile up new dirty clothes in the general area where the basket's supposed to be, but that's, uh, kind of what happens around here.) Yonatan wanted the basket, and started to grab it from Shir. I told him no, reminded him that we don't take things from the hands of other people. Yonatan threw a small fit, crying that he *wanted* it, and tried to take a swing at me. I felt the irritation rise; it certainly didn't help that I'd been up half the night with his sick brother. Why was my older child being so petulent about something so insignificant? I told him again that we do not take things from people's hands. His tantrum started to escalate.

Finally, through the exhausted fog, I remembered, What are you going through? I looked at him and said, "It seems like you're frustrated and disappointed and that you really wanted the basket." Through the annoyance and grumpiness, through my desire that this child just please *get over it* because I did not deem this to be important and I was tired and didn't feel like managing it . . . through it all, somewhere in there, I was able to find the question—to see the child on his own terms, not on the ones I so very much wanted to impose on him.

The moment I related to him with love, with a willingness to see him, his attitude changed completely. He chilled out almost instantly and wandered off to play with something else. I was able to retrieve the laundry basket from the toddler and even to complete the small task I had set out to do. Dirty laundry in the hamper! (For twenty-four whole hours before it's turned into clean laundry being ignored!)

In the Garden of Eden story, Adam and Eve eat the apple from the tree of knowledge of good and evil, even though they were told not to. When God goes looking for them, they freak out and hide, like pretty much every kid who screws up. And God calls to them: *Ayeka*—where are you? As parents, we try, in our best moments, to go looking for our children. Even when we kind of don't want to. Even when we're exhausted and frustrated and wish our children would just hand us the damn laundry basket already. But still, when we can, we seek them out—to understand where they are, to see if we can find them.

The twentieth-century Jewish theologian Martin Buber makes the distinction between what he terms an "I-It" relationship and one that is "I-Thou." In an I-It relationship, he explains, the other person is little more than an object at your disposal—the waitress is the object who brings you your food, the cabdriver is the object who brings you from one location to another. Your relationship to the object is a pretty limited one. Even if you were consciously aware of the waitress as having talents, longings, sorrows, and a complex history, her full selfhood isn't really your main interest in the relationship. You want to know whether your food will take an hour to arrive and if it will already be cold by then, or not.

An I-Thou relationship, on the other hand, is one in which the other person is fully seen, and fully accepted— regarded as a whole being, full of hopes and dreams and selfhood, and, if this language makes sense to you, created in the divine image. The relationship is not limited by a more utilitarian, you-do-for-me-I-do-for-you attitude. I-Thou relationships are ones, in other words, in which we endeavor to see the other, and to accept them for who they are, right now, in this moment, today. Ones in which we ask: Where are you? What are you going through?

I-Thou relationships are about authentic connection. When we're able to encounter another person (as fully as any of us ever can), the relationship comes alive, animated by concern and caring. It feeds us—not only because we all desperately need to be seen, but because beholding another person opens the channels that are so often blocked in our own hearts. I personally believe that the work of seeking and finding one another, in all of the complexity and wholeness that meeting someone else always demands, is the crux of what we're all meant to be doing on this planet.

Of course, it's not necessarily easy to live this kind of relationship on the ground with anyone, and children present their own challenges. For example, Shir has always had a hard time going to bed. He never wants to say good night because that means All The Fun Stops Always And Forever. One evening when he was still in the crib, for example, I managed to lullabye him, grumbly and resistant, into bed, but I could tell that we were keeping a fragile peace. And sure enough, the minute I got more than a foot away from his bed, toward the door, he began to scream for milk hysterically, in that young toddler tone that implies that all doom is coming to pass. I weighed my options and considered the data points I had—including that he wasn't supposed to have milk in his crib and that letting him cry himself to sleep was unlikely to succeed, given that he often screamed until he barfed as the ultimate trump card in these situations.

I tried the obvious things, like offering him water from the sippy cup that was already in the room. In this moment, truly, I wasn't seeing his selfhood in full flower. I wasn't thinking about how great it was that I had a new opportunity to extend myself. I was mostly thinking of him as the shrieking object that I wanted to be asleep. The object keeping me from getting on to other things.

There are a lot of moments in my parenting life, in which, to be honest, I fail the Buber test. But . . . maybe not completely? If I was only thinking of Shir as the It that I no longer felt like dealing with, I might have resorted to tactics that aren't OK by anybody's standards. Part of me, even in the screaming, was able to make out that there was a whole other human in front of me.

So I sighed, pulled him out of the crib, handed him the sippy of milk that he had spied in the back pocket of my jeans (yeah, it's a very chic look), sat with him while he drank it, and sang a little "Wheels on the Bus." And then I saw him again. Here was Shir. My little bear, feisty and vulnerable. I felt that feeling that we think of as "love," that tenderness and mushiness. The one that's expressed in drawings of Bugs Bunny with hearts in his eyes. Here was my snuggly little Thou, a mysterious world unto himself.

But what if Fred Rogers was right, and the love we have for our children is found not just in really seeing them, in Buber's sense, but in the *effort* we make to see them? What if the love is in the striving? In the fact that, though part of me was irritated with Shir for not behaving exactly as would have been most personally convenient for me in the moment—in spite of all of it, I went looking for the actual child underneath the hysterical flailing? Those moments when we get the cartoon heart-eyes are great, sure. They're a heck of a pleasant reward, but that's not the manifestation of love. Love is in the search. It's when we look to find them, when we choose them, frenzied howling and all.

The love we give out doesn't only flow in one direction, though. When we extend ourselves to help foster others' growth, when we engage in the striving necessary to accept them as they are—that impacts us, too.

When my friend Michael's daughter, Yonit, was about ten months old, her parents took her to a family bat mitzvah—a long weekend of celebrations, services, and gatherings. During lunch, she began to get fussy; her mother figured that it meant she wanted to nurse, so she took Yonit out of the social hall to a quieter room where she thought they'd both be more comfortable. But nope, she didn't want to nurse—she was suddenly happy, just wanted to play. Later that evening, at the party, she once again started to melt down; her parents assumed she was tired and ready for bedtime, so they brought her back to the hotel. But her mood changed as soon as they got to the room—she became once again content, pleased to engage with her parents and in no particular hurry to sleep. That's when her parents realized that, most likely, little Yonit had been feeling overwhelmed by all the people and the noise; both times, the corrective was quiet, not food or sleep.

For Michael, choosing to really see his child—and thus understanding these breaks from stimulation as a genuine need of hers, as necessary for her as food and sleep—was something of a revelation. For, it turns out, he often also felt exhausted and overwhelmed by too much noise and too much socializing, but had never looked very closely at that feeling, let alone given himself permission to act on it. However, if he was required to take Yonit's need seriously—to regard her, even as just a baby, as a person with legitimate demands—well, maybe that meant that he was allowed to take his own self-care seriously as well? He began to consider what it might mean to take a time-out in the middle of a social obligation, or to not go, or to leave early, in order to look after himself. In his act of love for Yonit, he began to rethink his own expectations for himself, and to open a whole other door of possibility for engagement in the big world—one that might not always come with maximal social approval, but one that might best nourish him.

So often the act of striving to love and accept our children takes us on journeys we didn't anticipate. Sometimes it's a forced recognition of our unmet needs, or it's a push toward new interests, insights, understandings, and ways of doing things. It's not easy—it requires that we go deep into ourselves, that we face the fear that can come with opening our hearts.

Buber says that I-Thou relationships have no pre-set boundaries. In my experience, when I am able to enter into I-Thou, it feels as if the hard lines between myself and others melt, that there's a possibility for something beyond intimacy. That is, we extend beyond the narrow boundaries of the self in order to enter into communion with another.

For Buber, I-Thou is the model of the relationship that we have with the divine. Through the work of doing love, through the act of loving, we raise the possibility of connection with all life, with all that is, with Love itself.

Giving love changes us and our children. Love is as necessary as air.

It's how we tap into one another, find each other; how we grow, and flourish, magnificently, together. It's inconvenient and it's maddening and it's frustrating and it's sometimes painfully difficult to love another person, even or especially our own child. But this love is our spiritual practice. It is our work and our task down here on this mortal coil. It is not only the oxygen that we offer to our children, it's what makes us able to breathe, ourselves.

My friend Wendi is a busy working mom—crazed, with the kind of job that demands long hours as well as evenings and weekends. A few weeks ago we were having lunch and she was telling me about baking cookies with her five- and seven-year-old children as part of an upcoming holiday celebration.

"It was my *korban asham*," she said, wryly, setting a piece of ginger on her sushi roll with her chopsticks.

Her *korban asham*: her guilt offering. In ancient times, the Israelites offered animal sacrifices to God from the Temple in Jerusalem. The book of Leviticus details the different types of these sacrificial offerings: There was the guilt offering, brought to atone for a variety of transgressions; the sin offering, to atone for unintentional, careless acts; and other kinds of sacrifices that were made as part of the daily workings of the Temple or when a person was feeling particularly grateful.

By referring to baking with her kids as a guilt offering, Wendi was being a little self-deprecating and sarcastic, commenting on the near-impossibility of working motherhood. But there's something profound about her use of that metaphor. She had chosen to squeeze out the time to do something with her children that would delight them as a sort of an offering to the divine. Or to them. Both, maybe. It was a sacrifice, literally. The night she baked cookies, as every night, she had a towering to-do list and was exhausted. She most certainly could have used that hour of dough-rolling to relieve some of her stress, or to get a little sleep, or even to reply to a few emails. But she chose to give up that time, and to make of it a gift of presence for her children.

The word for "sacrifice" in Hebrew is *korban*, and derives from the verb "to draw close." Back in the Temple days, *korbanot*—animal sacrifices—were how the Israelites drew close to the divine. There are a lot of reasons for this. Principally, the animals served as a substitute for us humans; it was as close as we could get to God short of offering up our own lives. Animal sacrifice was also a means of bringing some intentionality to the act of eating meat; sacrifices were often the occasion for a big, holy barbecue, and the underlying message was that taking a life was a big deal, one that should be undertaken with humility and reverence.

At a certain point, daily prayer became a substitute for the sacrifices, but I wonder if we shouldn't also see our acts of love and service for our children—and maybe the other people in our lives—as sacrificial offerings, as holy acts. When do I give my children my time and attention, because, like Wendi, I'm concerned that maybe I might be close to, or even over, the line of attentive, loving parenting? What do I offer when I'm pretty sure I've screwed up and I feel a need to make amends? How do I show up? What of my heart and presence do I give them after I've been impatient, grumpy, resentful, taking my crap out on them, not listening, not taking their needs seriously? What do I give them as part of our routine each day? What are the offerings we make, what of ourselves do we put on the altar to serve and care for them?

Ilana Kurshan, a friend who's a writer and teacher living in Jerusalem, stumbled on the same set of questions one morning. A while after my conversation with Wendi, I discovered a blog post Ilana had written about her Talmud studies, which was taking her knee-deep into the laws of sacrifice. She wrote,

> I had woken at 5 a.m., eager to steal the only quiet moments of the day before the kids roused. I stood there putting away yesterday's dishes while listening to my [daily Talmud] podcast. The [section I was studying that day] mentioned trumat hadeshen, the first ritual activity performed in the Temple every morning, which involved clearing away the ashes from the previous day's sacrifices. I thought about how trumat hadeshen is not unlike emptying the dishwasher, a ritual that links the day that has passed to the day that is dawning. I froze the breast

milk I had pumped the previous day and cleaned out the bottles, and then I set up [my son's] place setting with his map-of-the-world placemat and his monkey sippy cup. These are activities I perform every morning; they are love's austere and lonely offices, and they are, in a sense, my version of the Korban Tamid, *the daily sacrifice offered every morning in the Temple.*[10]

What are the daily acts of service, the things that we sacrifice on a regular basis, as offerings to our children?

It's one of the funny things about parenting that the more of the mundane work you do, the closer you are to your kids. It's tempting to hand off the routine stuff—the bath times and the meals and the corralling them to clean up their toys and helping them put on their socks—to someone else. This is what grandparents say is so great about their gig, right? They're freed from everything but storytime and playtime, and don't-tell-your-folks-but-let's-get-ice-cream time. Parents are stuck being the discipline enforcers, the lost toy locators. But when we do these things—each pair of socks, each bath, each messy dinner, night after night—we draw close to our children. We are brought close to them. The more we give over of ourselves, the more we have of them.

It's exhausting, to be sure. But it's how it works.

I had to learn this the hard way.

My first pregnancy wasn't exactly physiologically fun times (I'm not sure whose is), but my second was even more special. The first trimester was pukey enough to merit drugs, and by early in the third, my nice hipster midwife was looking at me pityingly every time I came in. The frequent Braxton-Hicks contractions got rolling earlier than I'm told is typical, and that last month I had painful actual labor contractions at regular intervals. I'd be sitting in work meetings and writing, discreetly on the side of the agenda handout: 11:08, 11:14, 11:20, 11:28, trying to gauge at what point I might need to ask a coworker for a ride to the delivery room. Then the contractions would suddenly stop and I'd zone back into whatever the meeting was about, knowing that they would just as suddenly start up again later. I think I was pretty damn professional about breathing through the pain quietly as my colleagues discussed upcoming programs and where we should hold the donor event.

Nir, knowing how exhausted and uncomfortable I was through much of this, stepped up in the childcare arena. Instead of us switching off who took care of Yonatan in the evenings, he started coming home every night in time to bathe our kid (since, after my belly grew past a certain point, I wasn't so good with the stooping over) and get him to bed. He was also on top of a lot of the physical, logistical stuff involved in getting Yonatan up, fed, and ready for preschool in the morning. I was, frankly, glad to have the excuse to engage in at least a little bit of my favorite third trimester sport: lying on the couch feeling miserable.

But it took a toll on my relationship with Yonatan. Between all the direct care that Nir gave him toward the end of my pregnancy, my stay in the hospital, and the amount of time I spent nursing the newborn Shir or sleeping or recovering from childbirth . . . well, I was doing a lot less of the on-the-ground work to care for my preschooler than I had been before. I started to feel myself losing him. It wasn't just that he had a preference for his father—at least in our family, the kids have bounced back and forth between being Team Abba and Team Mommy now and again—but that he began to float away from me. Children change so quickly, and the needs of the Yonatan of that time were different from those of the Yonatan of a month or two prior. I didn't know exactly how to deal with the current child's food fussiness or potty issues; I wasn't even sure what he would find fun. The solutions that bloom from seeing the gap between yesterday and today were harder to find, because I had missed a few days in a row. The sense of camaraderie and shared intimacy wasn't as close to the surface. I became less and less sure how to find my son.

It was hard, and perplexing, and painful. And I was exhausted from childbirth and middle-of-the-night feedings, and, of course, as Nir was taking more care of Yonatan, I was taking more care of Shir, so I knew better how to soothe the particularities of his tiny baby cries. And we were in the middle of moving from Boston to Chicago and ending jobs and starting jobs and overwhelmed in about six directions at once. So for a little longer than we should have, we let this double imbalance continue. It was just . . . easier to do what was easier.

And we all paid the price.

Yonatan most of all, I'm sure.

It was only after we moved, once I was able to get into more of a routine, that things started to shift. Nir worked late a couple of nights a week, and I'd be with both Yonatan and baby Shir. Slowly, I was able to carve out more one-on-one time with Yonatan, more time in which *I* was the one preparing the snacks and taking him to the potty and answering his questions and enforcing disciplinary measures. Things started to shift; he and I began to find one another again. Each sock. Each snack. Each bath. They build, and build again. They make something—they are our offerings, our sacrifices, our acts of devotion and service. They are holy, these acts of intimate care, and they are part of how we love our children. We sweep out yesterday's ashes to make space for everything we can offer up today. And when we perform these acts of care, we find ourselves drawing close to our kids, being brought near to them. Again and again and again.

A while ago I saw a documentary on the American guru Ram Dass and his recovery from a stroke. He talked about a near-death experience he had had, and how, at the crossroads of his existence—that critical moment right before crossing over—he thought about his family instead of about God. He looked at the camera and told us, with no small amount of sadness in his voice, that he had failed the ultimate test.

This man, known worldwide as a great contemporary spiritual teacher, was sure that thinking about specific people he loved proved his lack of enlightenment. He wished that, instead, when he was on his deathbed, he had been grooving on some more abstract experience of the universal beyond.

For Ram Dass, his family was a distraction from a more transcendent priority. He figured that the sweat and care and heart-exploding love that happens down here on Earth was a mere trifle next to a *true* spiritual experience. Dass seemed to be saying that love—and loving others—was not a path to the great divine unity.

Well, I think that's crap.

Rather, I suspect that our love for our closest people is actually the window through which we might be able to see everything that matters.

I used to think like Ram Dass. I get it. I spent more than ten years before Yonatan was born chasing glimpses or glimmers of the transcendent; those brief moments in prayer or meditation when I felt a fleeting sense of unity with something beyond my small self felt *really* good. I spent my twenties reading books about how to get outside the particular limits of our individual consciousness in order to experience that fantastic oneness. And, I will tell you, that oneness, when you can get it . . . it's like being briefly granted the keys to the gate of the heavenly castle, and getting to even maybe peek into the windows, maybe even get inside for a second before you're booted back out. Once you get in, you want to stay in there, and you want to figure out how to get further in next time. No question.

But then I became a mother. And now I can't conceive of an Everythingness that suggests that my children's specific selves don't really matter. Because they do, in all their particularity and uniqueness. It's not just that people matter, that humanity matters. It's that *Yonatan* matters. *Shir*

matters. These little humans, each with their distinct person-
alities, needs, and ways of being in the world, are inherently
of consequence. The transfixed delight of my contemplative
firstborn when I read him a new story. The insane laugh of
my little daredevil when we flip him upside down. Their importance in the world is in their specificity, in the unique
makeup of their little souls, in the fundamental truths of
who they each are. And more than that—the desperation
with which I love them is full of attachment and desire and
all the other stuff "real" spiritual people are ostensibly supposed to shed or transcend. As I see it, the burning particularity of my love for them is not the problem.

And it's not a means to an end, either. Carol Lee Flinders
is a scholar of mysticism who once wrote, "When your three-
year-old breaks up your meditation, you groan and wonder
when you'll be able to pick up the thread again, but here,
now, are love and laughter and cheeks like flower petals
that won't be here forever. Look again, *she* is Parvati. *He* is
Krishna. And if for a moment you all but lose yourself in loving one of these small deities, chalk it up as . . . rehearsal."[11]

Flinders is a feminist, deeply engaged in the conversation
about women's experience and spirituality. But I can't get
over the sense that this particular comment, intentionally or
not, sounds like a softer version of the Ram Dass thing,
which comes up again and again in a lot of religious and
spiritual thinking. Right? Religious scholars so often seem
to tell us that we think about our family to help get us
thinking about God. We love our preschoolers as practice
for loving the divine.

No. Just no.

When I mentioned this Flinders comment to a teacher and friend,[12] he immediately countered, "What if it's the other way around?" That is, what if loving God—who- or whatever that is—and doing all the serious spiritual work to get present in the moment and tap into the big unity of all things and experience a glimpse of transcendent reality is actually just a set of exercises to better enable us to love the actual people in our actual lives? Are our lives supposed to have some secret other meaning that's deeper than the tenderness and care that we help to nurture down here?

Rabbi Akiva, one of the greatest ancient rabbinic sages, once said that the greatest principle of the whole entire Torah is *V'ahavta l're'echa k'mocha*—"You should love your neighbor as yourself."[13] Love others. That's more important than keeping kosher or Shabbat, more important than fancy ritual acts of devotion, more important, even, than, "You should love God your deity with all your heart, all your soul, and with all your might."[14] The most important act of spiritual service that you can do is to love other people with all the compassion and engagement that you would wish someone else to offer you, that you would offer yourself.

Sometimes we are able to give this by simply working the muscle of empathy. And sometimes, being clear on how we would wish to be loved—whether or not we are, in fact, loved in that way—makes us even clearer on what we need to be giving out. My friend Ella grew up with working parents, the kind who couldn't easily take off for a sick kid, and they didn't have a lot of local support in the form of other parents or friends who could help out. As a result, for much of Ella's childhood, if she happened to get sick, she had to go to school anyway, because there was nobody around to look after her. It was difficult. She reflects,

> *I always resented it. Going to school with a still-resolving UTI or a cold so bad I could hardly breathe made no sense, as I wasn't learning anything, and my mother's vague, resigned sigh and "you'll be all right" didn't explain her ambivalence or worry to me, just her disinclination to deal with the problem at hand.*[15]

Now, as a mother, she's militant about offering her children exactly the kind of care she wishes she had received years ago. It's giving to her daughters as she would give herself. For, she says,

> *Nothing, and I do mean nothing, that I do as parent— one who is humbly aware of her own flaws and who is more pragmatist and less fun-oriented than the average suburban mom—gives me more pleasure and sense of familial well-being than seeing my sick kid cheerfully park it on a couch at home for the duration of a school day. They don't get sick often—we are very fortunate— but knowing that those little glassy eyes are at least at home, those fevered bodies comfortable as they can be made, and those uneasy minds are distracted by mindless television rather than attempting to function through*

a miserable day in a place where no one cares about their discomfort, is a deep pleasure for me.[16]

There are two categories of commandments in the Torah: those between people and the divine, and those between people and other people. The Ten Commandments is said to be split straight down the middle—the first half is all about not committing idolatry, not taking God's name in vain, keeping Shabbat, and so forth. The last five—don't steal, don't kill, don't commit adultery, don't desire what isn't yours—are all about how we can create community together. When people describe someone as religiously observant, they usually mean that she prays on a regular basis, keeps kosher, observes the Sabbath and holidays in a traditional manner—all that "between us and God" stuff. Whether or not this person engages in malicious gossip, whether or not she gives as generously to charity as she can, whether or not she relates with care to strangers and guests. Whether or not she takes time from professional pressures to coddle a sick kid who might need some extra TLC that day. It's a mistake to downplay the importance—both the holiness and the religious significance—of this work that happens between and among us.

The interpersonal love that we offer, the acts of devotion and service, the moments in which we extend ourselves in order to foster another's growth, are, Rabbi Akiva tells us, the main point of this whole thing. If we pray piously every morning and then, after leaving synagogue, walk past the homeless person on the corner as though he isn't even human, what kind of spiritual life is that? What kind of life is that?

When we do spiritual work that forces our hearts to open, our hearts become open. When we practice extending ourselves in love and care, we learn better how to love and to care for others. And it might even be that when we let ourselves go down, deep down into that love, that we can meet the transcendent there. Maimonides, the twelfth-century philosopher and legal scholar, wrote, "What is the way to love and be in awe of God? . . . As the Sages said regarding love, through *this* you know the One who spoke and [created] the Universe."[17] That is, we know God through love. Our acts of love are the path in. They're not practice, not rehearsal, not the second-best consolation prize. They're a good unto themselves that can offer us access to ultimate wisdom—*if* we take our love and those we love seriously, and engage them on their own terms. If we allow ourselves to go deep down into the specific, attached love that we manifest with and through our children . . . down there, in that deep, pulsing, desperate love, is the door to the holy: the access-point to Love itself, the whole universe, transcendence, the divine. (I actually suspect that this is what Flinders meant, even though her choice of language—the suggestion that loving your kids is practice for loving God—still rubs me the wrong way.)

I wonder how Ram Dass's mother would have regarded her son after his stroke (if she was still around—I don't know if she was). I imagine she might have been full of tenderness and an urgent hope for him to be safe and cared for. And she would have let that tender feeling expand, bigger and bigger, until she didn't just want goodness for her own son, but for all the people in her life, and maybe all the people in her neighborhood, or her town. And if that love and care and concern expanded, it might have bloomed into a wish for all of us vulnerable beings to flourish, to be happy, and to live out our bright, beautiful potential on every level.

Maybe that's how we can access divine love. Perhaps the great interconnectedness of all things doesn't ask us to push aside our particular love. When we love deep into the particularities of the people in our lives—our family, in all the many senses of the word—and we allow ourselves to be carried into that fiery place reserved especially for our children, we may find ourselves standing at the gates of the great Everythingness.

If all of our spiritual efforts are aimed at loving these people better—well, that alone is and should be enough. And, as it happens, if we're able to go deep into that specific, aching love for these particular people, with *these* smiles and *that* laugh and *that* sweet face—something else might happen as a natural consequence of it. Maybe, as our hearts overflow, we find that the love can, naturally of its own accord, extend wider, until it encompasses caring for all things, and connection to everything—until our love becomes Love itself, the very flow and force of the universe.

CHAPTER TWO

Sweeping Cheerios from the Floor

Finding Inspiration in the Mundane

———◆———

There's no denying it, childcare involves a lot of repetitive labor.

At first, there are diapers—so many diapers. There are endless hours of feeding, whether by bottle or breast. There's a significant uptick in laundry. There are endless circuits picking up items from the floor—whether to babyproof or, later, to keep yourself from breaking your ankle on the dump truck left in the hall. There's an extended ritual of cleaning up after a messy baby or toddler who's thrown most of her meal on the floor—cleaning of both baby and floor, of course. Over and over and over: cut grapes, wipe noses. Pick up the dump truck. Wipe nose again.

Even acts that are generally considered the best parts of active parenting—like reading to your child—can have a skull-crushing repetitiveness to them. That first time through *The Very Hungry Caterpillar,* most parents engagedly read the story as something of a conversation: You see, that's the caterpillar there. Do you see the sun? What color is it? Do you like to eat pears, too? By the time the kid is demanding to hear it for the nine gazillionth time that hour, many of us have gone on autopilot. Because, frankly, the reiteration that a developing mind craves in order to feel safe and to gain mastery over new concepts can be pretty boring to the average adult.

There are a lot of aspects of parenting that have the potential to be, well, kind of numbing. And an exhausted mom or dad who's been up half the night with a fussy or sniffly kid can easily become a zoned-out zombie while engaging in the same tasks, again and again, whether alone or with a small companion who's not quite up to an adult level of discourse.

Aaron Traister began an essay about this phenomenon for *Salon* by saying, "I don't know if parenting makes you chronically stupid or just temporarily slow, but after four years of child rearing, most of them spent as a stay-at-home dad, my intellect has been dulled to a nub."[1] Much of the rest of the piece talks about his extended entanglement with diaper cream, *Hippos Go Berserk!,* and safety scissors.

Frustrations with this work should not be trivialized. Betty Friedan famously referred to "the problem that has no name," in *The Feminine Mystique*—which, while not about the drudgery of childcare exclusively (but, rather, the stifling of women's capacities when they are relegated, without other options, to the hearth), the tedium of parental labor was certainly a big part of the picture. "As she made the beds, shopped for groceries . . . ate peanut butter sandwiches with her children, chauffeured Cub Scouts and Brownies . . . she was afraid to ask even of herself the silent question—'Is this all?' "[2] History—and, well, sexist oppression—is paved with centuries of arguments that women's rightful place and deepest spiritual and emotional fulfillment should come from the tasks of caring for child and/or home, whether or not she likes it.

And parents who work outside the home (even those who consider themselves fulfilled professionally) still do a tremendous amount of the repetitive labor of kidcare when they're with their offspring in the mornings, in the late afternoons and evenings, on weekends. More to the point, even parents who happily choose to stay at home with their kids, who love doing so, and who would not want to be anywhere else—well, they, too, as Traister notes, can sometimes experience the millions of small acts necessary to care for those children as tedious and draining.

But I wonder if it's possible to make at least some of the work a little less monotonous. The Jewish philosopher Max Kadushin talks about "normal mysticism"[3]—that is, an engagement with the holy that permeates every activity. The daily tasks are part of our time on this Earth, and there's nothing in doing them that's mutually exclusive with a life of depth and meaning.

Rather, the goal might be to carry out the basic menial tasks of life with a different mindset. For example, some Buddhist teachers talk about "beginner's mind":[4] a sense of openness and complete immersion in the task at hand. When we do something for the first time—whether playing guitar, walking in a new part of town, or whatever else—we pay close attention. Keeping track of what's going on demands a lot of our bandwidth; zone out, and you could turn the wrong way on an unfamiliar street or screw up the notes you're playing. As we get more used to the neighborhood, say, it becomes easier to walk around while spaced out, thinking of other things, without getting lost—you know to take a right over by the flower shop and can do it even without thinking about the fact that you're turning. Autopilot, in other words.

The challenge that many teachers of spirituality set forth is to live every little experience as though it were an absolute novelty. If you stopped to enjoy the gorgeous flowers in the window of this shop the first time you passed by, the theory goes, ideally you would feel the same amazement at their beauty every single time—you would not become inured to them as they became a familiar, known entity in your daily routine. It's not only about trying to read *The Very Hungry Caterpiller* with the same genuine enthusiasm after the nine thousandth go-through, but to feel completely absorbed in the cutting of those damn grapes.

But how do we do that?

The basic idea is that it requires focusing the full self on the activity. Meditations abound for, say, washing dishes—as you wash, be aware of how your feet feel on the floor; notice the weight of the pot in your hand; note sensations in your hand of pressure, slipperiness, the temperature of the water. Observe the sensation of your breath as it enters and leaves your body. Most importantly, notice the thoughts that rise up, but rather than getting sucked into them, let them fall away—if the need to write a grocery list pops into your head, don't say, "Oh, yes, the grocery list!," and saunter off into a reverie about onions and tomatoes. Rather, the idea is to keep breathing, to refocus on the sensations in front of you, and to trust that the grocery interest will fade of its own accord. Be immersed in the act of washing.

As the Buddhist teacher Thich Nhat Hanh put it,

> *To my mind, the idea that doing dishes is unpleasant can occur only when you aren't doing them. Once you are standing in front of the sink with your sleeves rolled up and your hands in the warm water, it is really quite pleasant. I enjoy taking my time with each dish, being fully aware of the dish, the water, and each movement of my hands. I know that if I hurry in order to eat dessert sooner, the time of washing dishes will be unpleasant and not worth living. That would be a pity, for each minute, each second of life is a miracle. The dishes themselves and that fact that I am here washing them are miracles!*[5]

A monastery is generally defined as a place for those who renounce worldly pursuits in order to fully devote themselves to spiritual work. In both Buddhist and Catholic monasteries, domestic labor has long been considered part and parcel of this practice—the chopping of wood, the carrying of water, the cooking of meals, and the scrubbing of the floor.

And yet. Parents have a unique challenge not usually found in Japanese monastaries or Jerusalem yeshivas: demanding small people. The deep, attentive space that it's possible to enter when one is doing dishes alone in the kitchen is harder to find when you're trying to simultaneously load the dishwasher and get the baby to eat the food on the high chair tray, or when cutting grapes brings you not only to an awareness of the knife on the surface of the fruit and the sweet smell wafting up, but also of the sound in your ears—a high-pitched, "Mommy *Mommy MOOOOOMMMMMY*!" Or when your attention is divided because you need to cut those grapes at the same moment that you're trying to make sure that your toddler doesn't start sucking on the marker or drawing on the walls, and all of this is happening right as it's time to nurse.

I'm aware that even opening up a conversation about embracing the drudgery has the potential to just make things worse. That is, parents are already set up for enough unfair expectations piled on their heads. Now we're not supposed to only feed our children morally superior food and stimulate them according to the most cutting-edge psychological research, but we also have to be "fully present" in the drudgery as well? Parenting is hard enough—and, for most of us, it's pretty much a win if we manage to get through the day in one piece. And if there's anything that can turn one's brain into mushy toast—as Traister notes—it's hanging out in kiddieland. Not to mention that the many pressures on parents—economic, sociocultural, psychological, and more—can add additional layers of frustration and distraction.

The truth of the matter is, I'm usually a mess: either harried and stressed or distracted and out of it. I haven't slept very many nights in a row in the last long while, thanks to a toddler who's going through a nightmare-having phase, our reoccurring friend the croup, an older kid who's been trying to come kick it (literally) in our bed halfway through the night, and my own insomnia, born of a brain often full of too many things and not enough time to decompress—since there's plenty of work to be done cleaning up the house every night, even after the munchkins go, finally, the f--- to sleep.

When my husband heard that I was writing a chapter about mindfulness and parenting, he actually *snorted*. "You?" he demanded.

I'm not very good at this stuff. I'm distracted and I fail, most of the time. I'm a great multitasker, but not a great doing-what-I'm-doing-and-nothing-else-er. I'm not usually in a magical place of flow in which I am able to engage each activity deeply.

But I have figured out a few things about what some people call "mindful parenting" that convince me that this is a good, and even helpful, model. That this is, can be, maybe even should be, our practice, when we are able to get there. And when we're not, we need to cut ourselves some slack, have compassion for ourselves, and give ourselves a gold star for getting through the day with the children more or less in one piece. That's OK, that's more than OK. Sometimes "being present" with your kids involves lying splayed out on the floor, half-conscious, at five a.m. while somebody plays Legos around your head.

But if you can manage to bring some of your intention into the picture on a particular day, this present-moment stuff has a lot to offer.

Here's one thing I've realized: If you are able to be in charge of dishes when the kiddies are asleep or someone else is keeping an eye on them, do it. As Thich Nhat Hanh notes, it's really a great opportunity to refocus. Even if it's only for a few minutes, it has an impact. When I do the meditation-dishes—that is, when I attempt, again and again, to bring my buzzing mind back to the thing right in front of me—I become more lucid. Calmer. Softer. More three-dimensional. More aware. Clearer on what I'm actually feeling. It's good medicine during days full mostly of hectic craziness; doing the dishes can serve as a spiritual palate cleanser. It enables me to live part of my life as I'm actually living it—not distractedly thinking of the past and future, not split in a lot of directions. And then, when I'm done, I'm a much better parent, and I'm much more able to show up with my full self to my kids. It helps.

And obviously it's not only the dishes. It can be folding laundry. (God knows there's plenty of it.) Or even wiping a tiny bum clean of poop. When I can, I focus on the sensation of the wipe in my hand, the softness of the tushy I'm cleaning, my feet as they're on the floor, and, yes, the cooing noises I might make to the human being whose bum I happen to be wiping. The intention to be present when doing mundane work with a child transforms, for me, my interaction with that child. There's just so much more of me there.

Which leads me to something else I've figured out: If the logistics of parenting make it impossible to do only one thing fully, sometimes you can do two things. That is, do two things and not any other thing. If you're loading the dishwasher and feeding the baby in her high chair, try to get yourself—in moments here and there, when you can—fully doing them. Those ten seconds that you run the cup under the faucet before putting it in the dishwasher? Look at the faucet, feel the cup, be aware of the action of putting the cup in the dishwasher rack. And then, a moment later, when you turn back to the child, put as much of yourself as possible into fully experiencing the action of attending to the child. Or, if you need to peel an orange and read a story, try to have as much of your awareness as possible in the several things happening simultaneously. Feel the weight of the kid in your lap, smell his hair, and at the same time feel the coolness of the fruit in your hands as they work, as you try to summon your very best Lorax voice. It's a lot of things at once, but that doesn't mean it's not possible to try, now and again, as you have the bandwidth, to experience as many of them as possible as they're happening.

I wonder if our homes can be a sort of monastery—a monastery in which our fellow monks sometimes throw horrific tantrums, a monastery that involves plenty of moments when we're honestly just too exhausted or frazzled to chop that wood with any real intentionality, but no less noble a place into which we can retreat from the big world out there, and in which we can practice, and practice again, being awake.

There's a story in the Talmud (Brachot 5b): Rabbi Yochenan goes to visit Rabbi Eleazar and finds him sitting on the floor, weeping. At first, Rabbi Yochenan is a little clueless, suggesting a litany of reasons why his friend shouldn't cry. Are you sad because you're poor? Don't worry, not everybody gets to be rich! Are you sad because you haven't invested much time in study? Don't worry, we all do what we can! Needless to say, this lame attempt at sympathy doesn't really help. Finally, Rabbi Yochenan gets around to actually asking Rabbi Eleazar why he's upset, and the answer is pretty amazing:

"I'm crying," he said, "on account of all the beauty that's going to pass into dust."

In other words, Rabbi Eleazar was overwhelmed by the exquisiteness of the moment, and at the same time he was bereft because he knew that, no matter what happens, it wasn't going to last forever. His awareness of life's transience both intensified how he experienced its magnificence and caused him to grieve for it at the same time.

There's a phrase in Japanese, *mono no aware*, that captures this. It translates literally as "the pathos of things" and refers to the understanding of impermanence that heightens both the appreciation of the beauty of all things and the slight feelings of sadness evoked at their inevitable passing.

When I'm able to look—really look—at my kids, to see

how quickly they've already grown and how quickly they will continue to grow, it's both magical and heartbreaking. When I can actually bring myself to take in the still-chubby preschooler with the squeaky voice, knowing that even in a few months he'll look to me less and less for reassurance and guidance, and to see the gangly kindergartner jumping on the couch while he sings with me, fully aware that he'll soon prefer to play alone in his room—the exquisiteness of who they are *now* is pulled up in sharp relief.

Kathleen Norris wrote a poem once that makes me a little weepy each and every single time I read it. It ends, "Now the new mother, that leaky vessel / begins to nurse her child / beginning the long good-bye."[6] *Mono no aware.* Use it or lose it. We're going to lose it either way—that good-bye is inevitable, somehow. There will always be plenty of time when we're distracted, harried, trying to parent while navigating a work deadline or having that semiconscious intimate encounter with the kid's bedroom floor at an ungodly hour. So why not try to find a few brief moments when we can savor the magic, really see the beauty in front of us?

When Shir was about a year old, we went out to brunch with some friends. This, in itself, was a noteworthy event—we left the house and went to an actual restaurant! Whoo. The waiter knew just what to do when he saw kids in his station; he brought over some crayons and paper and two of those cold drink takeout cups—you know, lid, straw—filled with milk, one for each kid. Yonatan sucked his beverage down in about a minute. Shir was at the end of the bottle era, early on in his entanglement with sippy cups, and he wasn't totally sure what to do with this weird object in his hand. But hey, he watched his older brother, and it's generally fun to put stuff in your mouth, so he stuck the tube attached to his cup between his tiny little lips. He started sucking— recreationally, it seems. I don't think he had any real expectation that something interesting would happen.

His face, as cold milk pooled into his mouth, registered shock, surprise, delight—and, best of all—wonder.

Kids live on the wonder channel a lot of the time. It can take me forty-five minutes to get Yonatan to walk a block because, wow, he just found a stick!! And the stick is very important!! And now he needs to beat it against the tree!! And what happens if he jams it into the cracks between the sidewalk?? It's a sword! It's a magic wand! And oh, hey, is that a truck? What kind of truck is that? Moooommmy!! Did you see the truuuuuck?!

Some of you may be familiar with this phenomenon.

A lot of the time my response to this kind of potchke-ing, as my mom called it, is impatience. After all, we are on the way to meet someone at an actual time over here in ex-ternal reality, or I need to get Shir home to nap or even, hey, watching Yonatan bash the stick against the tree is kind of boring for me and did I mention that I need to pee? I get antsy, and I tend to check out of actually engaging with him and, rather, just do what I can—beg, borrow, steal, wheedle, coerce—to get the next thing to happen.

The twentieth-century rabbi and theologian Abraham Joshua Heschel wrote a lot about "radical amazement,"[7] that sense of "wow" about the world, which he claimed is the root of spirituality. It's the kind of thing that people often experience in nature—at the proverbial mountaintop, when walking in the woods, seeing a gorgeous view of the ocean. But it's also, I think, about bringing that sense of awe into the little things we often take for granted, or consider part of the background of our lives. This includes the flowers on the side of the road; the taste of ice cream in our mouths; how groovy it is to suck on a straw and get milk in your mouth; or to find a really, *really* good stick on the ground. And it also includes things we generally don't even think of as pleasures, like the warm soapy water on our hands as we wash dishes.

The real master teachers of radical amazment are, of course, kids. And we can let our children move us—we can feel vicarious joy in our baby's face, full of shock and delight. And when our kid finds that stick when we're walking, we can climb on that radical amazement train and ride it for a moment or two as opposed to dragging them away from it to whatever Very Important Place we're trying to get to. We can try to remember that having that whole long fight about how it's time to drop the stick and get going, no, really, I meant that *now*, please, usually takes about as long as it does to just have a little damn wonder.

Our willingness to experience radical amazement will not only help us to transcend the monotony and mind-numbing repetiton of parenting, but will probably also help our kids in the long run. The conservationist Rachel Carson once wrote, "If a child is going to keep alive his inborn sense of wonder, he needs the companionship of at least one adult who can share it, rediscovering with him the joy, excitement and mystery of the world we live in."[8] We can be the people who either crush or cultivate our children's sense of awe as they enter a world that doesn't necessarily foster it. When we choose to experience wonder, we help our children retain the tools to keep doing so as they get older.

The more we practice seeing the world—and our kids, and our lives, and all the boring, frustrating stuff we have to do—with a lens of awe and mystery, the easier it becomes. And each time we go there, it becomes just a tiny bit more like a habit. This is true of radical amazement, and it's true of the mindfulness practices—like the dishes—that Thich Nhat Hanh recommends. As my friend Laura put it once, "Does meditating magically give you a happy life? It doesn't magically get you a boyfriend or a job. But it does train you, the more minutes you rack up in that state, teaching your nervous system it can be that [calmer] way; eventually that state becomes something you can reach out for when you need it, and it helps you handle challenges better and welcome opportunities easier. And when a situation feels very *not* like that," that is to say, when you feel distracted and pulled in multiple directions and stressed, "you notice and you don't want more of it." Slowly, over time, and when you can, you start making different choices.

Basic awareness meditation and finding the delight and awe in whatever's happening now aren't always the same things. After all, sometimes we have to face emotions we've been running from—we discover in the present moment that we're angry, or tired, or sad. And sometimes we find amazement and wonder. But they work similarly, I think. Each time we can show up to what's right in front of us, we stop sleepwalking for just a little bit and experience our actual lives as they're happening, in both their exquisite beauty and their transience.

Natalie Goldberg, in her classic book *Writing Down the Bones*, recounts that, for a time, she was studying intensively at her local Zen center—until one day, the master said to her, "Why do you come to sit meditation? Why don't you make writing your practice? If you go deep enough in writing, it will take you everyplace."[9]

Couldn't this also be true of parenting? Are we brave enough to go that deeply with our children? Are we able to sit with the crushing boredom that can come, sometimes, with childcare, to find out what might be on the other side of it? Are we willing to find out why we can be so easily triggered into frustration and sometimes anger when our kid is determined to do things at her own pace, on her own terms? Are we comfortable really allowing ourselves to understand the extent of the need and vulnerability our kids have for and with us, and to meet this responsibility with a full heart? Or are we going to allow ourselves to check our phone (again) when we get fidgety, to let our kid play on his own rather than trying to actively engage with him—because engaging feels loaded, because it pulls back the veil on all of our gross, squirmy, unresolved stuff? It's terrifying and fraught, it really is.

And yet.

In those brief moments when I'm able to be really, fully

with my kids—and myself—I feel a great love opening up and pouring through me, through them, binding us one to the other. Even if inevitably the moment gets broken a second later when Yonatan tries to grab something sharp and Shir starts crying and the usual chaos is reset in motion. But I also find that when I'm able to feel that love, I get brittle much less quickly. When I am able to be present, to experience them, and even sometimes the "wow," I'm often also able to let go and allow things to happen within their own time frame, at their pace—I can turn getting them to the bathroom or to the dinner table into a game instead of a battle of wills. It all opens up. But yes, it happens infrequently.

Being present with our kids is scary. Because it brings us face to face with our lives as they are now, rather than with the story we've been telling ourselves about them, or the reveries we construct about how great things might be in some alternate reality. It forces us to confront our own discomforts, sadnesses, anger, and pain. It forces us to sit with the reality that if we choose to be with our kids, at least for a little bit, we have to let our to-do lists lie fallow for a few minutes—and to let all our anxiety about that rise up and fade out. It's the only way that we're able to actually offer our children the attentive love they so desperately crave from us.

Needless to say, the reason that religious traditions refer to this as spiritual practice is that it is a practice—something that is rarely, if ever, perfected, but which must be done again and again and again, constantly trying to be better. Mostly we screw up. But we try, and try again.

If, usually, your dish-doing time involves thinking of all the things that you're grumpy about and concocting various fantasies in your head about where you'd like to be at that moment—well, if you're able to be totally absorbed in the dish-doing for a moment or two, to feel the sponge in your hand, to watch the water falling from the tap, to let your mind be full of the sensations and actions of your hand moving the sponge around the shiny silver bowl, feeling its weight in your hand as you slosh water over it—that's huge. And, if each time you do dishes, you try to bring yourself a little more to that state of presence, not even thinking about the outcome of clean plates, but rather to be in the act of washing—well, that's spiritual practice. And if you can bring yourself to that moment for even a brief second as you're cutting the grapes and hearing the kid scream—well, I daresay that could change your life.

The messy repetition of life can, perhaps, bring us to the sacred. As Rabbi Emma Kippley-Ogman put it, "Changing diapers and doing laundry are not," on the surface, anyway, "challenging theologically the same way that illness and pain is." And yet, in the seemingly never-ending nature of these tasks, deep in the grit of what it is to be a human being, she says, there is a deep teaching: "I get a sense of what the infinite is about from these processes." Those diapers feel endless. So does the laundry, and the dishes, and the wiping of runny noses. Of course, they're not really endless—someday we will not be changing this child's diaper, someday she will know how to wipe her own nose, someday the kid is likely to do his own laundry and eventually live somewhere else. *Mono no aware.*

And yet, for now, these repetitive, mundane actions really do demand our attention again and again and again. But this diaper change or load of laundry can be our portal to the infinite. The thirteenth-century kabbalist Moses de León wrote,

> [T]he sublime, inner essences [of infinity] secretly constitute a chain linking everything from the highest to the lowest, extending from the upper pool to the edge of the universe. There is nothing—not even the tiniest thing—that is not fastened to the links on this chain. Everything is catenated in its mystery, caught in its oneness.[10]

Certainly, even just thinking of that pile of laundry or this sink of dishes as a link to the infinite can sometimes pull you out of the mindset of boredom and into a more interesting headspace. But the Jewish mystical tradition has another line of thinking that I find useful as well. Some traditional texts talk about how every act has the potential to release holy sparks—aspects of the transcendent—into the universe. For example, Rav Abraham Isaac Kook, an important late nineteenth-/early twentieth-century kabbalist, wrote,

> We constantly aspire to raise the holy sparks. We know that the potent energy of the divine ideal—the splendor at the root of existence—has not yet been . . . actualized

in the world around us. . . . As we become aware of [this] ideal, absorbing it from the abundance beyond bounded existence, we revive and restore all the fragments that we gather from life—from every motion, every force, every sensation, every substance, trivial or vital. The scattered light stammers in the entirety, mouthing solitary syllables that combine into a dynamic song of creation.[11]

In other words, everything in the world, and every action, has an aspect of the sacred within it that can be unveiled and added to the "dynamic song of creation." How does one do this? As with the Buddhists, for the kabbalists, it's all about intention. Are we eating and drinking to gobble and glug, or are we bringing a sense of blessing, a gratitude for the sustenance that we are lucky to have and a humble awareness of its source? Are we washing dishes in order to get done with an annoying chore and get to dessert sooner, or are we washing with a sense of awe at the warm soapiness in our hands and a will to link this action with the great dance of life unfolding? Can we even hear the love and longing from the pint-sized voice screaming in our ear for our attention as we try to clean up the food on the floor while also wrangling a squirmy baby? Can we find some tiny specks of light scattered somewhere within ourselves to help us when we respond? Can we find the holy spark inside the action of picking up those half-chewed peas? The critical issue is about performing these actions with the mindset that they are a humble form of service.

Benedictine oblate Kathleen Norris writes, "It is a quotidian mystery that dailiness can lead to such dispair and yet also be at the core of our salvation."[12]

When we offer up the grapes and the dishes and the diapers as spiritual service, when we conceive of our homes as our monasteries, when we commit to doing routine work as an intrinsic part of the care we provide for our families, we bring holy sparks into the world. When we conceive of our repeat performance of *The Very Hungry Caterpillar* not as a burden but as a mantra, or liturgy, we can reconnect to the great love that binds us to our children, to everything that lives, and, perhaps, to the transcendent. We are transformed, for the good, in the process. We are brought into communion with the great, gorgeous shape of our lives. Most of us might not be able to live in this place of mindful awareness all the time. But when we can get ourselves there, however briefly, when we can be present in even the most mundane of acts, we're able to live our lives as they're actually happening. This work, these quotidian mysteries, can bring us into the dynamic song of all of creation.

CHAPTER THREE

Frustration! Anger! Desperation!

Transforming Hard Feelings

———◆———

The other day, Nir left for two weeks of work in Germany.

The boys and I, after seeing their dad off, sunscreened and set off into the Sunday afternoon. There were bubbles, a game of catch, some sort of Jedi duel that involved Shir perched on my back. We stopped into a local eatery for hush puppies and lemonade while we watched half an hour of the World Cup and I tried to keep Shir from smearing ketchup all over everything. Then we went to meet a friend of Yonatan's and his parents at the park nearby. But oh, wait— there was some miscommunication and I had to coax the kids back onto bike and stroller so we could schlep to the other park. And then the usual hassles: Shir trying, repeatedly, to make a break to the street, Yonatan and his friend having some sort of fight and Yonatan getting sullen and noncommunicative, that moment of panic when it seemed like Shir had actually fled the premises, and the livid relief when it turned out he was just briefly out of sight.

We finally made it home. I gave them some decompressing playtime. I gave myself decompressing downtime. I bathed them. I read them a story while they were in the bath. I got them out and dressed.

We went into the kitchen.

"OK, what do you want to eat?" I asked Yonatan.

He gave me the death glare. "Pasta," he said.

It had been a pretty carb-y weekend with them. And I knew that there would be pasta meals in the future, when I was *really* too exhausted to deal. That night, I had to raise the banner for more complex nutrition.

"Not tonight," I said, feeling the annoyance rise. I was tired. I really just wanted this to be easy. It wasn't going to be.

"Paaaaasta," he whined.

"No, sweetie. How about an egg? Do you want it fried, scrambled, or hard-boiled?"

"PAAAAASTAAAAA."

Somehow, I got him to agree to a hard-boiled egg. Shir, all this time, had been shrieking in my ear various requests for various foods that didn't constitute dinner by any index—cookies, chocolate, and so forth. Finally he started screaming, "Cottage cheese with honey! Cooоottage cheese with hooooney!!!!" I tried to bargain him down to cottage cheese with raisins instead. He wasn't having it. I poured myself some wine. I set cottage cheese with honey down in front of both of them. Stress hormones buzzed through my body.

I was irritable. I was grumpy. I didn't feel like dealing with this, didn't want to be a responsible parent just then. I didn't actually feel like being around anybody, honestly— after a full day of human interaction, I was itching for a hit of solitude like a junkie in need of a fix. I had already been making dark jokes at my friends earlier about firing the toddler after he tried to bolt from the park for the third time, about Nir coming home to find the children feral in the living room and my resignation letter on the table. But over here in actual reality, it was dinnertime. And the children needed to be fed.

They ate, in relatively good spirits, for a couple of minutes, and I went to take the eggs off the stove and peel them. My back was turned, and as I finished the first egg and started on the second, I called to Yonatan to tell him to bring his plate for his hard-boiled egg.

Except, oh, wait, he'd gone into the other room to play. I called him back in to eat, and reminded him that we weren't done with the dinner portion of our evening program. He didn't want to come. There was a . . . process. Finally, I got him back in the kitchen.

"I don't want a hard-boiled egg. I want a fried egg."

The waves of anger rose up from within me, emanating like heat. But as I looked up to argue with him, I noticed that Shir had dumped both his cottage cheese and his water on the table and was splashing his hands in the mushed-up mess.

I ran over and did what I usually do when he gets into food-throwing—I pulled the chair back quickly so that I could separate the child from the gross before the former made more of the latter. Except: Shir had recently grown out of his booster seat so he wasn't strapped into anything, something I hadn't considered in my fast reaction. He toppled over with the force of the chair being yanked back and got conked on the head; I only managed to partially catch him on the way down.

So Shir was howling in my lap, Yonatan was still yelling at me about the eggs, and I was full up on guilt and frustration and despair. I was kissing my frightened toddler and mopping up the water and cottage cheese on the floor and trying to retain composure at least insofar as my kids could tell.

I got the cottage cheese cleaned up and Shir back in his seat. Yonatan and I bickered for a few more minutes about what he had to eat before he was allowed to go play—and I closed the kitchen door so that he was at least symbolically trapped. I fried some eggs—I just didn't have another go-round about the hard-boiled in me, we'd eat them at some point. Yonatan started whining about how come he couldn't have one fried and one scraaaambled? I thought unkind thoughts. I bit my tongue. I scrambled one of them while it was still mostly uncooked, in the pan.

I remembered, finally, to take a deep breath when I served their food. My nerves were raw around the edges. And then, after he took a bite, Yonatan said—actually said—

"Mommy, sing me 'Dayeinu.'"

His timing was impeccable.

"Dayeinu" is a song we sing at the Passover seder, one that goes through all the great stuff that God did for the Israelites during the Exodus. At the mention of each miracle, we sing *dayeinu*, meaning, "it would have been enough." It would have been enough if you had just taken us out of Egypt. It would have been enough if you had taken us out of Egypt *and* split the Red Sea. It would have been enough if you had split the sea and gotten us onto dry land. And so forth. It is the ultimate song of counting one's blessings, a song intended to remind us that sometimes things aren't perfect, but what you've got is already something to be grateful for.

Little bugger.

I mean, this is pretty much my experience of parenting. Just when I think my kids are going to finally break my sanity once and for all, they do something that regrounds me in my love for them so deeply that I start to wonder if it's all part of a premeditated, calculated game on their part. But the fact is, sometimes I do it to myself, too. Right before their bedtime that night, I was so desperate to have them asleep that I was about to go out of my head with it. Then, once they were down, in the quiet, I could remember how much beauty there had been in the day: little boys laughing with their bubble wands, squealing on the tire swing, shrieking as they chased after me to put me in "jail," shoving their little faces full of hush puppies and giggling as a player hit the soccer ball with his head. Even over dinner, once they got settled, there was sweetness.

"Mommy, blow on my eggs! You always cool them off the best."

They love me. They want to be loved by me. And I love them.

So why is it so hard sometimes? And how is it that caring for them can bring out the worst, most complicated feelings in me?

The feminist poet and author Adrienne Rich wrote in her journal, in 1960:

My children cause me the most exquisite suffering of which I have any experience. It is the suffering of ambivalence: the murderous alternation between bitter resentment and raw-edged nerves, and blissful gratification and tenderness. Sometimes I seem to myself, in my feelings towards these tiny guiltless beings, a monster of selfishness and intolerance. Their voices wear away at my nerves, their constant needs, above all their need for simplicity and patience, fill me with despair at my own failures, despair too at my fate, which is to serve a function for which I am not fitted. And I am weak sometimes from held-in rage. . . . And yet at other times I am melted with the sense of their helpless, charming and quite irresistable beauty—their ability to go on loving and trusting. . . . I love them. But it's in the enormity and inevitability of this love that the sufferings lie.[1]

I-Thou is a lot of work sometimes.

But so often it feels like I'm not allowed to say this. When I speak these feelings out loud, part of me steels myself to hear "What kind of mother *is* she?" Aren't mothers supposed to be paragons of effortless, virtuous love at every moment? Aren't we supposed to take all the challenges in stride, encompass them in our limitless grace, unfettered by the pettinesses and complexities that, let's face it, are part of so many other aspects of our lives? Aren't we supposed to be, in the end, those Victorian angels of the house?

Who we are with our children is supposed to be somehow disconnected from who we are in every other aspect of our lives. Parenthood is supposed to magically transform us.

I mean, it transforms us. Just not magically. The transformation is damn hard work.

But we can't do the work if we can't name the challenge, if we can't talk about how difficult loving our kids really can be. When it is named, it's usually in little whispers at the park or at playgroup, or among the parents after they've put their kids to bed. We murmur about how many ugly feelings our kids can inspire in us. We feel that we can't say it too loudly, because it challenges all of our cultural assumptions—still, even at this late date—about what parenthood is and is supposed to be.

But when we pretend that the hard feelings aren't there, they stay put. They live, insidiously, in a corner of our brain, sucking out some of our bandwidth and holding us back from living in integrity and truth. When we name them, we drag them out into the light, where we can see them more clearly and, maybe, make some more thoughtful decisions about how to handle them.

And on some days, you know, *dayeinu*. That's enough.

———

My friend Dan is a sweet, lovely guy, and the proud papa of a fifteen-month-old.

"I saw your talk, finally," he said, referring to the online TED-style talk I gave about some of the ideas in this book. "I liked it, though I watched it after I put Lev in bed, and he was screaming his head off the entire time. So, you know. Parenting and spirituality." He laughed wryly and shrugged.

Parenting is, obviously, not all magical mindful moments, warm fuzzies, and feeling high—the stuff people think of when they talk about "spirituality." A lot of parenting takes place while our little dears are yelling, crying, shouting, forgetting to use "gentle hands," or smearing the inside of a banana peel all over the window screens. On a regular weekday afternoon, just in the four or five hours between picking up the kids and them finally falling asleep, I'm capable of feeling frustration, impatience, irritation, anger, joy, bemusement, boredom, despair, more frustration, love, affection, more impatience, accomplishment, antsiness, and whatever the feeling is that goes with the repression of swear words.

And that's a regular evening, not one with massive meltdowns or something really, truly epic happening in the potty-related arena.

Kids are hard. Independent of everything else, they're little beings with underdeveloped capacities for rationality and self-restraint who bounce between dependence and independence, the desire to assert their will and a need for our imposed structure, a suicidal curiosity and their own hyper-strong emotional range. Jane Lazarre wrote in *The*

Mother Knot about a friend of hers who would say, "I can't wait until tomorrow when it is your day to keep the children . . . but I dread leaving them in the morning."[2] Motherly love, Lazarre says, is found in being able to hold the contradictions, the longing for our children coupled with the more complicated feelings they sometimes evoke in us.

And, despite what my friend Dan implied, the hard moments are legitimately "spiritual." That is, real spirituality isn't only about moments of blissed-out love and radical amazement, but rather also encompasses the anger and the frustration and the ambivalence. Though the language of spirituality has been co-opted over the last twenty or so years by people trying to sell you aromatherapy bath candles and twelve-point guides to making your life simple, pleasant, and eternally smooth, that's never been what spiritual practice is all about. Warm and fuzzy is good for business, as we see in millions of popular titles of books and articles and seminars that promise to remove every obstacle from your life, to give you only good feelings, and to remove the bad ones forever. You don't see a lot of books out there with titles like *In the Present Moment You Cry Sometimes Because Being a Person Can Be Hard and Painful*. People want their spiritual experiences to come without the grueling work of confronting their demons, when we've genuinely messed up, or, yes, the baby is screaming in his crib. The market follows what people want, so the media ends up telling a false story about what it is and is supposed to be.

Spirituality—the real deal, the impulse undergirding every religious tradition out there—isn't about the easy and the sweet. Yes, radical amazement is part of it. But so are all the sorrows and challenges that come with bravely facing the world—and ourselves—without flinching or turning away. As my friend Laura puts it, spirituality is the work of "forgiving the world for being imperfect and consenting to live in it anyway, with an open heart." Even when it makes us furious or sad or frustrated or full of longing. And part of the work of parenting, maybe, is in forgiving our kids for being needy and complicated and difficult and crazymaking sometimes, and loving them despite and through it all. And forgiving ourselves for letting the challenging moments get to us—for sometimes being angry, impatient, exasperated, even despairing. It's about fighting our way to that open heart, even or especially when all we want to do is shut down, numb out, and close up shop. There's enough forgiveness and compassion to go around for all of us.

A lot of seminary students, at some point in their studies, do at least one unit of clinical pastoral education (CPE)—that is, train as chaplains in hospitals, nursing homes, hospices, or prisons. Much of this training involves working directly with the patients, residents, or inmates in these settings; helping folks who are struggling with serious, sometimes life-or-death, questions and issues. The real work for CPE interns, though, is about getting clear, crystal clear, on what's keeping them from being maximally present with other people.

It's excruciating, really. Part of the process of reflection with the supervisor and other chaplaincy interns involves going over detailed write-ups of some of the intern's pastoral encounters and asking major questions about them that force the intern to consider really, truly, why he responded as he did. Why did he ask the questions he asked? Why did he decide to sit down at this point in the conversation? Why did he follow up on one verbal cue but drop another? This process holds up a mirror onto how interns see the world—their assumptions and fears, their unconscious concerns. The meta-question that CPE training asks is, really, "What's preventing you from having a fully I-Thou encounter, from responding today to the needs of today?"

Fascinatingly, in these reflection sessions, interns will start talking about their parents' divorce, their relationships with their fathers, the beliefs they hold that could get them ostracized by their church communities, their fears of inadequacy in the face of someone else's willingness to be vulnerable. The specific way in which a CPE supervisor helps a chaplain trainee review his or her past encounters is designed to force what's so often unconscious to the surface—what the intern might be bringing into the room, and the interaction, unawares.

This certainly played out in my own supervisory group, when I trained at a hospital during rabbinical school. Why did one seminary student offer a prayer just when her patient was starting to make himself vulnerable to her? Pushed to think it through, she admitted that she just didn't believe that her raw, compassionate presence was worth anything without the religious bells and whistles. Why did another trainee change the subject when the patient he was working with started talking about how much she was suffering? After some help examining the question, he realized that his own suffering was never taken seriously as a kid. I went under the microscope plenty of times, like when I went to extraordinary lengths to get a dying cancer patient permission to go out and sit in the gardens with me for a bit. It seemed urgent, somehow, that he have this experience (which, I note, he hadn't asked for or indicated he wanted), and it was not an easy moment when I realized that I was trying to facilitate for him the "good" death I wasn't able to give my mother when I was twenty-one.

The purpose of the training is to help hospital chaplains to understand how their experiences in their families, cultures, and life impact how they show up and respond to patients—and how, sometimes, it can interfere with an authentic encounter with the person in front of them. My colleague who didn't believe that she, herself, had anything to offer a patient without an "official" reading or prayer had been raised to feel as if she had to prove herself over and over again; it was a revelation for her to realize that what this patient probably needed from her was just for her to listen and respond from a place of intuition and concern, not for her to pull out her prayer book and recite a piece of liturgy.

The reason the unresolved, difficult, and vulnerable spots in our own lives come up when we're trying to help someone else face illness or incarceration or death is because, let's face it, they impact how we move through the world on so many levels. One person's fear of conflict or another's feeling obligated to appear super-competent at all times have deep, deep roots. My colleague's need to bring a prayer instead of just listening was informed by a childhood of being praised for her actions and accomplishments, and never quite feeling like she was good enough just as she was, without something to show off. This feeling was so deep that it colored her engagement even with someone with whom she didn't have a long-standing personal or charged relationship.

So if it's true that chaplain interns bring their past into their interactions with patients they've just met, how much more is it true of parents, since our own experiences of being parented and loved are *obviously* going to manifest as we parent and love our children? I mean, it's almost a given that we will project our own selves onto these little humans who are (whether or not we're biologically related to them) *ours*. And the same question that they ask in chaplain training applies: What filters or blinders are keeping you from seeing this moment clearly? What's preventing you from responding to the actual need in front of you, instead of playing out your own fears and hurts in ways that aren't relevant or useful?

My friend Lucy's first marriage was abusive on a number of levels, including emotionally and verbally. She was manipulated, randomly attacked, inconsistently judged, and made to doubt her own intuition. She lived in vigilant fear of the next explosion, and organized her life, as much as possible, around avoiding her ex's wrath.

Eventually she got out, thank God, did a lot of work to

heal from the abuse she had suffered, and went on to meet a great, loving guy. Together they had a beautiful son who she loves desperately.

But her little boy is, of course, just a child. And it turns out that, despite the very major work that Lucy did to try to heal from the damage inflicted on her by a very angry man, there are some buttons that are hard to uninstall.

One day she wrote to me,

During the years I lived with [the ex] I once went to a counselor. She asked me what I was coming to counseling for—what I wanted to change. I said—I make a lot of stupid mistakes all the time. I lose my keys, I park the car wrong, I say the wrong things. I don't know if I have a brain tumor or dementia or what, but I just do things wrong all the time.

I think I saw her for six weeks. She taught me a centering visualization. At no time did she ask me how I knew that everything I did was so wrong. The answer would have been: I can't seem to stop enraging the man I live with.

Thirteen years after my last sight of him: Another century, three states later, married ten years to a gentle and patient man, raising a longed-for child who is all heart and snuggles and lively energy.

And multiple times a day I am going along feeling like everything's fine, and something goes off script. Begins to go off. My child asks a civilized question and I give him a civilized answer that is not what he wanted and instead of speaking he wails. . . . [Or he snaps at me for] not reading his mind and knowing he now wants something completely different from the last thing he said he wanted, which he didn't bother to articulate but the first I hear of it is that he's already indignant that I'm proceeding with the previous plan. . . .

And for me, every time—the electric sensation of slippage between realities. I thought we were in the safe peaceful normal place. But surprise! Roll the dice for random attack! HOW DID I NOT SEE THIS COMING??? Must Improve Hypervigilance! Aooooogah!

The vitriolic self-excoriation for having let down my guard AGAIN is more painful than whatever is actually going on. I said to [my partner]—so most people don't have this experience of life, that interactions with other people are like . . . you're playing a pleasant game of chess, and every so often masked men with assault rifles burst in and kick over the chess board, and you have to go, oh, crap, I was going to say "bishop to king's 4" but I guess the answer is "hide under the table" now.

"No," he said. "Most people don't experience ordinary life that way."

Lucy's son is engaging in behaviors that are normal and developmentally appropriate for his age: not being sure what he wants, getting petulant and tantrummy when his parent is unable to read his mind (even when he's changing his mind fourteen times a second), getting emotionally overwhelmed and having shouty outbursts as a result, sometimes out of the blue. But Lucy's history of trauma makes her sensitive to the expectation that she is supposed to read minds and to being on the receiving end of sudden, loud emotional outbursts. So what might be exhausting to the average mom triggers my friend's post-traumatic stress disorder, and can make her shut down, utterly, in an instant.

But she's self-aware about it, which makes all the difference. She had written to me in order to blow off steam and refocus—to remember that this little boy was not her abusive ex, that his shouting didn't signal imminent danger to her self and being. Once old traumas are triggered, it can be really hard to flip the switch back to the present day. Lucy has done some incredible work around trying to identify and dismantle her internal minefields, and continues to. She knows that her son's emotional health and sense of safety depend, in part, on having a mom who doesn't shut down every time he expresses an emotion, every time his reaction isn't what she was expecting.

But man, it's not easy.

There are so many ways that pain gets passed on down the generations, so many ways that our own buttons get installed. Lucy's button was about a damaging ex; someone else's might be about a long and complicated relationship with food and body image, or growing up feeling like a second fiddle to a sibling, or being tacitly expected to be the caretaker for other siblings or even a parent, an undiagnosed learning disability that impacted self-esteem or school performance, or one or more of many other possible dynamics or experiences.

And even if there isn't some defining challenge or issue that a person can point to as formative, there are still legacies—the particular psychic mold of your family tree, the norms of the culture in which your parents and grandparents were raised, how that one thing that happened three generations back continues to imprint your family's emotional map.

We all have *stuff*. Sometimes how our stuff shows up is clear and obvious, and sometimes we, or our kids, are just lumbering through the day when *BAM!*—we smack into some reaction we weren't expecting to have quite at that moment. And, probably most common, and most insidious, is how our expectations of, and responses to, our kids are colored by messages that we aren't even aware we picked up. Maybe they're straight hand-me-downs from our parents (or grandparents), and maybe they're an unconscious reaction against our own upbringing that we want to reject. But we all received, and pass on, messages—about what level of perfection needs to be attained to earn love, or whether or not certain kinds of fun are excessively indulgent, whether rules are mandatory or stifling, what consequences are reasonable, and where the line is between helping kids be independent versus abandoning them.

There's an old joke about a woman who cuts the end of her brisket off before putting it in the oven. One day, a friend asks why she does that, and she says, "I don't know. My mother always just did that." She asks her mother, who says, "I don't know. *My* mother always just did that." The woman goes and asks her grandmother, who says, "Well, the pan I used to cook the brisket in was too small for the whole thing!"

I think that, a lot of the time, our family emotional legacies are like that. There's a certain way of doing things, and we don't even know to ask whether or not there's a coherent reason for it that has anything to do with our present-day reality. Let alone whether there might be other possibilities for responding to stress, encouraging compliance, navigating conflict, or expressing affection. Sometimes preemptively cutting off the end of the brisket is totally fine—or at least neutral and inconsequential—and other times we don't even see that we (or our kids) would be much happier cooking some totally different way.

But these small humans live in our homes and receive all of the rough edges of our unworked-through bits. Their experiences of safety, growth, care, and neglect are shaped by our interactions with them. They learn how to be a person from watching how we move through the world, and much of their selfhood is constructed through their interactions with us. Humblingly, as author Peggy O'Mara puts it, "The way we talk to our children becomes their inner voice."[3]

The responsibility we hold in shaping their hearts and minds, and the necessity of being a positive model for them, makes it all the more urgent that we listen when they show us—or when we see for ourselves—all of the places where we still need to heal and grow. Our kids, and our experience of parenting, can force us to face how we were not parented well. Maybe we were abused or neglected, or maybe our parents were just imperfect people who fell short sometimes in meeting our almost bottomless needs. How do we name and grieve what we didn't get in order to consciously choose differently, in order to not repeat their story? It isn't easy—it's hard and painful. And, of course, every parent is fallible. How can we acknowledge our own inevitable failings while striving to be better?

My friend Melanie has discovered, for example, that the faults she finds in her teenage daughter are all too revealing when she's willing to look more closely at them. When she gets an urge to criticize her daughter's appearance, or eating habits, or study habits, or relationships, she tries to pause— to resist saying what's on the tip of her tongue and to see what comes up for her, internally. When she does that, she says, she "can get an indication of where [she] internalized criticizing voices as [she] grew up." Perhaps not surprisingly, the things that bother her most about her daughter have some sort of long-buried personal resonance for her. And understanding that this is the case is a great motivator. She reflects,

> I see myself as a shock absorber. I have a reaction, and instead of moving ahead with the criticism that comes up, I stop myself and have to feel the pain that came up for me about that [particular issue] when I was her age. Then I get to heal my past and I get to hopefully interrupt passing on the same chain of hurts.[4]

How can we parent our actual children, and not ourselves as children? Or our abusive ex? Or our regrets or fears? How can we become attentive to the ways in which our story interferes with engaging our kids and become as present with them as a chaplain does with someone she's serving? If we admit that our children's needs are real, we might have to admit that our own needs weren't met as kids or later in life, and to feel the grief around that. What do we need in order for this to be possible?

The thirteenth-century Persian Sufi poet Rumi once likened being a person to being a guesthouse. Emotions show up as "unexpected visitor[s]," and, Rumi implores us, we should "Welcome and entertain them all! / Even if they are a crowd of sorrows, who violently sweep your house empty of its furniture, still, treat each guest honorably. / He may be clearing you out / for some new delight."[5] That is, when a feeling shows up, we should give it some space to do its thing. Rather than trying to push our anger and frustration aside, we should allow them in, and acknowledge them. We should trust that they won't stick around forever once we let ourselves actually experience them—and that even our most intrusive of sorrows may clear us out for a "new delight" that we can only experience after the pain is fully felt. (In my experience, the emotions we don't give ourselves permission to feel are the ones that linger and linger until they're given proper attention.)

That doesn't mean we indulge those emotions—feeling

anger and acting in anger aren't the same thing. But if Shir just smacked me in the face, pretending that I don't have a reaction to it will make it impossible to reconnect with him. The anger will be there, arms folded, fuming, and blocking my access to the love and compassion underneath. Allowing myself to say "that hurt, I'm feeling angry" at least acknowledges that there's something else in the room. And when logistics allow (true story: sometimes they don't), if I can take a minute to just feel that anger and breathe through it, all the better. The anger gets attention and then, inevitably, gets bored and goes someplace else. As far as I've been able to discern, this is the fastest means of getting back to seeing my kids as Thou, being present with them—to make space for whatever's showing up in my proverbial guesthouse, to name it, and to give myself a minute to feel it. Who knows what it's clearing out?

This is true of the frustration, anger, or desperation that any normal person would feel in routine parenting situations—the baby screaming in his crib, the two-year-old who goes ballistic because she was given the wrong spoon, or the six-year-old who suddenly becomes militantly defiant in his refusal to put on his shoes even though school just started and mommy has to be at a meeting in twenty minutes.

And it's true of the old stuff, too. That chaplain who felt inadequate to hold her patient's suffering has probably been keeping that fear and inadequacy at bay for a long time. What if she invited those feelings in, allowed them to sit down and have some tea? What if she honored them, had compassion for them, gave love to the part of her that didn't get whatever she needed a long time ago? What if, instead of shoving that fear into a corner again, she said, "Hey, you're here, OK. What do you have to teach me?" For as Rumi tells us, every feeling has been sent "as a guide from beyond."

If we remain resolute in the idea that feeling pain will destroy us utterly, we'll never find out what we can learn from that pain and fear, and what's on the other side of it. Feeling pain won't destroy us. But running from it might.

As meditation teacher Sylvia Boorstein puts it,

> *If I say to myself, "This is painful, but it's O.K.," and I stay there, then it's just what it is and then it changes. But when I run away from it or I push it away or pretend that it's something else, that is the suffering. All those maneuvers that we do to avoid saying, "This is true. This is what's happening"—the maneuvers themselves are the suffering.*[6]

When we can really make space to experience all the feelings we've been keeping at bay, well, that can open us up in unexpected ways.

When I was in my early twenties, I went to a meeting with my rabbi, Alan Lew. I was participating in an intensive meditation practice period with him, and meeting regularly was part of the deal. This particular day, I was upset about a few things happening in my work. He asked me a few questions, and then concluded,

"So you feel like a failure, in other words."

Uh, yeah. I guess so. Thanks, I feel better now.

Then he softened. "Of course you feel like a failure. Everybody does, deep down." He instructed me to embrace those feelings until I got to the place where my failures merged with everybody else's failures, with all the failures of the entire world. I went home, and I sat. I watched my breath, and I allowed this dark, nasty, swallowing fear to rise up and overtake me. As it came up I descended to meet it, like a swimmer pushing toward the ocean's floor. Eventually, somehow, I got down into a place where my own loss and grief and fear and disappointment merged into Loss and Grief and Fear and Disappointment, into fundamental facts of the human condition. Deep in that place, I felt, somehow, connected with all of those millions of people out there feeling these things—not because of the specifics of these emotions, but because of our shared sweet, vulnerable, messy humanity as a whole.

The meditation enabled me to plug into a picture much bigger and much more important than my isolated, solitary woes. Suddenly, I was only a bit player in a much grander drama. I was all the more normal because I felt like a failure sometimes—not special, or weird. And that, in itself, was strangely empowering.

When our kid is screaming in our face, we often react the best that we can in the moment. Sometimes we can make out the vague outlines of the Thou in front of us—just enough to dial down the intensity of the hard moment. Sometimes we can let ourselves breathe into the frustration, to acknowledge its presence, so we react with the knowledge that the frustration's in the room, but we don't let it drive our response. And sometimes, maybe, we can get our specific frustration to be a universal feeling of frustration, to remember that the fact that we want to tear our hair out because the toddler just dumped an entire bowl of yogurt on the floor or the preschooler who adamantly insisted that she *didn't* need to use the potty then peed on the living room rug just makes us human and connects us with everybody everywhere—most especially all the parents, maybe even including our own. It plugs us into the big picture and reminds us of our own beautiful fragility, and makes it easier for us to see everyone else's, as well.

And sure, sometimes we have to wait to really feel that frustration properly (because the preschooler now needs to be carted off to the bathroom for the apparently imminent poop, because the toddler's about to climb down from the chair and fingerpaint yogurt all over the walls). But until we give it space to come out, that feeling might be careening around our internal living room, knocking things over, waiting for some damn customer service from our head and heart.

And even more than that, Rabbi Kalonymus Kalman Shapira, a Polish rebbe who eventually taught from the Warsaw Ghetto, reminds us that giving some space for these feelings can help us remember, too, that we are not our emotions. He writes,

> *A person . . . is a mere inn for the thoughts of the world that are passing and returning, going and coming, and the essence of the person is not to be found. . . . Just*

as time and the world change, so do they [i.e., her thoughts]. . . . First they were bad guests and now they are good, [revolving] according to the world and the day. . . . If a person is [truly] present in her house and in her essence, then it must be that joy will not take control of her mind and worry will not direct her so much.[7]

The more attuned we become to these guests, and the way they check in and out, the more easily we can remember that we are not them, and they are not us—that the anger and frustration are temporal, as are the joy and delight. The more we pay attention to our feelings' arrival and departure, the more we can remember that we don't have to be defined by them, or to assign more significance than necessary to the fact that they're in town at the moment. When we're able to understand the power that we have as hosts, we can be more magnanimous with the irritation and sadness when it comes, but feel less and less driven by it, more in control of our heads and our hearts.

The more we can internalize this idea, the more we will be able to offer our full selves—and not our emotional reactions—to our kids. When we honor our feelings as invited, honored guests, we find that new doors may be opened in our relationships with ourselves, our children, and maybe everyone else out there, too.

Usually giving space for our own feelings will bring us back from regarding our kids as The Object That Just Drew on the Walls or The Object That Just Threw His Brother Off the Couch, and help us see them as Thou again. But sometimes it helps to take a minute, in the fury and the exasperation, to remember just how vulnerable they really are.

Over the years, my friend Julie developed a practice of doing what she calls "calling the angels" for her daughters (now aged five and seven) when they go to bed. She invokes by name the angelic presences that are part of Jewish lore—calling, and speaking to, Michael, Uriel, Gabriel, and Rafael—in order to bring the spirit of protection and comfort and inspiration into the room. She reflects and reframes her daughters' experiences that day, sometimes tailoring the blessings she asks the angels to bestow according to what's going on in each child's life.

One evening, they were out at an event and Julie had a major conflict with her seven-year-old. The girl was, Julie said, "being absolutely horrible. A whole other level from the usual crap." That night, as Julie went to tuck her daughter in, she found that she "couldn't call the angels for her. I hated her. I absolutely hated her." Julie was carrying so much animosity after the rough evening that she couldn't engage in the openhearted practice she usually used to connect with her girls. Her anger was blocking her.

So she sat there for a moment, closed her eyes, and took a few deep breaths. And then she began picturing her daughter as a tiny baby. She remembered how helpless and dependent she was then, and how clear that little girl's need for Julie's nurturing was. There, at her daughter's bedside, Julie started sobbing; the shell of her acrimony had been cracked open.

She was able to call the angels then, and included a wish to them for her daughter to understand that her mommy was doing her absolute best. Even if it was hard sometimes. And that she loved her very much.

We live on the third floor, and have a little balcony. When Yonatan was four, he took to throwing things—toys, pillows, books—off the balcony. It really wasn't OK, and he knew it. He also knew that if he threw toys, he wouldn't see them again for a while, and that there was likely to be some other consequence to boot. But a four-year-old's impulse control is not so hot and he was testing boundaries.

One morning I asked him to share the toy he was holding with his little brother, so he ran halfway across the apartment in order to throw it off the balcony. It was a clear eff-you: If I can't have it, nobody can have it. It was the last straw of a frustrating morning, and I shouted at him, really screamed, as I put him in a time-out.

There are a lot of reasons why I don't want my children to grow up in a home with yelling. I have a pretty firm commitment to raising them to feel loved, safe, and not afraid in their own home, and a screaming adult is terrifying to a small person. So to have slipped in a way that's human and understandable but still, well, really not great—it's a terrible feeling. That was one morning (not the first, not the last) when I failed my son and I failed myself.

Every Rosh Hashana and Yom Kippur, rabbis start talking about the work of the season, *teshuvah*. *Teshuvah* is usually translated as "repentance," but it literally means "return." It's about coming back to where you need to be—emotionally, spiritually, ethically, interpersonally—and repairing any damage you've done in your relationships with others, and perhaps with God, when your actions strayed from your ideals. There are several steps to making *teshuvah*. You have to acknowledge what you did wrong (whether or not it was intentional). You have to take actions to correct the mistake, if that's possible. If it was an interpersonal hurt, you have to go apologize to that person—up to three times, if they refuse you at first. You have to make amends, if possible. (There are certainly things that people do to one another that are beyond amends.) And you need to invest some time working out how things can be different next time. After all that, *then* you can work on making things square between you and the divine.

The classical literature on *teshuvah* talks about *cheshbon ha-nefesh*, the accounting of the soul that happens as part of this process. That is, you have to spend some uncomfortable time figuring out exactly how and when you've failed to be the person you want to be. Essentially, you can't return—make *teshuvah*—until you have some real understanding about where you've gone; you can't make amends until you're clear on how you've messed up.

Luckily for us parents, we are offered ample opportunities to see our failings. All we need to do, probably, is to pay attention to how we are with our children for a couple of hours—a week max—and we'll get a lot of telling information. When are we attentive? When are we dismissive? When are we pretending to be engaged but are actually checked out? When are we manipulative or deceitful with our kids, even with little things that ostensibly "don't matter"? When do we run out of patience, and what does that look like? Children are, among other things, powerful little mirrors, and not all of what they reflect back to us about who and how we are is necessarily comfortable or fun to see.

The good news is that if we can untangle the places where we're stuck and broken as parents, it can powerfully impact our entire lives. My rabbi[8] used to say that during the month leading up to Rosh Hashana, a person should watch his behavior (including decisions, motivations, and emotions) around food, money, or sex, and he will see all of the neuroses and problems of his life illuminated—the universe in the grain of sand, if you will. Needless to say, I think a hard look at our parenting can do the same thing. Our relationships with our kids offer an easy-access on-ramp to all of our laziness, pettiness, and unresolved stuff, if we're willing to look. Just as the chaplains' patient interactions shone a bright light on a whole lot of things that had nothing to do with the hospital, fixing this one little corner of our lives can shift things around everywhere.

The medieval sage Maimonides defines perfect *teshuvah* as that moment when you come to a situation in which you had previously acted badly and, this time, do it right. Whether it's the second, fifth, or twentieth time around when you finally behave concordantly with your values and ideals, that moment when you finally get there—that's *teshuvah*. But a person might reasonably ask: How could it be that you might be back in the exact same situation as the one in which you had previously screwed up? Who gets an instant replay like that?

Rabbi Lew used to say something like, "Well, if you haven't done the work, you'll get back there." That is, if you haven't faced down your problematic traits and unhealed wounds, you will undoubtedly manage to find yourself in some variation of the same situation over and over. It's only when you do the work necessary to become a different person that you, naturally and organically, make a different choice.

Fortunately, kids continue—over and over and over—to offer us the chance to try again, to do better. The intensity of these bonds are indeed an enclosed spiritual space in which to do the work that we need to do. It's tricky, sometimes, and inelegant, but if we choose to face who we are with intention and humility, there's the possibility for us to grow into the people our children so desperately need us to be.

A student once asked Menachem Mendel of Kotzk, a nineteenth-century Hasidic rabbi known as the Kotzker Rebbe, about the language of the *V'ahavta*,[9] a central piece of liturgy that is recited twice a day. The *V'ahavta* says to place "these words"—that is, the commandment to love the divine—"*upon* your heart." Why, the student asked, does it say *upon* your heart? Why not place the words *in* our hearts? The Kotzker Rebbe answered, "So often, our hearts are closed. When we place these words upon—on top—of them, they will stay there until one day, our heart breaks, and the words fall in."[10] There are truths—experiences of the transcendent, capacities for love—that are only available to us when our hearts are broken open. When we're determined to stay on lockdown and not feel the hard feelings, we keep all that light at bay.

My friend Tamar has learned this all too well recently. She and her partner had decided to enter the foster system with the hope of adopting, and were thrilled when they were told that their first placement—a sweet one-month-old girl—would never go back to her mother. She reflected, many months later, "Though I never carried her in my body, I do feel a primal connection to [this baby]—something deep and true. She is my daughter."[11]

Initially, she says, she "thought of [this baby's] mom as someone who was, frankly, dumb, and didn't really care about her child. She smoked and used drugs while pregnant—I would never do that, I thought." But over time, the mother's behavior changed; she "started to really get it together." And, Tamar said,

> I could see how hard she was working for her daughter—
> how much she loved her and wanted to care for her as
> best as she possibly could. At first I really tried to keep
> my distance from her mom, but I realized that parenting my foster daughter means parenting all of her, including the part that connects her to her mother.[12]

She slowly opened herself up to a relationship with the baby's mother, knowing full well that, in doing so, she was making herself vulnerable to grief and heartbreak—but also knowing that it might equip her to better and more fully love the child that had entered her life and her heart. In order to truly care for this little girl, she had to be willing to push herself far past her own comfort zone, into a place of risk. She reflects,

> *In the past few months I have really bonded with her mom, and am so proud of the progress both mother and daughter have made. It's going to be totally devastating to give our daughter back to her mom, but the whole experience has brought so much richness to my life. I feel like a completely different person than I was before she came into our home—a better, more compassionate person.*[13]

Our kids offer us a chance to see ourselves, and to do the work to become different people. When we take them up on it, we discover that the things we have feared and loathed most about ourselves, the pain we have run furthest from, isn't going to kill us. Rather, the cracks in our heart—our broken, vulnerable places—allow in the most radiant light. They turn pain into compassion and love. And then, each time we attempt to draw closer to these tiny, vulnerable beings in our care, we become a little bit more the people they need us to be.

A couple of our very dear friends are frequent guests on Shabbat. They don't live within walking distance of us, so about once a month they just come and stay over for the whole Sabbath. We have dinner together, they sleep in our guest room, we all walk to the synagogue in the morning, and then they come back to our house for lunch and stay until it's dark out Saturday night, and the Sabbath ends.

For a long time they asked: Are you sure this isn't an imposition? Is it OK? Isn't it too much to have us here *all Shabbat* once a month? And I've had to explain, over and over again, that of course it was OK. We love having guests, we're delighted to have meaningful time with them in particular on a regular basis. My friend's concern was finally set to rest when I explained to her that, actually, it's a lot easier with the kids when they're around than when they're not.

During the midafternoon Shabbat witching hour, particularly when the weather doesn't permit a trip to the park, the kids start to get bored and antsy, and Nir and I are usually ready for a break. But if our friends are staying over, one of them will happily read them books, and the other will let them pounce on and climb all over him. They love our kids, think they're cute and fun, and it's a novelty to play with them. Pretty much everybody wins. And frankly, just having other human beings in the room changes the energy—even if the adults are all just lying around talking, the kids are somehow more relaxed, more likely to be able to entertain themselves. When Nir is out of town at a conference or something on Shabbat, I make a point of having guests for lunch—even though it's more work with the cooking and setting the table and cleaning up and everything—because the other-people-around factor makes such a huge difference in my, and my kids', experience of the day, and everybody's mood.

Because, of course, feelings are hardly a fixed thing. In our house, and for a lot of parents, who's in the room has a big impact on how we experience what's happening. How I react to a meltdown, a mischevious boundary test, or even a request for my attention if I'm trying to focus elsewhere will definitely vary depending on where my head is at, and whether I'm on solo or if I have other grown-ups around.

As in many two-parent families, there are a lot of moments in which our kids are with one parent, not both. One of us is with them and the other is frantically trying to catch up on work or maybe (maybe!) sneaking off to get some exercise or something. And as is the case for a lot of parents, it's a lot harder when it's just one of us with them. We love these little muppets more than either of us could have imagined loving anyone or anything, but their needs are so relentless, so endless. Parental isolation, and its impact on everybody's emotional state, is a real thing.

Anne Neville writes powerfully about the challenges of being a stay-at-home mom in an essay for the website Hip Mama:

> *Who decided that the two of us should be each other's only companions for ten hours in a row?*
> *Here's the thing that's hard: my son has learned to walk, run, climb, throw, smear, and dismantle. He has not yet learned to construct sentences or follow instruc-*

tions. He is not autistic, or developmentally disordered, or emotionally damaged. He's just two. He wants to be Doing Something every second that he is awake, and he does not want to do any of it alone, and he does not want to do any of it sitting down. If I start him stacking blocks, and I walk into the other room, he leaves the blocks and follows me. If he is sitting at the table eating lunch, same thing. There is no autopilot with a two-year-old. He is doing what I'm doing.

And sometimes, if she tries to focus on something besides him, he gets desperate and tries to seize attention, sometimes by hitting, which might lead to a time-out. But, she writes,

after two minutes [of time-out], the cortisol in my bloodstream is at pretty much the same level it was right after somebody hit me in the eye two minutes ago.

Who decided this was safe? Am I saying I'm a danger to my child? Am I saying I'm an unfit mother? Am I saying I'd better fill that Prozac prescription? Am I seriously saying that a forty-year-old woman with a graduate education in a helping profession cannot handle two four-hour blocks of interacting with her own beloved, long-awaited child?

I'm saying that by the time his father comes home at night, I'm so dissociated all I want to do is curl up in an office chair and drink margaritas until I fall asleep. . . . In our current culture, every family is still an

island. Though I have co-workers and neighbors, and
even a church, I still find most days my son and I are
stranded without relief boats in sight and I am past
the point of caring whether they arrive with on site day
care or anti-depressants, as long as they arrive.[14]

For Anne, the isolation she feels when alone with her son is almost crippling—the intensity of his needs, and his limits as a toddler, push her past the place where she can be present with him, day after day. As challenging as this is, though, she does have a partner who comes home in the evening and is able to take over to some degree—whether helping with bedtime or cleaning up the dishes.

Lauren, on the other hand, is the single mom of a six-year-old with special needs, so she struggles not only with the same hard feelings that a lot of parents face, but with the unique logistical and psychological challenges that come with doing this particular hard thing, alone. She reflects,

Isolation takes over a lot when you're a single parent—
and especially as a parent with special needs, and a kid
who has attachment issues on top of other things. "Why
don't you just leave her with a friend?" [My daughter]
needs to be watched in her house, by a consistent baby-
sitter, so that's a lot of money—and when she is watched
it triggers some of her other issues.

If she's had a bad day at school, or if she's getting to
me and my buttons, I can't just go to the grocery store or
to a friend's to let off steam—I'm stuck with her. And

I have to be very careful in terms of what activities we do; going out to dinner after work and school doesn't work, because she needs to be in bed on time. We can't do home playdates because it's too stimulating for her.

There are times I'm able to walk away and go into my room to cool off when things get hard, and times when I've thrown a plate down in anger. I've never hit my child and I never will, but I'm not the mom that I want to be because of all this. My threshold is pretty low, and my reserves are gone.

Given all of this, the other people in her life—the ones who have really made an effort to understand where she's at and what she needs—have become much more important. Sometimes she relies on email and texting as an outlet, and sometimes her community shows up with the help that it can offer. She muses,

Sometimes someone will let me know that they're going to the grocery store, can they pick anything up for us? They can't necessarily help with my daughter, but they can help in other ways. Overall, I need to rely on people in a way emotionally that I'm not used to. But through all this, I've built up a great support system.[15]

It turns out that the so-called African proverb that titled Hillary Clinton's 1996 book, "It takes a village to raise a child," isn't actually a literal translation of anyone's aphorism. But it does echo something the Jita people of Tanzania say, which might translate a little more accurately to, "regardless of a child's biological parents, its upbringing belongs to the community." Not as snappy for a book title, but the sentiment is the same: Ideally, there should be a whole extended network of people caring for and helping to raise our kids.

Some folks have that in the form of local family who help out and make a huge difference not only in the logistics, but in helping them feel connected and supported—grandparents who handle school pickup when parents are at work, cousins who come by for a standing Sunday playdate, or the newborn's aunt who stays over once a week to be in charge of nighttime feedings and let *both* exhausted parents sleep. Some family members are less hands-on but offer advice or even financial assistance, and also serve as part of the network of people who love this child desperately, and who take part in raising him to adulthood.

But not everyone has that physical, daily embeddedness with siblings and parents and cousins and cousins' kids. Many of us leave the nest and then fly off to seek our fortunes wherever they may be—and wind up living far from the people who would help us in that way. Others of us have more complicated relationships with our own families or for whatever reason our families just aren't able to give us the sort of help—whether logistical, emotional, or both— that we need as parents.

And that's where other forms of community can come in. Sometimes these connections manifest in simple tasks, like sharing carpooling duties, or making a google doc to help set up meal delivery, childcare shifts, or whatever's needed when someone has a baby, or gets seriously ill, or loses a loved one. It's not that big a thing in the grander scheme of things, but it can bridge, just enough, logistics that had seemed unsustainable during a challenging time. As the Talmud teaches, "If you lift the burden with me, I will lift it too. But if not, I will not lift it either."[16]

Sometimes it's just about having people in your life who love your kids and who are happy to play with them on a Saturday afternoon, right when you need an hour of downtime. Sometimes it's just about feeling like you're not stranded on an island, but rather sitting at the edge of a beach full of love and laughter and people who are a regular part of your life and adore your kid nearly as much as you do. It's not for nothing that a lot of people I know use the language of "family of origin" to denote the folks who raised them, to differentiate from "chosen family"—since our adult bonds sometimes feel thicker than can be encapsulated through the word *friendship*.

When we're lucky enough to have communal networks in our life, it's certainly good for our kids. For example, the National Longitudinal Study of Adolescent Health, involving some ninety thousand teenagers, found that "connectedness" emerged as the factor most likely—by a significant margin—to help protect kids from emotional distress, suicidal thoughts, and risky behaviors including smoking, drinking, and using drugs.[17] Dr. Christine Carter, executive director of the University of California at Berkeley's Greater Good Science Center, suggests, "We know from 50 years of research that social connections are an incredibly important, if not the most important, contributor to happiness. And it's not just the quality, but also the quantity of the bonds: the more connections your child makes, the better."[18]

I had already been religious for about ten years before I had kids, so my default community, for a long time, has been through Judaism. The people I see in synagogue, the people with whom I celebrate holidays, eat with on Shabbat, the people whose baby namings and houses of mourning I attend—that's a core, though not the only, part of what I think of as my community. Of course, there are lots of kinds of communities, and they're not all based around one's religious life: The queer community. The volleyball league. The local craft scene. Great coworkers or professional colleagues. A close-knit neighborhood. People who've been working together for some time on a shared cause. Whatever the external form, the kind of community I'm talking about is one that's proximate—that is, it's comprised at least mostly of people who don't live inside your computer—and is made of people that you see on a regular basis, people who are or could be woven into the ongoing fabric of your life.

Of course, online community, and the relationships that can be forged or maintained online, are real and sometimes crucial—a few of my dearest friends and closest confidantes fall into this category. But, unfortunately, friends who live elsewhere can't give my kid a ride to camp or hang out with us when I'm a week into solo parenting and ready for some three-dimensional support. This isn't to denigrate the kinds of kinship that can take place online, or that are first created online.

But that's not the kind of community that takes place when there's time for conversations to unwind however they may, for laughter and touch and tears in one another's physical presence. And even if your community isn't a "spiritual community," in the sense that it's based around a faith or religion, I'd suggest that living in community is a spiritual endeavor. Living in interdependent connection with other people is powerful and profound. It forces us to be open. To be vulnerable. To try to hear those with whom we don't necessarily or immediately agree. To bravely excavate sites of potential conflict and commit to transcending separateness, rather than brushing over differences. To be impacted by the joy and suffering of others. To allow their destiny to be ours, and to allow them into our own. This is what we do when we parent, but it's a different endeavor when we allow other adults in. When we allow ourselves to be not in charge all the time; when we ask for help.

As Catholic theologian Thomas Merton put it, "Souls are like athletes, that need opponents worthy of them, if they are to be tried and extended and pushed to the full use of their powers, and rewarded according to their capacity."[19] Other people help us to be our best. Our kids offer that all-too-worthy opposition, but there are other kinds of extensions of our power (including our power to make ourselves vulnerable, to live in uncertainty) that might require interface with other adults.

When we're able to weave ourselves into a web of community, it makes parenting easier—the hard moments, the funky moods, and the logistical craziness are often mitigated when others are able to be a part of our lives. It enriches our kids' lives to have other loving grown-ups around. It helps us model a certain kind of giving and connection to our kids—whenever I bring meals to a friend in need or help out in some other way, I make a point of telling my kids or bringing them along, so that they grow up understanding that part of our job as people is to care for one another.

And being embedded in community can give us a vitamin that we desperately need, something that can sustain us through the inevitable despair, frustration, loneliness, ambivalence, pain, and discomfort that's simply part of the experience of parenting. As Rabbi Arthur Green once put it, "As humans who are creatures of love, we receive the divine life-flow in the form of love, turning toward it and being fulfilled by it just as naturally as plants stretch towards the light."[20] This is the love that we offer to our children, even through the difficult, even through the muck. This is the love that our children give us. And when we have more people in our lives to love and who love us, we all grow taller and stronger as a result.

CHAPTER FOUR

I Have So Much Control Over Someone's Life, But Ultimately I Have No Control

Rethinking Power and Powerlessness

———◆———

Some of my kids' favorite games go like this: Shir tells me he's excited about driving the fire engine at the park, "But it's just for kids. Not for you," he admonishes. "Please, pleaaaaase? Can I pleaaaase drive the fire truck?" I'll beg. He'll squeal: "No! No! NO!" The harder I beg and the more he can shoot me down, the happier he is. Or Yonatan will come and "kill" me with his cardboard sword, and he's most gleeful when I die expansively, flailing and begging for mercy. "No, no. No mercy! You're dead now!" he'll cackle, delighted.

These moments live in stark contrast to so many of our other interactions, when I tell them whether we can go to the library or if today we have to run errands instead (and I said *no running* in the store!), when I start counting to three because it's time to stop playing and go get ready for the bath, when I decide whether they can wear sneakers, or if it's still so muddy out there that it's got to be boots, or, most recently, when we told them that we'd be moving temporarily to live halfway around the world while Nir was on sabbatical. My children feel keenly how much power I have over them in both small and large respects, so the games they play where they have power over me carry a particular charge. They love being able to tell me "no!" because mostly, in the real world, they can't.

The irony is that, for the most part, my kids don't see how I really have power over them—as far as they're concerned, it's just a parent's job to dictate when it's time to play and eat and bathe. But for us grown-ups, it can be terrifying to ponder the extent of our power. We determine what environments will be good for our children, and how they spend their time. We teach them how to respond to challenges and how to interact with strangers on the street. We show them, in all sorts of conscious and unconscious ways, how to get our attention. We are tasked to safeguard their physical safety, to keep them fed and clean, as well as feeling emotionally safe. Their interactions with us determine whether or not they see the world as a benevolent or hostile place, whether they regard themselves and others as capable and worthy of love, whether they feel they have permission to dream.

Psychologists tell us that we even have the power to craft our children's memory—that toddlers who report on what happened at the zoo will only mention things that their mothers explicitly pointed out during the visit.[1] Like, if a monkey jumped on the kid's shoulder and sang him a song, and mom didn't say anything, he won't think to recount it later—but he will tell the interviewer all about the elephant's trunk, because mommy had mentioned it. We literally have the power to decide how our children experience their own lives, to show them what is important and to create the filters with which they regard the world. Is the person on the street corner scary? Someone to rush past awkwardly? Someone with whom we have a friendly interaction? Someone we can and should help? How? With what tools? Our kids' understanding of what's reasonable and possible comes almost entirely from us.

William Makepeace Thackeray wrote in his nineteenth-century novel *Vanity Fair*: "Mother is the name for God in the lips and hearts of little children."[2] And I think, at least in part, that Thackeray is talking about this, how we are our children's everything—their judges and comforters, their providers and boundary-setters. We determine if they will receive the proverbial rain for their harvest or if they will suffer hunger and drought. Whether they get their basic needs met. Whether they will receive the love that they spend their whole lives seeking.

God is portrayed as a parent up and down traditional religious sources—mostly as a father, but not exclusively. The metaphor is burned deep into our collective cultural psyche, and it reveals a lot about how we think about parents and children, power and powerlessness. At the same time, though, it also challenges some of our conventional thinking about parenting and power. The way the somewhat anthropomorphized character of God is written in the Torah can offer us a unique way of understanding the weight of this responsibility—as a partnership with, rather than control over, the small people who are dependent on us in almost every way.

In the Book of Exodus, the critical moment in the development of divine authority and power takes place not long after the Israelites leave their servitude in Egypt. Over a period of weeks, they journey from the Red Sea to the base of Mount Sinai, where the giving of the Torah will take place. But before this happens, we are told that this moment will involve the creation of a covenant.

A covenant is a binding agreement, a pact between two parties, confirmed by oath,[3] sacrifice,[4] or other means. What exactly is being agreed to varies widely by context; it has its origins in ancient kings' contracts, laying out the obligations of a ruler to his people and the people to their ruler. In the Exodus story,[5] though, the concept of a covenant is turned from a mere contractual relationship into a sacred bond of mutual obligation and care. "You will be," God tells the Israelites, through Moses, "my treasure."[6]

The Hebrew word for covenant is *brit,* which is derived from the Assyrian word for "bind," or "fetter."[7] There's a sense of permanence to it—that even though one or both parties might change over time, they're bound together, regardless, through it all.

The Israelites, who play the role of children in our story, are not always perfectly well behaved. They freak out and rebel when they want attention,[8] they throw tantrums because they don't like the food they're served,[9] they whine and complain even when they're shown a wonderful gift meant to be theirs.[10] Through it all, God—sometimes needing a little persuasion from Moses, to be sure—remains loyal to the terms of the relationship. There are punishments and consequences for the Israelites' bad behavior, of course, but the covenant is never broken. Even after the Isaraelites are given a time-out in the desert that lasts for forty years, God and the people Israel are fettered, one to the other, in it for the long haul. The promise is not broken, despite some really exquisite boundary-testing on the Israelites' part.

I try to tell my kids on a regular basis that there's nothing they could ever say or do that would make me love them any less. I may find the behavior unacceptable, but they are loved, and that's never going to change.

Just as God-the-metaphorical-parent forges a covenant with the people Israel, so, too, can we choose to think of our relationships with our children as covenantal, a sacred pact of obligation. When a covenant is forged between a ruler and his people or the divine and a community, it's not necessarily a symmetrical relationship—and neither is a parent-child relationship. Despite the asymmetry, though, covenantal relationships presume that both parties have obligations to one another and that each party can impact the other. As novelist Rebecca Goldstein put it, it's about "the knower and the known, always susceptible to each other's influence."[11] In other words, two parties—even with different levels of power—are able to be in the kind of relationship together that matters deeply to both, that influences and transforms both.

"The knower and the known, always susceptible to each other's influence."[12] As parents, we can be the knowers in our covenants with our children; we can look deep into them and meet their needs. This isn't a static kind of knowing; so much parental work is about endeavoring to see and understand—and thus to respond to—the child in front of us, who has perhaps grown and changed from who she was three weeks ago and what she needed then. We have to encounter our children constantly anew, as the Thou that they are, full and complete and complex and constantly growing. This is God's challenge dealing with the sometimes irascible Israelites, and it is ours, as well. It is our willingness to be "the knower," to listen and listen again, that underlies the covenantal relationship.

But we are also "the known" in our relationship with our kids. In some ways, they can see and understand us more clearly than anyone else in our lives. Sometimes it's maddening, to be sure, because they know exactly how to push our buttons, to make us crazy, to maybe even manipulate us—but also how to get deeper into our hearts than perhaps anyone ever has, how to touch us and move us. Intuitively, they understand when we're anxious, or stressed, or distracted, and also when we're happy, or approving, or connected. They can understand us better than we might even know ourselves. They are astute observers who watch us closely in order to learn how the world works, and how a person should behave in it. We are their keys and their guides, and we create the framework with which they interpret everything else. But, both consciously and unconsciously, they also understand who we are.

I see this all the time with my kids. I think I'm being present with Shir and he—even before he was two, before he was really talking, he would do this—would literally take my head in his hands and reposition it so that I was looking directly at him. I'd drift off into a reverie without even noticing, or reflexively check my phone—and he'd drag me back to him. Yonatan's behavior will often ebb and flow with my own internal moods; even when I think I'm being great about keeping my own exhaustion, frustration, or sadness under lock and key, he knows. Sometimes he bounces off my grumpiness by acting out and getting hyper, and sometimes he's surprisingly attentive and loving, as if he's trying to take care of me. When I give myself time to sit back and reflect, it's clear that his behavior changes the moment my mood does—even, again, when I think I'm keeping it contained or am not even conscious of the shift myself until after the fact.

Because, after all, I screw up all the time. I don't always keep my half of the bargain. My weaknesses are laid bare. The analogy between divine covenant and our own parental one can only go so far—we're not God. Even if mother is the name of God on the lips of the children, the children are wrong. My power is far from infinite—very far. But my commitment to trying to be accountable to them, as much as I can (despite the copious mistakes) is covenantal.

Covenant means allowing all this knowing to matter. To change you. To allow this relationship to alter you. "The knower and the known, always susceptible to each other's influence."[13] I have to be willing to hear them when they tell me—directly or indirectly—how I impact them. And to make decisions about what I might need to change about how I am with them, or in the world in general, so that I can better care for them.

In some ways, though, maybe the analogy is flipped. In a lot of respects, we as grown-ups have more power than our children, like God. But on the other hand, sometimes we're like the Israelites, in that we buy into this pact even before we fully understand it. After the Torah's initial revelation, Moses reads the "record of the covenant" to the people of Israel. They reply, "All that God has spoken, *naaseh v'nishma! We will do and we will hear.*"[14] There's a commitment to doing, to being in this relationship, even while knowing that the project of listening, hearing, and responding is continual, ongoing, ever-unfolding. We know one another, we see one another, we are vulnerable to one another—in the words of Kathleen Norris, covenant is about being "willing to say 'yes' long before we have a clear idea what such intimacy will cost us."[15] *Naaseh v'nishma*, "We will do and we will hear."

We sign on for parenting even before we totally grasp what it will demand of us. And once we say yes, we commit to being in it for the long haul. Sure, most parents make jokes about returning their kids to the baby store (and last night, between the two of them, I was woken up three times between midnight and five thirty a.m. so, yeah, it's a little tempting to look and see if I still have the receipts lying around somewhere). But obviously the jokes are jokes—and what underlies them, I think, is our need to process what all this intimacy is really costing us. Parenting is hard. The price is not trivial. But when we have a covenantal relationship with our kids, we say: I am willing to hold steady through all of this with you, no matter what it demands of me, no matter how I am changed in the process.

For writer Cynthia Ozick, covenant is about "duty, and . . . deed . . . secondary to subjective longings."[16] That is to say, a covenantal relationship is one in which the rubber hits the road, in which we do what we've committed to doing—whether or not we feel like it on that day, whether or not we're in the mood. In our covenantal relationships with our children, we need to meet them where they are, and do the work needed to care for them, even if we don't particularly feel like it on a certain day. Because, sure, we all have days when we would rather curl up on the couch with a great novel than wipe a poopy tush, or take a sweet, luscious nap rather than be drafted into participating in the dinosaur wars. We have plenty of moments when it'd be nice not to feel like we have such a big and heavy responsibility, to not have to decide what school to send the kid to in the fall, or to patiently and compassionately referee yet more sibling squabbles.

Acknowledging the nature of this covenant is a way to make sense of the mind-boggling dominion that we have over our children's hearts, minds, and souls. It's important to own it; when we feel that we have no power, or when we don't know the impact that we have, we behave badly. Scared and out-of-control parents who deny that they have choices and impact can frighten and hurt their children. We need to face the extent of the authority we possess over these little loves, and the implications of that.

Of course, not all parents have the same amount of power in relation to their kids, and that needs to be named, too. Some parents struggle to keep their children safe and fed, with a roof over their heads. Some parents grapple with the expectations—gendered or otherwise—of a family culture or community culture, and the impact that has on their autonomy. Sometimes parents are trapped in an abusive situation. Sometimes they lack power because of governmental policies or systemic cultural bias, such as racism or homophobia.

But all parents have some amount of power over their children, and there is a deep responsibility that comes with this power. When we think about this responsibility as covenant, it gives us a framework for it—a means of, perhaps, experiencing its weight as profound, as holy. This doesn't necessarily make the responsibility any less scary, of course, and it's not like I don't question myself a million times a day in all the ways I control my kids' experience of the world. Should the decision about whether they have dessert tonight focus on their nutritional needs or a little fleeting joy? Where's the line between attentive presence and stifling helicopter parenting? Between being absentee and giving them independence? Between squabbling and bullying? Will a particular new experience give them nightmares when they're thirty (and should that impact the decision today, or not)? It's not like the answers are so obvious, and it's not as if I'm clear about what the right answers are, or what the implications (if any; honestly, mostly my parenting approach goes with the "as long as you love them, they'll probably be OK—at least, I hope" philosophy) might be down the road.

Our covenantal relationship with our kids is one that can and should never be abrogated—no matter what they do. As the medieval commentator Ibn Ezra suggests, God says of Israel, "Even though they have broken My covenant . . . I shall not break My covenant with them, for I am God."[17] Part of how we make sense of our power is in honoring our covenant with our children, no matter what. We need to commit to those tiny little selves, and to letting them change us as much as we change them.

Every night, when I put Shir to bed, I lift his little body into my arms, he puts his head on my shoulder, and I sing him his lullabye. It's a beautiful Israeli song from the late seventies called "Layla Tov" ("Goodnight"), and includes the line (in Hebrew), "it's already late, but tomorrow we'll get up and see how the day arrives at the end of each night."[18] Intentionally or not, the language echoes, to me, the *Haskeveinu,* a traditional prayer—"lay us to rest, our God, in peace, and rise us up, powerful one, in life."

As I sing to my son, I feel his tiny heart beating against mine. It is a miracle that this organ works. That each minute, his body successfully pumps blood, again and again and again. When I think about how many different ways there are for a body to go wrong, I am humbled and astonished by the fact that most of us manage to go to sleep successfully and wake up successfully and make it through the day in one piece.

Sleep was considered a dangerous time to the ancient rabbis. It's a time of vulnerability, of loss of control—sort of a practice death. A dalliance with whatever creatures of the night lurk in the corners of the forest or of our own subconscious.

I don't fear sleep anymore. I did, for a long time—I had a nice healthy stretch of insomnia for years after my mother died. But now that I'm a parent, exhaustion tends to win out. My own sleep is a welcome gift. Yet there is a fear that still lingers, a different kind. When I go in to check on my kids when they're sleeping—to adjust the temperature in their room or pull up their covers before I put myself to bed—I check to make sure that they're still breathing. Every single time.

I once mentioned this to a friend in his early sixties, the father of three twentysomething kids. "How old are they when you stop checking to make sure they're breathing when they're asleep?" I asked. He shot me a penetrating look. "You never stop," he said.

As much power as we have over our children's lives, as much as we are able to control who they are and how they will be in the world in some respects, there are certain important things that we can't control. Ever.

I try not to get too spun out about this. I mean, first of all, probability indicates that they'll wake up in the morning, that their sweet little hearts will keep beating like they're supposed to for a long time, that they won't have an aneurysm or get hit by a drunk driver or become addicted to heroin or fall—or choose to jump—many stories from the roof at a college frat house. But more to the point, I try not to get too in touch with the abject terror that I always carry with me, somewhere, because being afraid can't change that outcome, not from here, not with the information I have now and maybe not even if I had more information with which to work.

It's a paradox, right? As parents, in some respect, everything we do matters, and can have real consequences for our kids—or, at the very least, can either support them into their wholeness or become grist for the therapy mill. From day one we're aware of the weight of the covenantal responsibility that sits on our shoulders: Is the baby eating enough? Where do we move the knives now that she can reach that drawer? When should we call the doctor about this fever? What does losing my temper teach my child about her worth, about her own sense of saffety?

But on the other hand, we have no power whatsoever.

For Rabbi Jeremy Kalmanofsky, this loss of control echoes powerfully with the metaphor of God as parent. But not the God who is in charge, responsible, forming covenants—rather, as Kalmanofsky writes,

> *Since my first child was born . . . the theological trope of God's parenthood speaks to me very differently. I hear its spiritual power—not through my experience as a powerless child—but in my experience as a powerless father. . . . For, God, I love these small people more than I love my own life. God, if I could only keep them*

from bullies and nightmares, unreturned love, leuke-
mia, bulimia, depression, bi-polar disorder, cocaine, car
accidents, flunking math, AIDS, rapists. . . . [19]

In a moment of profound fear about his children's fate, he prays, "God, keep us from the wrong place at the wrong moment." He listens carefully for the answer. The reply he hears, somehow, from the divine is not a comforting one: "*I cannot do that.*"

The God in which Kalmanofsky believes isn't one who can magically protect us from our own mistakes, our own misuse of free will, from the laws of nature as they've been set in motion. As much as Kalmanofsky aches to be able to protect his children, he cries, as he hears the God in whom he believes cry, "*I cannot do that.*"[20]

Ultimately, we can't control everything. Or most things, maybe. Terrors come and creep into our bedrooms while we're asleep, and sometimes there's nothing we can do about it.

There's a certain kind of heartbreak in parental love, I think, even in the most privileged, optimal situations. Even now, with my small children, I wonder how much of their lives is hidden from me. I wonder how much fear and passion and ecstasy I don't or can't see. I wonder what happens in their minds and hearts when they're not with me. Shir is almost two as I write this, and even though he's starting to talk a lot more, and even though I can understand his nonverbal language when he's anxious or secure, happy or off his game, I still can't ask, "How was your day? What did you experience? What do you dream about at night? What happened that felt thrilling and new and what made you feel weightless and terrified?" I can only guess, infer, to witness along with him the best I can when we're together, and to know that I'll never have the full picture.

And Yonatan at five is able to articulate more clearly if he wants to, but he's still building the emotional vocabulary to do so—it's part of my job to help him with this, of course. But even so, he's an internal processer. There are corners of his life that he just doesn't *want* to open to us. He's a sociable kid, but, at heart, he's the sort of introvert who doesn't always feel like sharing. Sometimes he does choose to tell me what's on his mind. But sometimes he informs me, directly and clearly, that he'd rather not talk about how his day was, or what he's thinking or feeling. And I know that part of my loving him involves not trying to break into his emotional space with a crowbar.

Even kids who are verbal processers don't tell their parents everything, at any age—God knows I didn't. Even the most articulate and engaged kids have an almost infinite number of experiences, perceptions, thoughts, and ideas throughout their day that they never really think to share, or that they ultimately choose not to tell their intimate authority figures. We'll never really know, fully, what our children go through, even when we love them with all of our heart, all of our soul, and all of our might—and we'll certainly never be able to control all of their experiences of the world.

Sure, we can try to instill our values and hope that they help inform how our children filter and respond to the things they encounter, but ultimately, it's out of our hands. One of the most difficult aspects of our work as parents is the letting go, acknowledging the limits of not only our power, but even of our understanding.

I think the recent generation of helicopter parents emerged in an attempt to try to stave off the terror that comes with admitting that, in the end, there's only so much we can control.

Bravely facing the fact that things will happen to and for our children that we can't control means accepting that we will feel sadness, hurt, anguish, frustration, or even joy on their behalf. Rabbi Abraham Joshua Heschel talks about "divine pathos,"[21] the sense of pity or sorrow that the transcendent feels in the face of human suffering. For him, the God who cries, "*I cannot do that*"[22] has to allow humans to muddle along with the circumstances they have been given and the world as it exists today, and feels the pain of watching the people Israel struggle with their side of the covenant. God, as understood by Heschel and Kalmanofsky, does not intervene in history, is not a genie who swoops down to prevent us from getting a flat tire or protect us when the Third Reich knocks on our door. The world has been set in motion, and the human condition, the frailties of our finite bodies, and our capacity to use or misuse free will are part of the package, for better or for worse. To some degree, even God has to let go and let the great dance of trial and error take place down here. The nature of human volition means, inevitably, that we will occasionally experience pain and affliction—and divine pathos means that that pain reverberates through the cosmos. "What is the image of a person?" Heschel asks. "A person is a being whose anguish may reach the heart of God."[23]

We're not God. But I think this sense of pathos is familiar to many parents. Perhaps the fact that our own children's anguish touches us deepest of all is reflective of our attachments, our limits as creatures of flesh and blood—but the anguish is there. We watch them grapple with self-determination, with existential fears and the constraints imposed upon them, and it reaches our hearts. And we, like the God of Heschel and Kalmanofsky, may sometimes be able to offer our children comfort and consolation—but sometimes we just have to sit with our pity and sorrow, and sometimes with the fear and uncertainty about what tomorrow may bring.

My friend John's twenty-four-year-old daughter lives at home with him. She has bipolar disorder, and for now her living with her dad is just for the best; John is hopeful that at some point in the future she'll be able to live independently, but not yet. It's hard, though. It's really hard.

One day last May, his daughter came home with blood gushing down her arm, crying that she had screwed up, she was sorry. She had tried to kill herself again. But she had a change of heart and made it to her dad in time, and thank God they were able to save her life.

Later, when he was alone, John finally had some space to let out all of his own terror and suffering and anger. He cried and he prayed, beseeching God for an answer. Why does his precious child have to suffer like this? *Why? Why?*

He wasn't expecting an answer, not really, but he told me that he heard one, coming from deep inside himself, like a boom, like a whisper. "It wasn't something I heard in my ear," he said. "It was the still small voice speaking into me, somehow."

What he heard, barely perceptible but powerfully clear, was, *The world was not made for you.*

"At first," he told me, "I thought, well, *that's* kind of harsh. It felt a little bit like getting slapped." He paused for a moment, and took a deep breath. "But as I reflected on it, I realized maybe it just meant, you know, I don't get to decide or understand how this all works. My job is just to love this girl unconditionally, and everything else just really isn't up to me."

The Book of Job tells the story of a righteous man who, for no reason he can understand, is suddenly faced with a number of tragedies. He loses all of his wealth and is stricken with a serious and painful illness. His children die. He spends most of the next thirty-seven chapters trying to figure out why this is all happening; his friends show up, each offering clever explanations, none of which really feels right. And then, finally, the character of God appears, out of a whirlwind, a mighty storm. And this is what God says:

Where were you when I laid the Earth's foundations? Do you know who fixed its dimensions or who measured it with a line? Onto what were its bases sunk? Who set its cornerstone when the morning stars sang together and the divine beings shouted for joy? Can you tie cords to Pleiades or undo the reins of Orion? Do you know the laws of heaven or impose its authority on Earth?[24]

The character of God goes on and on in this vein for some time. The message is, basically, "Listen, if you didn't create the universe, perhaps its logics and meanings (if, in fact, there are any) might be beyond your grasp." We have science, but even so, science can't explain everything. It can't explain the mystery—the mystery of what, and most certainly not the mystery of why.

Sam, the son of my friends Phyllis and Michael, was six when he started complaining about pains in his leg. Eventually they found out that the culprit was about as bad as it could be: leukemia. Sammy was a bright, wonderful boy with every privilege and access, beloved not only by his family but by an expansive international community. His parents asked everyone they knew to send superhero photos to his hospital room so that the boy could understand how many people were holding him in their hearts. Almost immediately, the walls were covered, floor to ceiling, with pictures. But even with care of all sorts pouring in, his illness and treatment nonetheless took a real toll on the family. Sam's dad, Rabbi Michael Sommer, wrote on the family blog:

For 18 months, I feared that my hands were never clean enough to be near Sam, that my runny nose wasn't just allergies, but was something that would force me to stay away from my Sam for an unforgivable week or more. I feared every bath, that I hadn't prepared him well enough, that dirty water would reach his central or picc line and complicate matters beyond our control. I feared that his chemotherapy would kill him, taking out his heart, a kidney or his liver. When he was microwaved, like leftover mac-n-cheese, for three days in a row in preparation for his bone marrow transplant, I watched and dreaded the cataracts the radiation would have caused if he had reached sixteen. For 18 months I lived in fear that I would somehow contribute to the cause of Sam's death. . . .[25]

So much was out of Michael's control, but there were a few things that he could control, and he did his best to handle those things with diligence—his own germs, the picc line, all of the factors in Sam's environment that might expose him unnecessarily. His anxiety was fueled by the vicious, overpowering love that he felt for his son.

But all the love in the world isn't always enough. As he wrote in that same post, despite all of his attention and care, the worst happened anyway. "Somehow, beyond our wildest dreams, we did everything right and yet Sam still died."[26]

Ultimately, we're powerless.

We beseech God in the *Haskeveinu* to lay us down in peace and rise us up in life because we're not so sure we're going to be able to do it on our own. The reason that the song I sing to Shir—"tomorrow we'll get up and see how the day arrives at the end of each night"—is such a powerful lullabye is because some part of us isn't totally certain that we will.

Maybe there isn't a why—a coherent answer to be found somewhere, in some corner of the heavens, about why a bright, loving child is beset with mental illness, or cancer, or one of many other horrors or even just everyday struggles. If there is, I don't know what it is. Regardless, though, John, and the voice that came out of the whirlwind to him, has it right. We're never going to be able to control everything, or to understand suffering, if indeed there is even something to understand. All we can do is to wrap up our fear and anger and pain and breathe it out as love for the children who have been entrusted to our care.

In the end, we need to be able to sit with the loss of control, to embrace it. We can't dominate the future—we have to submit to it. Would I make different parenting decisons if I knew what challenges my kids would face next year, in five years, in fifteen years? Absolutely. I mean, presumably. I mean, I don't know.

But it doesn't matter. We only have the information available to us right here, right now, and the knowledge that the future is unsettlingly uncertain. Being afraid about tomorrow will only make today harder and inhibit our ability to be with them and parent them now, according to the needs and demands of this moment, right here. My job, each day, is to do what I can to uphold my half of my covenantal relationship with them and to help protect them, nurture them, and equip them for the big world outside. To treat the uncertainty as a gift that propels me to try to embrace all of the now with both hands, to whatever degree I can—knowing that part of the realistic truth is that I'm going to be bored, distracted, and frustrated with my kids sometimes, because that's part of parenting. And that I'm going to take plenty of moments for granted, and that I have to be compassionate with myself and to know that this is how it goes.

Part of living in the now means not carrying that heightened awareness of the uncertainty of the future with us everywhere. Ugh, that would be terrible, and really, really not good for our kids—a clingy parent who relates to them from a place of fear that maybe they'll get cancer someday? That would be awful. So we need to own the fact that we don't know how this story will go, to admit that if we're not driving this car, we really shouldn't be trying to steer from the passenger seat.

Our kids need us to let go of what we cannot control. As Kalmanofsky writes, "We want our children to become fully realized human beings, living embodied images of God. They can attain this only if our power to protect them is limited, even as our love is infinite."[27] We need to sit back, to let their story unfold—and to let our children discover for themselves the extent and limits of their own power. They can't grow if we're micromanaging their present and future. We have to parent them, to love them, and to know that we can't control their story—either the glories or the sufferings. As much as I (truly, actually) wish that I could . . . I cannot do that.

The poet Rainer Maria Rilke wrote, "We need, in love, to practice only this: / Letting each other go. For holding on / Comes easily, we do not need to learn it."[28] Accepting our powerlessness as parents is heartbreaking. And terrifying. But facing it honestly frees us up to be here in the now, loving our actual children today as they need us, today.

For better or for worse, that's all we've got.

CHAPTER FIVE

Speaking on Your Heart

Prayer as Lullabye, Lullabye as Prayer

◆

Back in the day, when I was a rabbinical student and then a new rabbi, flush with a sense of mission as a Servant of the Lord and feasting regularly on Torah study, I wrote and spoke often about the importance of a regular spiritual practice. I preached (literally) and lived the principle that a meaningful, regular discipline was necessary to live in connection with and in service to the divine everythingness that flowed through and bound us all. For me, that meant praying the fixed liturgy three times a day, as is traditional—morning, afternoon, and night.

Then Yonatan was born. My prayer life tanked. I just couldn't—didn't—open the prayerbook. I couldn't figure out how to cross some imagined divide between myself and the practice that used to anchor me. I was a working mom in the first year of a new job, and even after Yonatan's sleep ostensibly evened out, there were always nighttime issues of some sort—growth spurts, teething, developmental funkiness. Even the ten minutes it would take to put on my prayer gear and do my thing just didn't seem to fit in the rush and push and exhaustion of our harried mornings.

I felt like a failure, a fraud with a dirty secret. The rabbi who couldn't figure out how to pray, the feminist clergyperson who quit when things got hard.

Adrienne Rich's classic *Of Woman Born* has a lot to say about how men's ideas about motherhood have hurt a lot of real, live women throughout history. At some point, in a section on the idea that mothers are supposed to be emotionally pristine—never angry or frustrated—she cites a nineteenth-century mothering manual that advises young mothers to pray when things get hard: "Do you say it is impossible to govern one's feelings? There is one method, a never-failing one—prayer. . . . The inward ejaculation of 'Lord, help me to overcome this temptation' may be made in any place and amid any employments. . . ."[1] Or, to put it in more contemporary language: Ladies, feeling resentful or frustrated? Just pray the bad feelings away! Then all your problems will be solved! Rich rips into this idea, citing it as a prime example of toxic messaging that belies the messy reality of caring for small children and sets women up for failure. Telling women to pray when they feel angry, promising that everything will just magically get better, denies the realness of their struggles and fails to give them useful tools for coping.

Not long after coming across this passage in Rich's book, I

was bathing Yonatan, who was about a year old at the time. Nir was out of town; naturally, my child intuited that his father getting on a plane was his cue to start projectile vomiting everywhere. The previous few days had been rough, and included doctor's visits and several rounds of schlepping both laundry basket and kid down the three flights of stairs to our building's washer/dryer to get the sick out of clothes and linens.

So there we were, in the bathroom, both of us exhausted from the illness and nighttime wakeups. He was being fussy and whiny and difficult and I was feeling like I had been stretched past my last nerve; I was on the verge of losing it. All I wanted to do was scream or run away or crawl into the Cone of Silence Where Nobody Needs Anything from Me—and then I remembered the Victorian manual's somewhat condescending suggestion to pray. And I thought: Well, heck. It couldn't hurt.

I whispered, almost inaudibly, *Help me.*

Suddenly, everything shifted. I could feel myself relaxing, and finding some compassion for my sick kid. I remembered that I loved him and that I was the grown-up and that we were going to be OK.

Did God (whatever that is) answer my prayer (whatever that means)? Did I, just by acknowledging the reality of my situation, effect within myself an attitudinal change? Is there any reason that the answer can't be "both"? This act of prayer reminded me that, as I understand the world, I wasn't totally alone—I was connected to something bigger than myself—and that this moment, even if it was difficult, wasn't mine to bear in isolation. And yet, I don't think that my experience contradicts Rich's critique of the troubling messages sent to mothers about what is or isn't acceptable to feel—the frustration and anger are real. But for me, at that moment, a retrograde handbook's chirpy instructions proved surprisingly transformative.

What is prayer? For me, the starting point in trying to answer this question is a biblical story that's actually, maybe not coincidentally, deeply connected to parenting.

The Book of Samuel tells the story of Hannah, a woman who, when we meet her, is in a state of deep depression. She's been struggling with fertility issues and she's feeling no small measure of despair—the text tells us that she was "bitter of soul."[2] At a certain point during a family feast, she gets up from the table, goes off by herself, and begins to cry, hard. I can only imagine it as that sort of deep, cathartic weeping, that moment when all the stuckness and pain crack, that moment when you hit the breaking point and just can't keep it together anymore. She's standing over to the side, sobbing, when she "increased her prayers before God. . . . Hannah spoke on her heart."[3]

In other words, prayer is speaking on the heart. It's a means to express something of our deepest selves, and not only naming it, but offering it up to the great beyond.

Whether or not you think of yourself as someone who believes in whatever might be called "God," I'd like to suggest that there is power to this. I don't think you need, necessarily, to know to whom or what you're praying in order to pray. Sometimes you can just . . . pray. And see how it feels.

If meditation can get us centered in the present moment, prayer can engage that presence, draw from or offer it up, or do both at the same time. Meditation is the work of the breath, of the stillness of the mind. Prayer is, as the Jewish tradition puts it, "work of the heart."[4]

This work of the heart often emerges from the hardest spaces. Sometimes it comes out of that moment when you're at the edge of your ability to cope and there's someone small for whom you are responsible who needs more from you than you feel you can possibly give. Sometimes it comes out of grief or despair or fear or anger or disassociated numbness, or an overwhelming feeling that doesn't quite have a name yet. Or from a bunch of those things all at once.

Hannah pours out everything that's been stopped up inside and allows herself to feel whatever she needs to feel—in this case, she lets herself cry. Perhaps all our prayers are open expressions of resentment, desperation, hope, gratitude, wonder, frustration, or many of the other things a person might feel when he or she is up to the ears in it. Rich objected to the Victorian manual because she felt it demanded that mothers push aside their hard, uncomfortable feelings. But real prayer doesn't do that. Nor will it magically fix everything. Prayer can help you to name what's happening, and to pour it out to the great transcendent beyond—to turn your isolated feeling into something that connects you, that binds you to something bigger.

It is this outward offering that turns "feeling feelings"

into prayer: We don't just experience them, we offer them up, to someone, something. We say, "Here, can you hold on to at least a tiny piece of this anger, frustration, and despair for just a second?" We connect our heart to the great infinite everythingness, the gushing, pulsing stream of life within and around us. We reach out. It's about tuning in to that which interlinks us all, that which is found within and between us.

Whatever it was that Hannah said, it was good enough. In fact, she's considered the greatest model for prayer in the Jewish tradition. Hannah didn't pray at a designated time; she didn't have a special language or formula for her words. She just said what she had to say, when she had to say it. And saying it helped her, healed her.

This might be something all people need. And we parents, whose lives are so governed by the needs and demands of tiny, snuggly little dictators and a myriad of factors out of our control, may need it even more. Most parents have woefully little time to sit in extended contemplation. Prayer—including spontaneous prayer, offered up for a brief moment while holding a baby in one's arms or bathing a fussy toddler—can offer a means of doing that work in a more spontaneous and ongoing way.

When you start to think of prayer like this, suddenly there's room for it in the corners of your life. During the chaos of the morning when you're trying to get everyone out of the house except *Where did you put my keys!?* At the grocery store, when there's a Mach Four tantrum happening at your feet. In the middle of the night, as you rinse the vomit off the beloved stuffed animal. When you're walking down the street with a baby in the sling on your chest, a diaper bag on your back, a sack of groceries in one hand and a hysterical older kid slung over your other shoulder. (Not that I'd know *anything* about that.) Those times when you most feel like you're at the last straw of your patience, when you just can't anymore . . . speaking on your heart can change the game. Even just murmuring the words "This sucks" can change everything. And when you do it with the intention of giving the feeling away . . . well, there's the door to spiritual transformation.

For me, after months of feeling guilty about not being able to pray in the way my tradition prescribes, and then having that moment of bathing Yonatan, I realized that I had, in fact, been doing something like prayer for a while. Prayer doesn't have to always be a plea for help, it can also happen when we speak our hearts in moments of wonder—those radical amazement moments, those times when we're able to look at our kids and think: Wow.

After all, in the words of Rabbi Abraham Joshua Heschel, prayer can be a "humble answer to the inconceivable surprise of living."[5] That is to say, a means of articulating the moments of awe.

And this manifests in all sorts of ways. I realized that the lullabies I would sing Yonatan over and over on the days when he was out of sorts, difficult to soothe, had taken on a liturgical quality. The repetition of these melodies created the same sort of hypnotic rhythm I was used to in my prayers, and that the same message—*I love you*—underlies them both. When I figured that out, I began to sing him (and then his brother, Shir, when he showed up) some of the one-line verses from Psalms, set to gorgeous music and meant to be repeated over and over as a sort of mantra. I sing them songs of hope and trust, of holding steady when fear is present and real. I sing them secular love songs that communicate the same things, and I offer these things to and through my sons, to the miracle that happened to allow them to come into existence as themselves.

In Genesis, it says that God created human beings *b'tzelem Elohim*, "in the divine image."[6] So to some degree, when I sing lullabies and liturgy of love to my children, I'm reaching out to the divinity within them—and perhaps, through them, to the divinity that encompasses but also transcends them, transcends us all. I want to teach my children about awe, praise, thanks, and how to ask for help, and I'm using resources both from within my tradition and from outside it in order to do that.

These days, my relationship to prayer—and my life in general—has a lot less structure and a lot more flow, and spontaneous expression, than I ever imagined would be the case. This pretty much goes against everything I had been trained to think about spiritual practice, both as a young adult and then, later, in rabbinical school.

Jewish tradition mandates a fixed prayer practice; the

silent, standing prayer that should be said in "serious concentration"[7] takes a number of minutes to complete, and should not be interrupted—"even if a king greets a person [while they're praying], he should not answer him, even if a snake winds around his heel."[8] I believe the liturgy was intended to force you to engage in a modality that most of us don't, naturally, on our own. It demands that we take time out of our own regular lives to step willingly into a mindset of connection, of reaching toward the holy—and to be changed by the process.

I took my prayer practice seriously. Even when I didn't make it to the communal morning service (which was, uh, a lot of the time), I would pray at home, with my prayer shawl and my tefillin (that is, phylacteries, special leather boxes containing parchment with Torah verses, affixed to one's head and arm via leather straps) and the words of the prayerbook would burn through me. It only took about ten minutes most days, anyway, and afterward I felt like it *did* something—as though my soul had just had its teeth brushed.

And then here I was, the exhausted mother of her first child, and I just couldn't bring myself to set aside the few minutes necessary for fixed prayers. It wasn't that there wasn't time—realistically, the child napped. It just wasn't what I chose most days. Some of this may have been that I was tired and overwhelmed, but I don't think that's all that was going on.

The liturgy, rather than feeling like a retreat from my battles in the big world, began to feel something like a prison—some of the time. The words just weren't always the solace they used to be. I mean, sometimes they worked. But sometimes I just couldn't bring myself to go there.

Rabbi Jane Kanarek articulated some of this when she said, of her infant son, "I feel so connected to Lev that I feel much less connected to the liturgy."[9] Another friend admitted somewhat sheepishly that holding a sleeping baby had begun to feel much more like worship to her than sitting with the prayerbook. For a lot of us, the irrevocable changes to our hearts and lives that come with having kids have major implications for our spirituality.

I don't think that necessarily means that "women's spirituality" or "mother's spirituality" is *necessarily* different, or is categorically different, from that of men's. I have male friends who, since becoming dads, have begun asking the same kinds of questions that I have about their prayer lives. I have female friends who still, after children, found tremendous depth and meaning in the same spiritual practices that had nourished them prior to becoming mothers—whether sitting meditation, regular prayer, or something else. For some of them, their relationship to that practice changed, as did what they pray for, but having that space to open themselves up on a regular basis was, as one friend put it, an anchor in a time when everything else was shifting so quickly. Their spiritual practice became a touchstone to find themselves and to connect to the divine—to clean out the copious internal gunk that accumulates when we're doing the hard, hard work of parenting, which pushes us to grow in so many directions at once. Some of my friends talk about saying the liturgy while nursing or bouncing a kid on their knee to keep the munchkin entertained, others talk about the precious time they take, sneaking off and stealing moments of privacy.

But the fact that some of my friends' external prayer lives stayed more consistent than mine did when I first had a kid doesn't mean that a lot didn't change for them, too. The experience of caring for children is transformative for a lot of people, and those transformations have implications that one doesn't always see in the classical literature—to say the least. The ideal and "required" forms of traditional religious practice don't necessarily work, or may not even be viable, for parents. If you're not allowed to interrupt your prayers for a snake crawling up your leg, what do you do if a baby blows out her diaper? Or is crying, or screaming for your attention? Or is about to do something dangerous or otherwise inadvisable? What's more important—your kid, or the conversation you're having with the divine?

Jewish law suggests that you should not hold a child during prayer, lest she disturb your concentration,[10] that you should not kiss your children in synagogue so as to instill in yourself the idea that no love compares to love of God.[11] If your child is crying, you should indicate to the child—without speaking—to stop crying, and if that doesn't work, you should walk away from her so that her crying does not disturb your prayer.[12] Another source reminds fathers not to hold a diapered child before afternoon prayers, lest he become soiled and miss the start of services.[13] All of this leads one Orthodox rabbi I know to remark that, as a result, he doesn't pray if he's alone with children.

Obviously, traditional Jewish law wasn't written for or by those who are in the trenches of intimate care of small children. There is a not-very-implicit assumption that someone else, somewhere, is in charge of the sticky, huggy, needy, emotional little humans that, evidently, impede a person's ability to live a life of spiritual service. Spirituality and children are placed in opposing, incompatible spheres, and women are relegated, along with the children, away from wherever it is that they're keeping the spirituality.

The idea that caring for children could be a core, crucial, even cornerstone aspect of one's spiritual and religious life, that loving and caring for them should be integrated, somehow, into one's spiritual and religious expression—well, it's totally absent from this thinking. And this absence isn't specific to Judaism. Rather, it's the norm in a lot of corners of the religious world. For example, a friend who is an Episcopal priest admits that "most of us Christian parents (at least during liturgy) try to shush our children to keep them from 'disturbing' us or others."[14] Some churches and synagogues make efforts to be "family friendly," offering toys in the back corner of the worship space, babysitting, or separate kids' services in a different room. I both applaud these efforts and make ample use of them myself. But it's true that they continue to perpetuate this notion that grown-up prayer—the "real" spiritual life—is something that happens only when the *kinder* are otherwise occupied, that this kind of intentional spiritual connection cannot happen with children, or as I'd like to suggest, through them.

Sure, there are exceptions—evidently Rabbi Shneur

Zalman of Liadi, the eighteenth-century founder of the Chabad branch of Hasidic Judaism, would pick up his crying grandchild during his own prayer and tell his son that a prayer which cannot hear the cry of a child is not a prayer.[15] But statements like this are aberrations, things about which a founder of a radical movement must instruct his son, since the culture in which they live doesn't take for granted that a distraught baby rightfully interrupts the recitation of liturgy.

Across cultures, more often than not, men have been the authors of authoritative rulings and women have been at home with children. In some places, women were part of, say, a monastic tradition, but then generally not mothering at the same time. The reasons for this are usually socioeconomic, but at the end of the day, there are a whole set of experiences, issues, questions, and types of thinking that come out of doing the work of parenting that have not been integrated into classical discussions of prayer and religious practice in general.

I wonder how various religious traditions might have formulated their approaches to prayer (and everything else) if they had been thinking about the realities of parenting small children from the beginning. And I wonder what these traditions could look like if the questions, challenges, and types of thinking that parenting opens up were taken seriously and brought into the conversation, even at this late date.

Liturgy scholar Lawrence Hoffman writes,

> *Imagine a continuum of spiritual behavior, with the normative men's prayers at one end. The official Jewish record of spiritual striving, that is the rabbinic literary*

corpus, records only that end of the spectrum. . . . *It is as if women walked through history carrying spiritual flashlights from which there emanated only infrared wavelengths, in a world where an automatic light detector recorded only ultraviolet. Whenever the flashlight threatened to reach the ultraviolet spectrum, it was deemed as malfunctioning and taken away by the light keepers in charge of ultraviolet transmitters. Meanwhile, a detached observer of social behavior in general would record (from time to time) traces of infrared radiation, but having defined light according to the other end of the spectrum, it would never occur to anyone to call it light, record it in detail or treat it seriously.*[16]

In other words, Hoffman suggests, the people in charge of recording and formulating Jewish religious expression—the folks articulating Jewish law and lore—didn't have the capacity to understand women's spiritual experiences, in part because they had already defined legitimate spirituality as something else entirely.

Part of me is ambivalent about this analogy—I'm not convinced that women as a category are spiritually different from men in some essential and necessary way. But on the other hand, for most of history, women's lives and experiences have been very different from those of men, and, as a result, their spiritual perceptions and expressions may have been, too. Of course, not all women in all times and places have been involved in the intimate care of small children, but many have, and for most women throughout history, that very work has characterized and shaped their experiences of the world. It's certainly true that the messiness, the complexity, the interconnected active loving and specific types of thinking that go with caregiving create glorious infrared expressions.

Some of these expressions have been recorded by history. *Tekhines*, for example, are prayers for women—and, critically, often by them—that were written in the seventeenth to twentieth centuries in the Yiddish vernacular. There were prayers that marked the daily flow of living, and others that consecrated moments in an early modern Jewish woman's life—prayers to be said while baking bread for the Sabbath, for a healthy pregnancy or an easy labor, for children at various points in development, to be said when one's husband was traveling. Yehudit Kutscher Coen, an eighteenth-century Italian Jew, for example, wrote a prayer asking God to "prepare sufficient milk in my breasts that I may nurse [my child], and grant me that I may raise him to be in awe of You."[17] And nineteenth-century Central European liturgist Fanny Neuda prayed for a son leaving home: "Spread Your protection over him, shield him and surround him in Your great kindness. Nurture and strengthen within him every lofty emotion, every good intention, every remembrance of paternal guidance that is imprinted on his soul."[18] Today, Jews of all genders find these prayers very powerful and meaningful as a lens for their own spiritual expression.

And, of course, some contemporary parents have composed their own *tekhine*-like prayers. For example, Hava Pinchas Cohen's "A Mother's Early Morning Prayer": "Grant me," she prays, "the courage to soften my expression / so that each of my children may / See his face within my face / . . . and the darkness that is ingrained / Within my face—cover it with light / that my patience not run out. . . ."[19] I know someone who keeps this piece posted on her fridge because she doesn't have time to pray in any traditional sense, but she has found that seeing this on a regular basis helps focus her interactions with her kids.

But as lovely and meaningful as these prayers can be, I still feel squeamish about the implicit idea that women have their own private, home-based spirituality while baking the bread and caring for the kids, and the so-called real action is over by the men and the more "official" means of holy expression. I'm also wary of simply adding, "and women's spirituality IS as valid as men's!" It's problematic, over here in the twenty-first century, to bind certain means of doing things to specific genders, and I'm not sure I like the notion that there's a spectrum of practice—that one is either infrared or ultraviolet—as opposed to the idea that our various expressions of spirituality can overlap, interact, and shift.

Obviously, these days, plenty of men parent and bake bread, plenty of women find their home in traditional ("public") religious expression, and same-sex couples and folks with all sorts of different gender identities both parent and connect spiritually in a myriad of ways. Some people with better time management skills than I manage to bake bread, parent, *and* make it to communal prayer services now and again—and, critically, may find deep spiritual gratification in all of these things, some of these things, or different things at different moments. There really isn't a binary, there doesn't have to be.

Sure, one could say that there's a tension. On the one hand, when people talk about religious disciplines, the implication is that a person has a practice—prayer, meditation, yoga, and so forth—that gets done every day (or three times a week, or whatever) no matter what, and that the practice Does A Thing: It changes you. On the other hand, well, what parents know better than anybody is that theories and principles are great, but when living the messy reality of life, they don't necessarily serve. And more than that, there might be profound truths to be learned from embracing the flux, the flow, as needed, as appropriate. What if there wasn't just one way to do this? What if a lot of ways were the right way?

In my case, I'd been carrying around the ultraviolet light, defining my religious expression by traditional rabbinic yardsticks, certain that it was the only possible option. It had served me well for a long time. But once I became a mother, I became more aware of other manifestations of light and discovered that, though sometimes my old means of spiritual practice still served me, there were other possibilities for connecting to the transcendent that, at times, spoke more deeply to who I had become, what I needed now.

Sometimes my prayer—offered up with intentionality into the great beyond—involves deep contemplation of my son's ear, or arm. Sometimes it can be found in just being present with him, in snuggles or smiles or games or fielding questions. Sometimes I manifest it in a tiny cry—"help!"— barely perceptible even to me, when my kids' needs are too big and overwhelming, when they're acting out, or even just when they're being normally spirited and rambunctious despite the fact that Mommy didn't sleep so well last night. Sometimes prayer involves other things—singing with them, singing words of liturgy to them, saying words of liturgy to God.

I don't think that how my prayer life has changed signifies that there's no wisdom to the tradition; rather, who I am and what I need has changed. Spiritual practice needs to be wide enough to accommodate expansions and contractions, shifts and changes in how we exist in the world. It has to be big enough for all the love we receive and give out. "You should not kiss your children in synagogue in order to instill in yourself the idea that no love compares to love of God"? Are you kidding me? There is enough room in our spiritual expressions not only for all of the love, but also for the hectic, distracted chaos that so often defines parenting, if we let it—if we are willing to expand our understanding of how much, how many kinds of, light exists in the world.

Every Friday night, after lighting candles and before drinking wine (or grape juice, really), I take each of my children's heads in my hands. I place my hands on the sweet and precious skulls of my little boys and whisper in their ears—as Jews have done with their children for centuries—"May God bless you and keep you. May God shine divine light upon you and bring you grace. May God lift you up and bring you peace."[20] And then I kiss their little heads, willing as hard as I can for my words to be true.

I think of prayer as a communication between me and the Great Everythingness; it's an offering up, and sometimes a sort of a receiving. Blessing, on the other hand, is something that we can give over to other people—something we bestow on one another, rather than on the divine. It has that same sense of lifting up from our deepest selves, that feeling of bringing something out from our heart—but instead of releasing it to the transcendent beyond, we give it to someone else.

For example, in some corners of the Jewish world, it's thought that a bride has unique powers to bless others on her wedding day. If you go to a traditional Jewish wedding, you might find the bride sitting off to the side before the ceremony, having little one-on-one encounters with her guests as they arrive—offering them her wishes that they receive grace, that they have a year full of joy, that they meet the spouse that is longed for, or that the child in utero develops healthily. That what this particular heart seeks, it will find. She might put her hands on their heads or their shoulders because something important is flowing. In Islam, travelers are considered particularly powerful in blessing—people will often ask a person to pray for them when he goes on the road. Muslims also consider those who are ill to be particularly full of blessing—to visit the sick is to be, as scholar Shabana Mir puts it, "enveloped in mercy."[21]

If prayer is about opening up yourself and offering yourself to the transcendent, blessing is about offering something to others. It's about allowing love and holiness to come from or through you, and letting it spill out onto other people.

It's about allowing our own divine image to reach out and touch the divinity in someone else.

I think we do this all the time with our kids, consciously or unconsciously. Like a lot of parents, I make up silly songs for my children, stealing the tune shamelessly from whatever kids' song, liturgical melody, or advertising jingle pops into my head. Sometimes it's because an obsessed-over toy needs a theme song, sometimes it helps me amuse myself and them while we're walking somewhere, sometimes it enables me to articulate for them what's happening right in the moment—which, by the way, is a great trick, because as I sing-describe what's happening now, I can also sing-describe what I want the kid to do next, and sometimes it actually works ("Yonatan is putting on his socks, putting on his socks, putting on his socks . . ."). And a lot of the time it's just how I express my love for them—this love that is so big and overwhelming that it spills out every which way, in hugs and whispers and songs and, sometimes, when I'm able to still myself, just breathing in the unspeakable magic of them.

Beyond my free-styled ditties, there are a few songs that have become canonical—in that I sing them to my kids a lot. Parents, of course, are controllers of the family canon. These songs have a lot of verses—one about how sweet they are, one about how brave they are and generous, loving, loved, beautiful, gentle, and nice. I started singing Shir's song when we were in the hospital together during his first day of life. I cribbed a melody traditionally sung on Passover, since he was born on seder night. It wasn't that I knew, objectively, that he was going to grow up to be kind and generous and brave and gentle and wise and loving (though, I mean, duh, he was obviously the most advanced one-day-old that had ever existed in the history of the planet). Rather, I wanted to bless him, somehow, with these attributes. To invoke, and to keep invoking as time passed, all of the goodness in the world, and for that love and power to be available to him, somehow. I didn't set out consciously or intentionally to bless him, but I now realize that's what I was doing, and what I continue to do every time I sing him that song or one of a million others that come out when my heart is popped open. I wanted to bless him and bless him again with strength and gentleness and generosity, to open myself as a vehicle through which something beyond me might be able to pour.

On a lot of levels, the impulse to bless my children is the same as my impulse to pray to the divine—that sense that there's something in me that needs to be released—whether in gratitude, in petition, in awe, in love, in hope, in joy. Regular, fixed prayer is about creating the space to do so when you maybe wouldn't necessarily have the time. And spontaneous prayer is, for me, anyway, about that moment when the proverbial pot boils over, or when I remember to lift the lid.

How does it work with blessing, though? Is it something that comes from within us, or can we be sort of a pipeline through which all of the love of the universe can pass? I tend to think of myself as a channel—I'm just the vehicle through which all the goodness arrives at my kids, or anyone else I can pour it on that day. My friend Laura says she thinks "it's more like a rain barrel. It comes from somewhere else, but it has to collect in you for a while." That collecting, she says, happens when you do things that fill up your heart and soul. Prayer. Meditation. Time with people who recharge your batteries, talking about things that matter. Listening to that one song that makes you cry a little bit with joy every time you hear it. Making art or crafting or that long walk out in nature.

The Sfat Emet, a late nineteenth-century Hasidic master, talks about the relationship between a cistern (*bor* in Hebrew—that is to say, a rain barrel), and a wellspring (*be'er* in Hebrew). He says that there is a "holy point into the very nature of every creature. . . . This is called '*your* cistern,' for it is attached to the body. The more you take the light of the soul upon yourself, drawing your deeds to follow this light, the more spirit and soul is added to you. This opens the wellspring that flows without end." That is to say, as we fill up our respective rain barrels with things that nourish us, and as our actions reflect our own light, we open up a wellspring—an endless, flowing source of this love and goodness, and we can draw from it and let it pass through us.

Sometimes parenting drains me, of course. Sometimes it's frustrating and hard and exhausting. But when my proverbial cistern is full, I'm able to be more present, more engaged, to think more creatively, even through the hard parts. And sometimes parenting fills me up—the snuggles and the laughter and the innocent sweetness just gets me, right where I need it to. And sometimes, when I am feeling most connected to my kids, most blown away by the sheer impossibility of them, I feel that wellspring open up. And that's when blessing, or something like it, starts to flow.

Sometimes what comes out is something that I offer to that which I call God—a thanks, a hallelujah. That's prayer. Sometimes it comes out as something I just want to pour over my children, in love and in joy. That's blessing. Maybe that which cascades through me, as a wellspring, or comes up from within me, as a cistern, is something that I give back to the great interconnected whole of everything. Or maybe I try to bestow upon the specific sources of my infinite love. (It feels infinite, of course, when I'm in wellspring mode—because it's coming through me, from Infinity.) Or maybe it's both of those things?

I wonder if the reason that the bride is thought to give special blessings is because, at this powerful, liminal, transformational moment in her life, she is more open than usual. A bride is a person in the chrysalis stage, melted down, poised on the edge between an old life and a new one. Her openness means the beneficence can flow more easily through her. If that's the case, then how our hearts are broken open by our children may fuel the power of our blessings as well. It's said that there is a tradition in some parts of West Africa of parents whispering into the ears of their sleeping children, "Become who you are."[22] That's blessing. That thing we do when we linger in the doorways of the rooms when they sleep, murmuring our hopes for their happiness and safety? That's blessing. And when we do it with intention, actually meaning to harness all of the exquisite, overwhelming love in the world and to offer it unto our kids? It's pretty darn powerful.

Giving blessing probably isn't the exact same thing as the

directing of spiritual energy, in the vein of the Japanese practice of Reiki, the Hindu practice of Shaktipat, Christian traditions of laying of hands, or in the customs of some North African and Middle Eastern Jewish kabbalistic masters. This energy work involves the directing of one's life force—the Chinese character for qi, this energy, alludes to the vapor rising from boiling rice. As Kirsten, my acupuncturist friend, describes it, it's "a fine essence emerging from and inherent to each thing that nourishes and sustains life." But maybe it's not so different, either. Reiki and other spiritual healing traditions use the language of serving as a conduit, and people who do this work talk about the cistern versus wellspring thing, meaning the difference between drawing from your own stores versus serving as a channel through which the energy of the universe can pass.

I took a Reiki class once, and the teacher claimed that the reason that it helps when we kiss our children's boo-boos is that it actually transfers our qi, our life force, to them, when they're a little depleted. That is to say, maybe the act of kissing our children when they're hurt is another form of blessing. In its own way.

This isn't to say that our blessings have the ability to keep our children protected from harm, that just because we whisper to them for health and happiness we can automatically make it so. Or even that if we intentionally draw spiritual energy from the great flow of all of life and offer it to our children we can protect them from illness or tragedy. I *wish* my theology worked like that. It's probably a more comfortable way to live. But I do believe that channeling that love in the direction of our children can help them to thrive and flourish, to feel, palpably, that they are the recipients of beneficence. It's not an inoculation against misfortune or suffering, winds or drought, but it is one means by which we can water the soil in which they are planted so that their tender little sprouts can arch toward the sun.

And the other reason I bless my children is because I can't not. It enables me to do something with all the overflowing love I have for them, to allow all my hopes and wishes for them to *go* somewhere, to let this profusion spill over into them. The love comes, it seems, to me from someplace outside my small self—this love is so much bigger than I am. It's like the way I find compassion even during those long, exhausting nights when it seems to be just about dried up. When I let it stream with intention, I am offering my children blessings. And hopefully, just as my own prayers help to nourish me, and fill up my own cistern, my blessings to them can nourish them as they make their way, inch by inch, as they grow and unfurl their gorgeous branches up against the sky.

Recently, I've found myself returning to traditional prayer.

I mean, I've been taking my kids to services every Shabbat morning since Yonatan was born. As soon as he was old enough to be mobile, I had to figure out how to focus on the service while he zoomed around me—I'd bring toys and books, and deploy them strategically to keep him amused during the parts of the service that demanded the most focus. Most of the time it'd go OK, though there was an anxiety in my praying that hadn't been there before, that vigilant feeling of knowing that he could start screaming or trying to do something stupid or dangerous at any second. That's still, so often, what my Shabbat looks like—Yonatan and now Shir get toys, I try to pray, if there's a kid's service or a playroom connected to the service we're attending (I've been part of a number of different communities in the years since Yonatan was born), we go to that after I get through with the most mandatory parts of the liturgy.

Even though it's certainly more hectic to bring kids to synagogue, I've never considered leaving them at home so that I could have a more focused experience. Nir has offered, a number of times, to forsake his own precious time of solitude (he's a secular Israeli, he's not so into joining us at services) to take them so that I could pray in peace. But setting aside the idea that I want my kids to grow up feeling like synagogue is one of the places where they feel at home, where they have cultural and ritual competence, it's really that I just *want* them there. It would feel weird to leave my heart at home when I go off to have a "spiritual" experience. Like, if I can't bring my little loves with me when I go to pray, I'm not sure my prayers could be what I'd want them to be. So it's distracting to bring the kids, yeah. But it's also centering and rooting.

Recently—now years after Yonatan was born, years during which daily prayer slipped away from me, when prayer became instead a more fluid, spontaneous, integrated thing—I've found myself returning to my daily practice. I've started pulling out my prayer shawl and phylacteries after dropping the kids off in the morning. I've been starting my workday not by checking email, but by connecting through this ancient, familiar process. I sit on our little balcony in the spring breeze, put on my ritual gear, and start in on the morning liturgy. It feels . . . good. Really good. Even with my mind, as always, bouncing around like a crazed monkey, struggling to find stillness inside words of praise and humility—still, prayer does its thing. And afterward, it feels like it used to. I am finding myself, now, choosing to pray again. My experience of prayer now is, in some ways, different because I'm different, but the muscle memory is still all there. I had missed it.

For me, after Yonatan's birth, formal prayer wasn't how I filled up my proverbial cistern, at least during the week. But now things are shifting, and I know they'll shift again. I can see how different forms of expression are going to ebb in and out of my life at different times, and I can trust the river to take me wherever I need to go.

There's a story about Menachem Mendel of Kotzk, a nineteenth-century Hasidic rabbi who became known as the Kotzker rebbe. As they tell it, he was walking down the street and asked the first guy he saw if he was going to put on tefillin—phylacteries—the following day. The man says, "Of course!" Like, of course he was planning to pray in the morning, what kind of question was that? And the Kotzker, known to be a little cantankerous at times, snarls, "Idiot!" He asks the second man he sees the same question, and the man gives him a nasty, defiant look and says, "No!" "Sinner!" cries the Kotzker. He asks the third guy, who considers the question for a moment and says, "Huh. Let's see, I mean, I put them on yesterday morning, and I put them on this morning, but . . . Well, I really don't know yet what tomorrow will bring, or what choices I'll make then." The Kotzker finally smiles approvingly. "This," he says, "is a wise man."[23]

The Kotzker Rebbe meant that every time one performs a commandment—as he most certainly thought one should—it should be a chosen, intentional action, not something done on autopilot. But this story also, maybe unwittingly, illustrates a broader point—that is, living a spiritual life with integrity requires us to be aware that we don't yet know what tomorrow will bring, or who we'll be then. We grow, we change, we need different things at different times. I was shocked when my daily prayer practice failed to compute, when it started to feel like a stifling burden. And I was amazed to find that having Yonatan helped me discover that there was a whole other room next door in which prayer and spiritual expression were full of a different set of possibilities—and that those possibilities would put my entire philosophy of Jewish law in the blender along with my practice. I'm not sure what will feel right tomorrow, whether I'll put on either literal or metaphorical phylacteries, or not. Or how I'll think about any of this stuff—alone, with my kids, through my kids. But I know that my love for them changes me, and that it has radically altered how I understand what prayer is, and can be. And that it has, utterly, inexorably, changed what I pray for.

CHAPTER SIX

Exhaustion and Poop

Finding Meaning in the Body Stuff

———◆———

When my friend Laurence had his first kid—a few years before I had mine—he shared one of his newfound secrets with me.

"You know you're a parent," he said, "when you find yourself saying, 'Oh my God, that's *SO* disgusting!!' at least once a day."

But not long after Nir and I became parents, we decided that Laurence wasn't right, not really. That is: Your definition of what's disgusting changes awfully quickly. Before kids I would have been pretty freaked out by coming in close contact with someone else's bodily waste. (I am, I admit, especially squeamish—pet owners, medical professionals, and many other kinds of nonwimps probably don't have this problem.) But even for me, these days, if I find myself saying, "That's *SO* disgusting!" it's because something really *special* has happened.

Parents of small children are pretty routinely deep in the muck of their kids' bodily stuff. After diapers (so many diapers), there is a whole universe of potty training, accidents, reminding or dragging a not-very-mindful kid to the loo on a regular basis, and the time it takes to get the hang of using toilet paper correctly. Not to mention all the days when a kid's digestive tract is just a little bit out of whack, or when the flu comes to town in force. There's the bloody nose that let loose all over the living room rug, the vomit on the couch, the boogers on the sweater, and I'd rather not think about what the kid with bronchitis just coughed into my hair. Caring for the next generation creates lot of reasons to have a good enzyme-based stain and odor remover handy.

It is, of course, just part of being a human being. We consume food, waste matter comes out. Occasionally it comes up the other end before it gets digested. Sometimes we get sick and the body produces mucus. Sometimes we get cut and we bleed. These are things that bodies do.

I had a revelation about this, though, when Yonatan was probably nine or ten months old. I was changing his diaper, yet again, and suddenly, some liturgical language asserted itself.

There are a lot of different kinds of *brachot*—benedictions of praise to God—in the Jewish tradition. We acknowledge the divine as the source for everything before and after eating, when going to the ocean, meeting an old friend, seeing a rainbow, hearing either good or bad news, meeting a non-Jewish king, before performing a commandment, and smelling a fragrant tree—just to name a few. One of the *brachot* that tends to make folks giggle the first time they hear about it is meant to be recited after using the loo—either urinating or making a bowel movement. (Yes! There's a potty blessing! There's a blessing for *everything*. We, as a people, are nothing if not thorough.)

This post-bathroom liturgy is translated as,

> *Blessed are you, God our deity, sovereign of the universe, who formed humans with wisdom and created within them many openings and many hollows. It is obvious in the presence of your glorious throne that if one of them were ruptured, or if one of them were blocked, it would be impossible to exist and stand in your presence. Blessed are you, God, who heals all flesh and performs wonders.*

It's a way of saying thank you for the fact that our body works well enough to do its business. This blessing encourages us to experience awe in the face of our physical complexity. It is an expression of our awareness of the myriad of things that have to go right in order for us to continue drawing our next breath—and the breath after that. The fact that we're able to eliminate waste is a wonder in its own right, a miracle worthy of our respect and gratitude.

It's fascinating to me that it took me as long as it did to make the connection between this blessing and changing diapers, potty training, and even accidents. I don't know of any sources that talk about what it might mean to say this benediction after changing a diaper—which is a pity, because this is yet another place where the tradition has a powerful, important tool to help refocus our intention as we perform the labor of childcare. But it's also another place in which the tradition's blind spots are laid bare; the people writing Jewish law weren't involved in the day-to-day care of small children, so perhaps it simply didn't occur to them to deploy this blessing in this way. Their limitation, though, doesn't have to be our own. The treasures of the tradition are here for us; it's up to us to go digging in the storehouse and find the light that's just waiting to shine into our lives.

Managing our kids' waste is sometimes smelly and sometimes unpleasant and sometimes a hassle, but when our kids poop, it's because things are going right—even though, for one of a thousand reasons, things could conceivably go wrong. Their bodies are working, and this is an extraordinary source of grace. There are so many levels on which we are helpless to keep our kids safe and healthy; for me, thinking of this blessing in the context of my kids' bathroom doings reminds me, once again, how vulnerable I really am. It's not necessarily a comfortable feeling, but it takes me into gratitude. There, in the midst of changing yet another diaper or dragging a reluctant toddler to the bathroom one more time, we can think of this benediction and experience a fuller appreciation for the moment at hand.

Of course there are still times when I find myself saying, "Oh, wow. This situation is *particularly* disgusting." But now, sometimes, I manage to remember that, even so, absolutely gross isn't so bad.

———

When I've shared the story of Yonatan's coming into the world with birth professionals—doulas, midwives, OBs, and the like—they always wince a little. "Ow. That must have *really* hurt," people who regard childbirth as totally routine often respond. That is, my body had forked over a particularly nasty combination of back labor—in which each contraction felt a little bit like an axe bludgeoning my lower back—and unusually strong, fast contractions that gave neither me nor poor Yonatan much chance to breathe. Even five and a half years later, I remember pounding the walls, screaming in excruciating pain that couldn't be assuaged by anything until the baby came out. Fun times.

Shir, on the other hand, did not put me through back labor. Compared to how things went with his older brother, bringing Shir into the world seemed, you know, doable. Not pleasurable, mind you, but during the couple of hours I was first unaware that things weren't progressing and then waiting during a hospital shift change for my new midwife, I was able to be a bit more engaged in the process than I had been the first time around.

As it turned out, my labor with Shir happened on the first night of Passover, the night of the first seder. While everyone else was sitting around tables of symbolic foods, retelling the story of the Israelites' exodus from Egypt, I was doing my best to actually breathe through the contractions that wracked through me in waves. I tried to use them as a sort of a meditation on the parting of the Red Sea; I tried to offer contractions as prayer. I became the waters parting impossibly, again and again. I sang a line from

Psalm 118 that appears in the Passover seder: "Open for me the gates of righteousness. . . ." As I labored, I got the intimation that the person inside me might be named Shir, or song—mostly for the Song of the Sea that the Israelites sang as they passed over the parted waters. We were planning to call him Ori (my light), but somehow the name Shir kept asserting itself as the waters of my body opened and opened again.

I know that I'm pretty unusual in that I had some time during one of my labors when I was able to—and chose to—think what might be easily classified as "spiritual" thoughts. Most of the people I know didn't much go there when the contractions were rolling, and, to be honest, I don't know if I would have thought to either if it hadn't been one of the biggest nights on the Jewish calendar.

What I do know is that, at a certain point, the "I" that I usually think of as calling the shots in my life was not in charge. My body, and the baby inside my body, were working together, and my own sense of will and self were merely along for the ride. I could bring my self onto the train that had already left the station, or I could resist, but that train was already careening, fast, down the proverbial track. Certainly, I'm lucky to be able-bodied and to have lived free from serious illness throughout most of my life—there are plenty of people who, for various reasons, have much less control than I usually have over what happens inside my body and where I put my mind. In labor, though, I was forced to engage with my body in a different way.

As my friend Rabbi Emma Kippley-Ogman puts it,

A lot of people say things like, "I found God in labor and delivery, that's the powerful presence of the divine." It was not for me—[labor] hurt and was hard. But it was a gateway into a different kind of experience of the divine that I didn't anticipate. Labor moved me into a physical space—it wasn't intellectual. I was out of my head and in my body in a way that maybe I was when I was rowing crew in college, putting all my energy into physical rather than intellectual activity.

I was taking a dance class yesterday, and I found that I couldn't do the steps correctly when I was thinking about other things. I had to put my mind away. Labor was like that, too. At one moment during labor, the midwife said, "take all that energy you're putting into your voice and put it into pushing." It wasn't disempowering; it was her way of saying: you can do this with your body, if you let it. For me, it was a transition into a very physical existence; I usually live in intellectual and emotional existence. My connection to the divine in these months [since my baby was born] has been in this physical experience.

For Emma, the relentless physicality of childbirth, and then, later, nursing, has been an opportunity to *be* in a more raw way than she was used to. Bringing her full selfhood into her body opened up, for her, unexpected aspects of living.

Obviously, there are plenty of parents—fathers and mothers—who were never pregnant with their children, who didn't deliver them, either vaginally or via cesarean, and many more who don't nurse, for a host of reasons. There are also people who get pregnant and give birth who don't identify as women, which invites other kinds of conversations about the physical and psychological experience of reproduction. In any case, for many of us who do go through pregnancy and delivery, it turns out to be a game-changer on a lot of levels.

For some, like Emma, it's about learning how to inhabit the body as they never had before. For others, gestating a whole new human being generates an awe and respect for what the body can do—its possibilities, and perhaps also its limitations. Sometimes that can be difficult, and painful. My friend Danielle had an emergency cesarean and, because of unusual medical circumstances, her son was delivered under general anesthesia. Rather than birth being a time of embodiment, she says, she "felt completely betrayed by and disconnected from [her] body." She reflects, "I had done my prenatal yoga, eaten organic, taken my natural birth classes—I followed all the rules and for the first time in my life that did not matter."[1]

My friend Judy learned the same lesson—that the body doesn't always follow the mind's plans—when she went into labor with her second child only twenty-five weeks into her pregnancy. Gavriel, like his older brother, was eventually delivered by cesarean, and for Judy, after a few uncertain days in the hospital trying to put off his entrance into the world, learning that he'd need a surgical birth demanded yet *another* level of acceptance. As she put it, "Labor is a lot about surrendering to the process, and then [given how premature Gavriel was] surrendering to something else that I didn't think was going to happen. At the moment when I thought I'd surrendered completely, I realized that I had to surrender to something else." This letting go, for her, required putting a tremendous amount of trust in her team of medical professionals—both those who delivered Gavriel and those who cared for him during the months he spent in the neonatal intensive care unit, before he could come home.

For Judy, this process of yielding to the reality in front of her—that her body was not doing what she had hoped or planned for it to do—has brought her new and surprising appreciations. For, she says, "I don't think my body is any less miraculous because it couldn't deliver vaginally. I had an ideal [for birth] that I thought I was going to have. Now I know that this is also a beautiful way for babies to come into the world that saves lives. It's let me see that the things that I didn't hope for in my life have been magical and precious and amazing."[2]

For Jenny, pregnancy was a watershed moment in being able to find respect for her body, perhaps for the first time. As she tells it,

> For many years, I had warred with my body for a variety of reasons. I have an intestinal disease. I had really struggled with how I was supposed to look. The experience of being pregnant, to me, was healing. I guess I felt that I was doing something important and that, in order to take care of this baby-to-be, I would have to be kind and compassionate to myself. That judgmental voice that was so amplified in the past softened. I found

I could direct a compassion that I had always directed outward more inwards.[3]

Even after preganacy, she was able to maintain that sense of compassion—to remember that her body did many things right, that it was a great gift, and that she herself was worthy of the same gentle caring that she usually offered to other people in her life.

For Mary Martin Wiens, too, her body's alterations through pregnancy became an exquisite opportunity for insight. She had struggled for some time with the aesthetics of her postpartum body—it was no longer lean and taut, as it once had been. One day, though, her three-year-old tried to pat her stomach, and she had a revelation. Rather than lamenting its squishiness, she invited him to feel how soft it was, to trace his fingers over her stretch marks. "Isn't it beautiful?" she asked. "Yes!" he squealed, in delight. Afterward, she reflected:

We journey from a seed in our mother's womb until we are planted in the grave with ever-changing bodies. Time scratches out its passage across my looks and the looks of all those I love. All our lives, our bodies manifest evidence of an existence marked by gains and losses. We gain and lose pounds, muscle, bruises, teeth, and hair. We lose elasticity and gain wrinkles. We gain scars. Our bodies process and carry our experiences, not without complaint, but with an unfailing perseverance that is worthy of both gratitude and honor. And one of the

*very great privileges of this life is to cherish the bodies of
those I love through all their gains and losses for as long
as I get to have them. We do not get to have those we
love forever. In that final losing, every turn of the head
and expression of the face becomes poignantly precious.
So, may I have eyes to see them now. . . .*

*My being here in this world in a body matters. The
touch of my hand on a shoulder, my hug, the soothing
sound of my voice, and the warmth in my eyes are ir-
replaceable to those who carry me in their hearts. Our
physical presence here matters, no matter its shape.*[4]

The lines of Martin Wiens's story are etched on her belly,
a testament to the love that she carried inside of her for nine
months and to the love she gives, and receives, today.

Our physical presence here matters, no matter its shape.

My brother is a marine conservation biologist. He did a lot
of his doctoral research on the Galapagos Islands, at the
Charles Darwin Research Station. Back when he was in
graduate school and I was in rabbinical school, we had a few
inane conversations in which he would try very earnestly to
convince me that evolutionary science was truth, and I'd
have to explain to him that, uh, I agreed with him. Religious
fundamentalism has so thoroughly co-opted the conversation in America that my own brother, when he saw me getting excited about observing the Sabbath and learning Torah,

assumed that I had thrown whatever information I might ever have learned about dinosaurs out the window.

Eventually I managed to communicate, in a way that he could hear, that my becoming religious didn't mean that I had stopped believing in evolution and the scientific method.

"Science and religion aren't mutually exclusive," I finally managed to get out. "They just deal with different questions."

We can't talk about the body without talking about biology. And sure, there are areas of religious thinking—particularly a few streams of Christianity—that distrust science, or that regard the body as problematic. But a lot of us religious folks, from a lot of different backgrounds, regard our embodiedness as a gift, and consider the things science can teach us about it to be crucial—even if science is limited, naturally, by its sphere of interest.

We're mammals. Babies are made when two cells come together, and then when that new cell successfully divides into other cells and eventually implants itself (or is implanted by doctors) in the uterus. A whole host of things then happen that are the result of millions of years of evolutionary processes. Cells divide and divide again, creating eyes, bones, kidneys. The pregnant body changes in order to support this life growing. If everything goes well, eventually a healthy new human being emerges, vulnerable but ready to take on the challenges of life on the outside.

It's all science, definitely. But damned if it's not also a miracle.

When I think about the number of things that have to go right in order to make a human baby, the mind boggles. But even more than that, it's that this *person* comes out as a *person*. And yes, yes, genetics conspire to give her this nose and that hair texture and possibly even this predisposition toward music or alcoholism. But there's something else there, something else that, to me, anyway, can't be explained coherently by science. It's something about the *spark of life*. The magic of this specific individual person's existence, who and how they are in the world, which can't necessarily all be charted on a genome.

Sure, maybe ten years from now geneticists will be able to explain why my firstborn child is a dreamy introvert and my second kid is the kind of nutty extrovert who's likely to be that last guy to go home at the end of the party in college. But I am skeptical of science's ability to explain why this child is *Yonatan*, this one is *Shir*, how they are themselves deeply and fundamentally, more than just a handful of traits lined up in order. Stuff about, I don't know, the soul? I don't have a very coherent idea of what that word means or whether or when to apply it, but there's something important about the process of us getting made, and the uniqueness of who we are, that, at least as far as I can tell, smacks into the realm of mystery. As the Talmud puts it, "there are three partners in creation: God, the mother, and the father."[5] Perhaps there's a spark of something beyond what we can measure with science, sperm and egg notwithstanding.

As the artist and activist Glenn Marla puts it, "There is no wrong way to have a body."[6] Rather, these fragile encasements in which we live may look like all sorts of different things, and may be capable of doing or not doing all manner of things. Not every body can walk. Not every body can digest certain foods without becoming ill. Not every body has an immune system that works optimally. Not every body can impregnate, or get pregnant. Not every body managed to make the difficult journey from zygote to fetus, from fetus into healthy baby. Not every healthy baby makes it to adulthood.

Of course, we need to grieve our losses, and even to grieve over what our bodies can and can't do, what they do and don't offer. We must allow ourselves space to feel sadness about the times our bodies, and the bodies of those we love, didn't or couldn't or can't do everything we wished that they could.

But for those of us who are here, now, our physicality is important. And there is no wrong way to have a body. Even the bodies that don't do everything we wished they would are a means of transmitting love and care and connection. When I remember my mother, I think of her hands. Her voice. How she was *Janie*, in her incomparable Janie manner, even when she was sick. Even when her body, riddled with cancer, was struggling to function. Even when she wasn't herself, not really, anymore. Her physical presence still mattered.

There's a Hasidic teaching: Another person's *gashmiyut*, physicality, is your *ruchaniut*, your spirituality. It's true in general, I think, and certainly for those of us who raise children. Our intimacy with our children is relentlessly physical. It's about their sleep cycles, and ours. It's about the kisses, the drool, the snuggles, the little tushy squeezes. It's about the raspberries we blow into their armpits. Are there other people in your life into whose armpits you blow raspberries?

When my kids were newborns, they each felt like an extension of my own body—an organ that could occasionally be handed off to others but was practically still part of me. (Research actually indicates that some of a fetus's cells stay on in the birth mother's body—cells travel through the placenta into her heart, lungs, kidneys, skin, and brain and remain there, part of her, for the rest of her life.)[7] And now, even though they're older, even though they no longer drink the food that my body once made for them, even though we no longer sleep in the same bed for all or part of the night (most of the time), the boundaries between my body and their bodies is still perilously thin.

They know exactly which crook of my neck or chest is theirs in which to bury their faces when they're in need of comfort. I know exactly how every patch of their skin looks, and will notice quickly if there's some rash or irregularity, or even a new beauty mark. Shir still sticks his fingers in my mouth, Yonatan climbs on my back, Shir pushes me from the front, everybody's tickling and wiggling in a pile. Yonatan still tries to get me to pick him up and carry him sometimes, even though he's getting heavy. Everybody thinks it's pretty funny to try to lick my cheek.

My friend Laura—who is an adoptive mom—encapsulates my experience pretty beautifully when she describes her own:

> Yesterday in church, Benjamin crawled up on my lap, all 7-year-old, 47 inches leggy 50 lbs of him, and tried to nibble my nose and suck on my fingers. I kind of can't imagine feeling any more raggedly or deeply inter-molecular with him. He touches my eyes. I can still adjust him so he kind of fits on my lap like a folded up lawn chair.
>
> And yet. Nursing, I don't know that one. Birthing, I don't know that one.
>
> But two a.m. yanked out of deep sleep by a rising pitch MOMMMMMMMMMMMM-eeeeeee like an ambulance siren, stumbling to the door, "what IS it baby," "I dropped my pillow."
>
> "Here you go." And then I bury my nose in his neck and hair for a minute in a combination of exhaustion and deprived REM and consolation and rage and com-fort. If I can't dream, I at least get to smell you.
>
> He treats my body like his personal jungle gym. Leap-ing off my bed to wrap arms and legs around me while I stagger not to fall down. Gentle with my body, please, baby. Easy on your old mom. That is not safe. Yes, I can still hold you up. Yes, I see how you're a baby possum. Om nom nom.
>
> Does he actually pull calories out of my body through my nipple? No. Is he feeding off my life force? Constantly. It's his job. It's my job.

He's used his fingers to open my eyelids. MOMMY STAY AWAKE! There's no boundary. He believes my body belongs to him. He'd live in it with me if he could.

Some days I would live inside my children's bodies if I could, make a nest of them and sleep down in the snuggle. Some days I desperately crave a bit of bodily autonomy, need to just not be touched and prodded and poked at, to live in my own skin alone for a moment. Some days they would live inside my body. Not always on the days that I would choose.

Our love for our children is profoundly embodied. The ways in which our physicalities are intertwined with theirs are just an outward representation of what happens on so many levels, of all the levels on which our lives and selves and their lives and selves become entangled, enmeshed—joyful, hard, wonderful, and complex as that so often is.

Walt Whitman wrote, "I sing the body electric / The armies of those I love engirth me and I engirth them. . . . And if the body were not the soul, what is the soul? . . . If any thing is sacred the human body is sacred."[8]

If anything is sacred, I think, it's the care and connection between bodies. The holy entanglement itself.

There is a pretty strong history of people engaging in physically demanding practices as a means of achieving some sort of profound spiritual state. Fasts, for example, are a feature of many world religions; walking on fire is practiced among some Hindu, Buddhist, and Taoist groups; throughout history, some Christians have engaged in various forms of self-mortification. Even something as small as the Jewish practice of binding leather straps on the arm can radically impact awareness during prayer. When you do certain things to your body, it changes your perception and your experience of reality in various ways, some more subtly than others.

One practice that's found in many traditions is that of sleep deprivation. Benedictine monks would try to limit sleep in order to maintain "spiritual vigor";[9] a number of Buddhist traditions use sleep deprivation as a technique on long meditation retreats to help practitioners attain unique states of consciousness, and even enlightenment.[10] The sixteenth-century kabbalists began the practice of staying up all night the eve of Shavuot, the holiday celebrating the revelation of the Torah, and engaged in various other kinds of night vigils, using techniques like studying with their feet in a pan of cold water to help maintain wakefulness.[11]

For most parents of younger kids (and a lot of parents of older kids, too), the prospect of voluntarily staying up all night—or even past ten p.m.—is one that could only inspire bitter, derisive laughter. Many of us were up last night, anyway—if not for a baby who still can't go eight hours without feeding, then for a two-year-old who was suddenly thirsty, a four-year-old who had to pee, a seven-year-old with a particularly unsettling nightmare, a nine-year-old with the sudden onset of a nasty virus. I'm grateful that, today anyway, I'm not in the desperate state of my friend Russ, who, as the brand-new dad of a newborn, just lamented, "What do you do when you have a gigantic tub of cold brew coffee in the fridge that you're scared to deploy because what if you need to sleep at a moment's notice? But *what if you need to be awake at a moment's notice?*"

Given that physically demanding spiritual disciplines are meant to push the mind into a nontypical state, might it be possible to think of the physically exhausting work of parenting young kids as opening up some sort of sacred gateway to the liminal? That is to say: We're getting up already. Might we be able to use that to our advantage, somehow?

The other night, Shir started crying around midnight, probably just as I was getting into the nice, juicy REM sleep cycle. I stumbled over to him, whispered in his ear, stroked his back. Nothing. Still crying, still asleep—a nightmare, probably. I picked him up and held him. He was still asleep, still upset. It was a warm, early fall night, so I carried him out to our little balcony, which for some reason has calmed him down since he was a baby. And, sure enough, once we got outside into the cool night air, he relaxed, tucked his head into that one spot on my chest. We sat there for a while, his little body pressed against mine, hearts beating against each other, out against the stars.

This sort of thing happens less and less frequently these days. During the day, he runs around like a maniac, stopping periodically to exuberantly hurl his arms around me, but he's gone almost as quickly as he has come. He doesn't really even want to be carried around. Even the times when it'd be more useful for him to be in my arms—like, say, crossing a busy street—require a whole negotiation about his independence and my requirements for his safety and whether he'd actually hold my hand the whole time or whether I should just grab him and haul him, squirming, to the other side of the road.

So the other night, we sat there outside for a while. I knew that it might be a very long time indeed until the next time I had him snoring lightly on me, fist curled into my hair. I looked at the stars. I breathed in the scent of my child, felt his chest rise and fall, took in the heavy quiet of the night and the tree and the sky. I was tired, but everything around me seemed both crisp and blurry. It was a moment of deep stillness.

Some of the literature on night vigils talks about the spiritual possibilities that they offer. For example, one of the first accountings of kabbalists studying Torah all night on the eve of Shavuot, in Adrianople, Turkey, in 1534, culminated when Joseph Karo, one of Jewish history's most important legal codifiers, entered a trance and a heavenly voice spoke through him, instructing him to move to the Land of Israel.[12] I never personally channeled anything during late-night Shavuot study, but interesting things did happen, I confess. Before kids, I was much more apt to participate in the full-night Shavuot program (after all, I could sleep all the next day and nobody would wake me or demand things from me). I'd join in with the teaching sessions my community would put together until some moment, around three or four a.m., when I'd suddenly feel a need to wander outside, alone, and meditate among the trees. Some really powerful things happened on those nights—undeniably mystical experiences, moments in which the gates of reality—or of my conciousness—seemed to open up, briefly, and offer me a glimpse of something on the other side.

Many Catholic thinkers place the value of the night vigils not in their ability to open you up to transcendent experiences, but to open you up to yourself, to God, on a different level. For example, Thomas Merton, the Trappist monk, writer, and contemplative, wrote about the ability of God to "search your soul with lamps and questions, in the heart of darkness."[13] A time to see all of the truths that we hide from ourselves, to lay them bare in the ringing silence.

With Shir, that night, and on so many nights, I didn't experience the skies opening up, an immolation into the divine. I also didn't feel particularly introspective; I didn't see it as a time to do deep inner work, honestly. But there's something else that night vigils with my kids allow me.

Merton, sitting watch in his monastery one night in 1952, beseeched, "God, my God, Whom I meet in darkness . . . I have prayed to You in the daytime with thoughts and reasons, and in the nighttime You have confronted me, scattering thought and reason. . . ."[14] Merton's rational thoughts had created a sense of order for him, a sense of his own priorities. At night, however, he felt much less clear: ". . . in this darkness I would not be able to say, for certain, what it was that mattered."[15]

I, too, am capable (some days, depending on the day) of feeling very certain and clear and rational during the day. At night, indeed, though, the urgency of my to-do list softens, and I see my life a little more holistically. But when I wake up with my children, I never, ever could find myself saying, "In this darkness I would not be able to say, for certain, what it was that mattered."[16] In the darkness, I am more certain than ever of what matters. This little heart beating against my chest. This sick child, cleaned up and consoled. This frightened boy, in need of my comfort, my reassurance, my presence, my touch, my love. My night vigils with my children are clarifying; my purpose is singular. I'm not trying to learn how their days went while I'm unloading the dishwasher, I'm not calculating how long we can stay at the park before we need to go. I'm not glancing at the ringing phone to figure out if it's a call I really should take. What matters is this little boy, with his head nuzzled into my neck, finally reassured, sitting with me under the stars. My night vigil is a vigil of love. It is, like so many other faces of my practice as a parent, a practice of love.

Brother Roger, the twentieth-century founder of an ecumenical Christian monastic community in Taizé, France, once said, "At times, prayer will be a burden to you. At those times, offer your body; your presence is your prayer."[17] Presence, I think, is often the prayer of parents.

Merton, on that long night in 1952, goes outside at some point. And he realizes something that I experience every time I get up to be with my children in the darkness: "Eternity is in the present. Eternity is in the palm of the hand. Eternity is a seed of fire, whose sudden roots break barriers that keep my heart from being an abyss."[18]

It's the palm of my hand that my children seek in the dark of night—my hand on their head, my body comforting theirs. The deep physicality of our relationship is part of its power, and part of what's sometimes so hard about it, too. Our selves connect through our bodies, and it is in the moments of touch and physical comfort that my barriers are broken, and that our intimacy feels most profound.

Probably there's some redeeming spiritual value to the exhausted hangover I feel the morning after an especially long night. Or maybe there isn't. But during those moments when they call for me—even when I'm so tired that I can barely handle another need, another call, even when I start to become convinced that my children nefariously coordinate the timing of their wakeups so as to obliterate my sleep completely—I am required, I am a comforter. I reach out for them, and somewhere, along the way, in the dark of night, I find their hearts. I find eternity.

CHAPTER SEVEN

Pecking Under the Table

*How the Magic of Child's Play
Can Infuse Our Lives*

———◆———

Nir and I had been dating for about a year when I joined him at his family Passover seder for the first time. His parents had moved the sofas out of the living room to fit enough folding tables to seat thirty people—grandparents, cousins, stray coworkers, whoever was hungry and wanted to come and eat.

The moment we walked in the door, my then-boyfriend was instantly buried under a pile of wriggling, giggling children who were all tickling him and laughing hysterically as he pretend-resisted and attempted to swing them in the air from his prone state.

Nir is That Guy. The fun one. The one who can wrangle one cousin's kid on his back while another is on his head, and make ridiculous noises while he hoists still more kids over his shoulders. The other grown-ups were sitting around, talking politics, gossiping, and checking their phones while Nir was flailing around, mock-begging for mercy.

He was like that before becoming a dad, and he's definitely like that as a dad. When he plays with Yonatan and Shir they all become delightful, rapturous lunatics. There is a freedom, an abandonment in how they are together—a full releasing of themselves into the moment, handing themselves over to hilarious spontaneity.

To be honest, I envy it.

It's not that I don't play. I've engaged in my fair share of elaborate scenes in which Monkey and Bear help Shir decide what to buy at the "store." I throw real and pretend baseballs with Yonatan; my legs have become airplanes for kids who fly above me in what is probably the closest thing to stomach crunches I've done in years. We tickle. We laugh. We build elaborate pyramids out of cardboard boxes.

But I think I have a harder time than Nir does in just fully relaxing into the play, engaging without worrying about how we probably should be getting to the bath now or whether it's time to take the veggies out of the oven. I just as often prefer to let the kids do their thing so I can have a few minutes to unload the dishwasher, which of course is legit— children can and should play on their own, test their own strength, resolve their own squabbles, and get lost in their own scenes without a grown-up hovering all the time.

But sometimes they want us to play, too—to not just let them find their own groove, but to participate with them. And too often I find I'm too busy, too calculating, trying too hard to multitask. I love the joy and freedom that happens when I finally get there, in play, with my kids. But what for Nir is second nature feels, for me, like something I need to consciously choose. And sometimes I really resist choosing it.

Psychologist Peter Gray reminds us, "Play should never ever be a duty; it should always be for fun. Play, by definition, is something that you want to do; so if you 'play' with your child without wanting to, you are not playing."[1]

I'm not the only one who struggles with this, it seems. I googled "play with my kids" today[2] and every single one of the results that came up on the first page had a title like "I Hate Playing With My Children!,"[3] "Play with my children? No thanks, it's far too boring,"[4] "Confession: I Hate Playing With My Kid,"[5] "Why Playing With Your Kid Can Be (Whisper It) a Little Bit Boring."[6]

Janelle writes a blog called *Renegade Mothering*, and she admits: *"Most of the time I **can't stand** playing with my kids."* One day she sat down to play Monopoly and found that:

> *Everything they do irritates the hell out of me. The way they slam the board when they're moving their tokens across it . . . the way they lean over and knock the money piles everywhere . . . the way Ava directs everybody's <u>every single move</u> . . . the way Rocket won't focus and rolls around constantly . . . the energy . . . the time it takes . . . all of it. My skin is crawling. I act terribly . . . telling them what to do, demanding they do things my way. . . . Demanding that they not act like kids. . . . As I'm doing it I hate myself.*[7]

A lot of her frustration is because her kids are just acting like kids. They don't keep the money piles ordered neatly, they get distracted, and their interactions aren't, well, very emotionally mature. The game doesn't proceed at an efficient pace. Janelle wants them to play, but on her adult terms.

Later, out of the heat of the moment, she recognizes this, and regrets the fact that her irritation interfered with enjoying the time with them. "I felt a yearning for that Monopoly game 5 hours after it happened," she writes. "I realized the beauty of what I missed *while lying in bed that same night*. Right now I feel the sacredness of playing a game with my non-stop director daughter and goofy distracted son. I feel it. I know it."[8]

Entering into play requires giving ourselves permission— permission to let go, permission for the game to not be played perfectly and for the money piles to get messed up, permission to be a fool, permission to let it be OK if we get to the bath a few minutes late today. It requires a willingness to jettison our usual goals and agendas to experience the process—it doesn't ultimately matter if we even get far enough into Monopoly to declare a winner. It doesn't matter if the tower is sturdy enough to stand unsupported. If it topples over, that's just an excuse to make a new one.

Getting into this mode is hard for a lot of us grown-ups, I think. I know it's hard for me.

As Tim Brown, CEO of the design firm IDEO, observed in a TED Talk about play, "when [adults] encounter a new situation, we have a tendency to want to categorize it just as quickly as we can,"[9] which, he observes, makes a lot of sense from an evolutionary standpoint. There were, for a long time, life-or-death stakes when we classified an animal as pettable or predatory, a plant as food or poison. These days, though, this tendency to classify can restrain us, inhibiting our sense of possibility. As Brown notes, when kids come across something new, they will "certainly ask, 'What is it?' Of course they will. But they'll also ask, 'What can I do with it?' . . . We've all told stories about how, on Christmas morning, our kids end up playing with the boxes far more than they play with the toys that are inside them."[10]

Kids are more interested in possibility than classification, in process than outcome. If we're having fun and don't actually finish the game, whatever, we had fun. If the box can be a boat, it's a boat. If it can be a train, or a stove, or a bed for Monkey, great. Spoons can become characters talking to each other, or swords in a swordfight, or airplanes. I have a very vivid memory of being six years old and stuck in the backseat of the car on a long drive. I picked up the umbrella that was rolling around in the back with me; it instantly became a very attractive doll, with a handle head, carrying strap hair, and a froufrou dress. She was an object within reach, and thus an available friend and playmate.

These days I find myself saying to my kids, more than I care to admit, "That's not a toy!" Usually it's because they've swiped my glasses or the filters I just bought for the heating system or are rummaging their sticky little hands around the cooking accessory drawer, and I know that soon there's going to be goo all over everything and if I turn my back it'll be a month before I find the can opener in the bottom of the toy box.

But still. When I reflect on it, I can't help but think of the first chapter of Antoine de Saint-Exupéry's *The Little Prince,* in which the narrator recalls a picture he drew as a child of a boa constrictor swallowing an elephant. He showed the drawing "to the grown-ups, and asked them whether the drawing frightened them. But they answered: 'Frighten? Why should anyone be frightened by a hat?'"[11] I try not to be *that* grown-up, the one who can't see the doll underneath the umbrella or the elephant inside the snake. But the truth of the matter is, I'm so often preoccupied by bedtime logistics or trying to remember that the broccoli is going to burn that I stop short of plumbing the depths in every drawing, in every kitchen utensil. I become the mom who tries to get her kids to play board games like adults.

But when we enter play with our kids—whether naturally or as a choice, as I so often have to make—we have the chance to shake off our habituated means of thinking and interacting in the world. We have a chance to see all the enchantment that can be found in a regular cardboard box. We can attempt to unselfconsciously release ourselves into the now, letting the wizard duel unfold however it needs to, engaging the Teddy Bear tea party on Teddy's terms, enjoying getting trounced and ridden on and throwing kids up in the air as they laugh and laugh and as you laugh and laugh. (And so what if the broccoli comes out a little crispy?)

Rebbe Nachman of Breslov, the late eighteenth-/early

nineteenth-century Hasidic teacher, sometimes instructed his disciples through allegorical stories. This one is known, for obvious reasons, as "The Turkey Prince":

A prince once became mad and thought that he was a turkey. He felt compelled to sit naked under the table, pecking at bones and pieces of bread, like a turkey. All the royal physicians gave up hope of curing him of this madness. The king grieved tremendously.

A sage arrived and said, "I will cure him." The sage undressed and sat naked under the table, next to the prince, picking crumbs and bones. "Who are you?" asked the prince. "What are you doing here?" "And you?" replied the sage. "What are you doing here?"

"I am a turkey," said the prince. "I'm also a turkey," answered the sage.

They sat together like this for some time, until they became good friends. One day, the sage signaled the king's servants to throw him shirts. He said to the prince, "What makes you think that a turkey can't wear a shirt? You can wear a shirt and still be a turkey." With that, the two of them put on shirts. After a while, the sage again signaled and they threw him pants. As before, he asked, "What makes you think that you can't be a turkey if you wear pants?" The sage continued in this manner until they were both completely dressed. Then he signaled for regular food, from the table. The sage then asked the prince, "What makes you think that you will stop being a turkey if you eat good food? You can eat whatever you want and still be a turkey!" They both ate the food.

Finally, the sage said, "What makes you think a turkey must sit under the table? Even a turkey can sit at the table." The sage continued in this manner until the prince was completely cured.[12]

The mastery of the sage is, obviously, in his ability and willingness to sit under the table with the prince, to peck and squawk together. That's how the relationship was forged, how they found a common language. I don't think we need to tease out all the pieces of the story—which was intended to be a parable of a Jew who had lost direction, spiritually—to see the implications for those of us who have been charged with the task of raising our own little princes, princesses, and occasionally mystifying turkeys. Sometimes the connection is only possible when we enter their worlds.

Shir went through a long phase recently when he would transmogrify, almost out of the blue, into a cat. We'd be hanging out in the living room or getting toward the end of dinner and suddenly he'd be on all fours, meowing intently. There was only one reasonable response: "Oh, *hello*, kitty! What a nice kitty! Can I pet you?" He'd meow and nod his head and come slinking up for scritches and snuggles. I don't know what the trigger was: whether he got bored, if he was feeling in need of affection or attention, or whether it was just, you know, amusing for him. These days he's more often a monkey—just as random, if a little bit less cuddly. He will just start answering questions with "Ooh ooh ah aah" and I have to figure out if I answer back "Ooh ooh ah aah!" or, if this time, instead of being mommy monkey I'm supposed to be mommy the human who loves this monkey—it depends.

Sometimes he's very directive. He's a monkey, but he'll tell me that I'm a horse—so I then have to assume the position and begin to whinny. Or I'm a tree for him to climb. Or whatever it is. When Shir is flying on my legs, he's really flying. The alchemy happens when I'm willing to enter his world, on his terms.

But in order for this to happen, I have to get down on the floor with him, to whinny or meow or woof or talk to Teddy or take building the Lego house very *very* seriously. I need to be with him under the table. That's how we find each other, how our common language is established and builds.

But I wonder if our relationship with our children is the inverse of Rebbe Nachman's story. Sure, to a degree, we're the sage who teaches the prince how to live in the world— we encourage our children to get dressed before leaving the house, to eat with their forks, and to do their toileting in the potty. We meet them where they are under the table and help them grow into the norms of our culture. But in another sense, maybe our kids are the real teachers, here. I learn plenty from sitting on the floor and meowing with Shir. I learn how to let go of my agendas and my classifications. I learn to be in the moment, in the silliness, to let it go off in unscripted directions, to enjoy the spontaneous acts of doing, without a goal, without some higher agenda. Shir, my little

Monkey-Kitty Prince, is, so often, my teacher, not the other way around.

When we're able to really let go and immerse ourselves in play, sometimes we can start to experience what's known as flow, that sense of being so fully engaged in an activity that everything else seems to fall away except what we're doing.

When we think about flow—being "in the zone"—and play, both, we often think of them as this effortless experience, something that just *happens* to us. We're just working or running or talking to someone and suddenly we find ourselves hyper-focused, super-engaged, fully immersed in what's happening. But psychologist Mihaly Csikszentmihalyi, in his book *Flow: The Psychology of Optimal Experience,* argues that much of flow's power is in the fact that we are almost *forced* to give our full attention to it. For, he writes, "The best moments usually occur when a person's body or mind is stretched to its limits in a voluntary effort to accomplish something difficult or worthwhile."[13] It's then that we're able to feel this immersive feeling of absorption. He explains,

> *When all of a person's relevant skills are needed to cope with the challenges of a situation, that person's attention is completely absorbed by the activity. There is no excess psychic energy left over to process any information but what the activity offers. All the attention is concentrated on the relevant stimuli. As a result, one of the most universal and distinctive features of optimal experience takes*

place: people become so involved in what they're doing
that the activity becomes spontaneous, almost automatic;
they stop being aware of themselves as separate from the
actions they are performing.[14]

In other words, what gets us into a powerful, pleasurable mental place is that we're facing challenges that demand our attention. And when we're able to give ourselves over to them completely, things start to flow of their own accord, to find a spontaneous groove, and we lose all self-consciousness. Those challenges can occur when you're pushing yourself as an athlete to go further than you have before, or are facing an opponent who is fairly matched for your skills. They can happen when you're working, in the process of trying to untangle a juicy problem. They can happen when you're dancing, when you try to push your body into the beat.

There are challenges in play, too: Your kid has to focus fully to use her developing fine motor skills to place that last block on the top of the tower without it toppling. Or to pay attention when throwing or catching the ball. To process her day in relational play, using Spiderman and Barbie's conversation to sift through frustrations, just as I sift through my own thoughts in writing.

But here's the catch: The things that are the upper-edge challenges that can help my kids' play become an experience of flow for them aren't, mostly, the same kinds of challenges for me. Some of the reason that I struggle to enter playtime with my kids is certainly that part of me is keeping track of what else needs to happen or because I have to work to see the doll in the umbrella, but maybe that's not the only reason. If I'm honest, a lot of the time I find my kids' play, well, *boring*. And from the looks of the titles of the posts I pulled up online, it seems I'm not the only one who experiences this. Maybe that's because I've become one of those awful grown-ups who doesn't care about the elephant inside the snake. I mean, it's possible. But at least in theory I do really value the flights of imagination, whimsy, and silliness that my children take, and sometimes take me on with them. In practice, though, I find that I may only have so much tolerance at a given moment for pretend grocery shopping before unloading the dishwasher starts to sound kinda interesting after all.

Here's why, I think: The personal resources that Yonatan needs to draw upon in order to build a car out of Legos or that Shir needs when he puts Teddy to sleep fourteen times in a row reflect where they are developmentally—emotionally, mentally, physically. They can find flow in their play because it's demanding "all their relevant skills." As a more-or-less adult, my needs and skill set aren't the same as Shir's, and the challenges that cause his play to be so consuming aren't challenges to me.

So, then, how do we enter into play with our kids? How can we find the flow along with them? Of course, sometimes we just do—sometimes when we're horsie to their monkey, sometimes when the pillow fight gets going, it feels easy enough. But other times, I wonder if it might be useful to remember that sitting on the floor was different for the sage than it was for the Turkey Prince. The prince was fully immersed in his turkeyhood, but any feeling of flow that the sage might have experienced wasn't as a result of believing that he, himself, was actually fowl. It was, most likely, because he was in his element as a teacher.

In order to find flow when we play with our kids, sometimes we need to be stretched and challenged, too. We need to find the point of growth for us, not to sit passively by as they grow.

Sometimes it's obvious how that happens. Yonatan is an early reader now, and I love, *love* reading with him. I find the experience absolutely enthralling—I can sit with him for hours at a time while he works through a beginner's book; I find it absolutely pleasurable and flow-inducing. What's so captivating for me, though, isn't that I'm personally challenged by the vocabulary, or that I'm wondering with rapt attention whether the kids in the story will succeed in building a treehouse (I bet they will). Rather, for me, what's exciting is both getting to witness Yonatan do this profound work, and figuring out how to help guide him along the process. How do I respond when he hesitates at a word? When do I help him if he's stuck, and what kind of help do I offer? What kind of encouragement will keep him going and what will annoy him or even shut him down? How do we have this reading experience together? When I read with my son, we're both engaged in a challenge that demands all of our resources—but our challenges are not exactly the same, and we're not using the same exact resources in the process.

It's the same thing when Yonatan and I duel, either using the cardboard swords I finally consented to help him make[15] or a plastic baseball bat against a stuffed tree. To what degree do I fight him fairly? When do I let him cut off my head and arms? When do I break out the rudimentary fencing moves I picked up in high school? When I do "slay" him in the chest, do I crow that I have won or just lightly call out, "Ah, gotcha!"? (Nir is much more likely to take the former tack; I'm more likely to take the latter.) When is our play just a fanciful time to pretend that we're knights? When is it a chance to help him learn how to lose gracefully? When is it a chance to let him feel powerful? I'm not necessarily thinking all these things consciously when we're sparring, but they're there, somewhere in the background, bringing more of me into the situation. I'm a gobbling, pecking sage— playing with my prince, but also aware of the bigger picture of his needs and growth.

And sometimes, honestly, what I find engaging about playing with my kids is less the act of play than the chance to be up close with them, to look at their pretty faces, to behold the strange enigma of their furrowed brows as they think, to steal a snuggle or just watch them in action. Sure, I'm playing and responding, but I'm less captivated by the game than I am by the quieter moment in which I can just witness, you know, *them*. I don't know if that would pass muster with Csikszentmihalyi's definition of flow, but loving them, in these moments—when I can remember to—feels like flow to me. Or maybe it's more radical amazement. I don't know that it matters what label we give it, as long as we're able to show up and experience the thing now and again.

I also find that watching them play, without the pretense

of participating, can be extremely flow-inducing. When I get to sit and watch Shir in the bath—when I'm not busy running to grab everybody's pajamas and put in the night-light and make sure that the water bottle is next to the bed, when I just allow myself the chance to hang out with him in the bathroom—it can be the most soothing moment of my day. It's calming, watching him be so fully absorbed as he diligently washes his baby doll, pours water over it and talks to it and soaps it up and splashes around in the soap bubbles. It's mesmerizing. In those moments, I feel everything I've been preoccupied with all day fall to the side as I'm able to be drawn into the exquisite show of watching him play.

Playing with our kids can also draw us in just by the fact of having to figure out who this kid is today—because she may or may not be the same person we put to bed last night. As psychologist Jean Baker Miller puts it, parents are

literally forced to keep changing if they are to continue to respond to the altering demands of those under their care. For an infant and then a child to grow there must be someone who can respond to the child. As the child grows, one's responses must change accordingly. What sufficed today will not suffice tomorrow. The child has come to a different place, and the caretaker must move to another place too.[16]

In other words, we must constantly grow in order to meet the growing child. And, as such, we have to figure out how to engage in play with the current iteration of this child. Even if our challenge in play isn't going to be found in sounding out the syllables of a word or using our developing motor skills to stack the blocks, we have to figure out how to reasonably connect with today's kid about these things, since yesterday's tricks might not work anymore. What Shir needs from me today when Teddy goes off to the grocery in our living room might be different from what he needed a week ago, and it might indeed require all of my "relevant skills" to figure out how to become the person equipped not only to parent today's child, but to play with him or her.

We have to extend ourselves to meet our kids everywhere they are, including in their play. When we do so, we find the possibility of entering a deep state with them that not only transports us, however briefly, but can transform us. Csikszentmihalyi holds that, when we play—or teach and play—deeply enough to enter a flow state, it can help us to grow. He writes,

> We found that every flow activity, whether it involved competition, chance, or any other dimension of experience, had this in common: It provided a sense of discovery, a creative feeling of transporting the person into a new reality. It pushed the person to higher levels of performance, and led to previously undreamed-of states of consciousness. In short, it transformed the self by making it more complex.[17]

Every time we're able to enter play with our children, we find a new opportunity to extend ourselves further than we've ever gone, and help our children do the same. Of course, there are plenty of times when it's not in the cards—when we're distracted, when there's too much else going on, when we just can't quite find that sweet spot that keeps us from being bored out of our gourds by yet another round of the Thomas the Tank Engine board game. That might happen a lot, maybe most of the time. But there's this other place, available to us, when we can get there. In that place, we can find not only the exhilaration of really letting go, and the sweetness of connecting with our kids, but feeling our own selves and theirs expanding from the pure pleasure of being immersed in the joyful task at hand.

Stuart Brown, psychiatrist and founder of the National Institute for Play, defines play as "anything that spontaneously is done for its own sake."[18] So there are two major factors: spontaneity, the sense that there's an unscripted, make-it-up-as-you-go feeling to whatever's happening, and that it's done *for its own sake*, without an ultimate goal to be met.

Which doesn't mean that there aren't outcomes in play. Children use play to process a myriad of emotions that come up during the day. Kids, after all, feel the fear and humiliation, the uncertainty, anger, jealousy, and disappointment that are part of being human, and certainly part of being a growing person who doesn't necessarily have a lot of power in relation to parents, teachers, or even sometimes peers. How many times do I hear Batman and Lego Man (while they happen to be in Yonatan's hands) working out a complex situation regarding who's inviting who to come play, or how Batman is actually mad at Lego Man because it's not fair what he did? And Shir has an amusingly transparent habit of forcing Teddy to endure whatever indignities he's had to suffer recently—whether getting a shot, clipping toenails, checking ears for signs of infection, or even just having to go down for a nap. Play gives kids space to feel their feelings, to make sense of them, to reexperience and release some of the hard stuff from a safe and manageable distance, with them, now, in control of how everything goes down.

And when kids play together, there are other outcomes. Whether roughhousing, building Legos together, or devising an elaborate game of Let's Pretend, they have to learn how to negotiate and figure out what the rules of the interaction are going to be.[19] Play has been associated with growth in memory, self-regulation, language development, and literacy-related skills.[20] And while elaborate fantasy play isn't necessarily common worldwide, it may be useful in "Western, information-based societies," where certain kinds of cerebral processing are valued.[21]

And most important, perhaps, in play, kids learn to develop empathy. As Stuart Brown notes, "[I]f you are in a rough-and-tumble situation, somebody hits you too hard, you know what that feels like. So you're not going to hit . . . somebody else too hard, because you know what it feels like. And that's the root . . . of an empathic response."[22]

The other night I was cooking when I heard Shir making a hard-to-categorize noise. It sounded like he was crying, but it would stop after a moment; it'd be quiet for a bit and then erupt again a little later. It definitely wasn't the sound of "I'm in serious pain," but I kept my ear cocked in case it started to seem like he needed me. It kept happening, though, so I finally left my post to investigate. There, lying on the floor of the living room, were Shir and Yonatan; Yonatan's foot was on Shir's head, and both of Shir's feet were on Yonatan's belly, and they were pushing each other and rolling around. They were giggling, mostly, and every once in a while, whatever Yonatan did evidently crossed the line into discomfort. So Shir would yelp, and Yonatan would move his foot two centimeters to the left, and it would be OK again, and they'd go back to giggling.

Yonatan was learning to adjust his behavior based on the cues that he was getting from Shir, and Shir was learning that if he communicated his needs, his brother would respond to them. They both, while laughing their faces off, were figuring out where the boundaries were, when a kick helped extend the play and when it might be the thing that shut all the fun down.

Sure, there are plenty of times when empathy doesn't seem to be in operation—yesterday, I had to actually say, out loud, "Yonatan, Shir is crying because you put stickers on his face. Perhaps this means that he doesn't want you to put stickers on his face, and that *you should stop now*?" There are times when they punch each other, and plenty of times when the desperation to get a certain toy trumps any interest in what the other sibling might be feeling. But sometimes, sometimes, I catch them learning and practicing empathy, perhaps most comfortably when they think nobody's watching.

Play helps adults grow in empathy, too. It can be hard, sometimes, to see inside the world of our children—they start off as these teeny extensions of ourselves that we pick up and take anywhere we need to. We push our grown-up agendas on them all the time: You have to eat your veggies, you have to clean up your room now, you can't watch TV until you do your homework, you can't go to the birthday party in only your underpants. We so often live inside our own personal episodes of *Parent Knows Best*.

But when we tickle a kid and then hear them asking us to stop—we have an opportunity to hear them. When we hoist them up, thinking they'll laugh like a maniac, but they express discomfort, we're pulled back into the gap between our perception and someone else's reality. When we see beyond the "just try it, buster" expression of a kid who is misbehaving and reach out in playfulness and love, we can sometimes access the part of them that longs to be treated with compassion and connection. Play teaches kids about this stuff, but it's not a bad refresher for us, either. And who knows—maybe when we practice this attentive listening with our kids, it can help us learn how to listen to the other adults in our lives with as much intentionality. Perhaps, if we practice noticing others' subtle cues, we might better understand when we've made an offhand comment that makes a colleague uncomfortable or that unwittingly presses a friend's buttons, or even pick up enough to know not to make that comment at all.

Empathy, of course, is a crucial trait to cultivate on multiple levels. When we're able to understand and share one another's feelings, a lot of things begin to happen. We love more deeply and care for the people in our lives more effectively. We are better able to hear the perspectives of those around us, and to understand that how we encounter the world is not the only possible way. We become more aware of how others may perceive our words and actions. We navigate interpersonal conflict more smoothly and with more sensitivity. We become more motivated to be of service, and to work for the betterment of others.

As Leslie Jamison wrote in her masterful essay "The Empathy Exams," "Empathy isn't just listening, it's asking the questions whose answers need to be listened to. . . . It suggests you enter another person's pain as you'd enter another country, through immigration and customs, border crossing by way of query: *What grows where you are? What are the laws? What animals graze there?*"[23] It's about being willing to try to understand another's experience, and being open to changing our actions based on the information we receive.

Empathy is at the heart of the Jewish tradition. The ancient sage Hillel was once challenged by a potential convert to recite all of the Torah while standing on one foot. He said, "That which is hateful to you, do not do to another. That is the whole Torah. All the rest is commentary."[24] Of course, the crucial nature of this sentiment is also echoed in Christianity,[25] Islam,[26] Buddhism,[27] and pretty much every other major religious tradition. Whether the emphasis is on loving one's neighbor, sharing in others' joy and mourning, wanting for others what you want for yourself, putting one-self in another's place, or sacrificing oneself in compassion-ate care of someone else, the message is fundamentally the same: Developing the ability to understand, and share, in the feelings of others is a crucial piece of our work as humans, and a life of spiritual service.

Empathy fosters a commitment to justice. The Torah tells us, in a number of places, "You shall not oppress a stranger, for you know the feelings of the stranger, having yourselves been strangers in the land of Egypt."[28] It's an important statement about how to set up a society, how to care for the most vulnerable, and what things should look like when you're in a position of power and privilege. And it all starts from remembering that if you don't like getting your head squished by someone else's foot, probably the other person doesn't like being squished by you, either. And in case you forget, a little yelp here and there can help you remember.

Some of the deepest, most important values that we can pass along to our children begin in play.

But even beyond empathy, problem-solving skills, or creativ-ity, play can bring us, well, joy.

Creativity experts Michelle Cassou and Stewart Cubley suggest that "to play is to listen to the imperative inner force that wants to take form and be acted out without reason. It is the joyful, spontaneous expression of one's self. The inner force materializes the feeling and perception without plan-ning or effort."[29]

The joyful expression of one's self. That moment of falling into laughter and silliness, to being a horse or a monkey or a dueling knight. I wonder if another reason so many of us grown-ups resist play is that there's some piece of it that is, frankly, kind of scary. After all, as Rebbe Nachman of Breslov has said, "Finding true joy is the hardest of all spiritual tasks."[30]

When we're feeling most things, most times, there's an element of distraction to it. We're sad about now and afraid about what might yet come to pass, we're angry about something that just happened because it taps into a whole host of things that happened a long time ago. We are so often bound up into a whole, complex network of thoughts and ideas from the past and the future. We manage, sometimes, to be both in the moment and somewhere else, in another point along the spectrum of time—torn, ever-so-slightly, in two or more pieces.

When we're feeling joy, on the other hand, there's only the moment of joy, and we take it in fully. In joy, we feel more sensitized, more awake, more alive. And it's that sensitivity, that openness, that can give us access to the transcendent, the holy, to the sacred stream of life that surges through us, connects us, surrounds us. The feeling of flow, of being in the flow.

Joy is the unknown. We don't always feel like we know who we are in the unfettered openness of now, what might give shape to our lives if not the recurring drama, the clinging to the past, or the crafting of stories about some vague, hypothetical future. But when we can get there, to that expansive space, it can bolster our awareness of our place in the cosmos.

Madeline L'Engle once said,

> *One of the greatest weapons of all is laughter, a gift for fun, a sense of play which is sadly missing from the grownup world. When one of our children got isolated by a fit of sulks, my husband would say very seriously, "Look at me. Now, don't laugh. Whatever you do, don't laugh." Nobody could manage to stay long-faced for very long, and communication was reestablished. When Hugh and I are out of sorts with each other, it is always laughter that breaks through the anger and withdrawal.*
>
> *Paradox again: to take ourselves seriously enough to take ourselves lightly. If every hair of my head is counted, then in the very scheme of the cosmos I matter; I am created by a power who cares about the sparrow, and the rabbit in the snare, and the people on the crowded streets; who calls the stars by name. And you. And me.*[31]

I matter, so does everything else. This moment is important, so are all the other ones. But if I'm just part of the great ecosystem of everything, then this sulky mood isn't anything bigger or more serious than anything else. And we may as well laugh. We may as well let go. We may as well embrace the vast exquisiteness of everything, of every tiny thing, the amazing joys available for us to have whenever we're able to let go enough to take them.

And it doesn't have to happen, necessarily, at a set-apart,

formal time; as we all know, play and laughter are often enough just shot into the rhythm of life with kids: When you beep-beep-beep someone's nose to get her to open her mouth so you can brush her teeth, when you and your kid start making up silly voices for each of the vegetables in the salad, when you walk someone to the bath by holding his legs in the air as he walks on his hands. When there's a tense moment that's about to become a power struggle but you diffuse it with a ridiculous face. Play doesn't have to happen only during time earmarked for Monopoly or pretend grocery store; it is often deeply suffused in our everyday interactions with our kids, when we're able to take ourselves lightly.

A lot of my more inspired play moments, actually, have come when I was getting close to the brink—the song I made up about Brussels sprouts when I was trying desperately to convince toddler Yonatan to eat some; the crazy, silly monster I turned into when really I just kind of wanted to start screaming; and most certainly the tickles when boundaries were being tested far past my patience level. When I'm able to channel my own frustrations into a silly or goofy or playful action, it helps shake up the energy in the room for everybody, and the kids respond to it. I remind myself that, in the grand scheme of things, it's not the world's biggest deal.

We can take ourselves lightly. We can reach out for the joy that's in the room right now. It may be hidden under a pout or inside our own distractions, but it's there, waiting for us, when we're ready to release it. Our self is ready for spontaneous expression—we just have to set aside everything preoccupying us, and let it rip.

The last chapter of *The House at Pooh Corner* makes me teary every time I read it, because it reminds me how our children, growing up in this culture, are so deeply urged to become the kinds of people who see a hat instead of a snake that swallowed an elephant. Who forget that the umbrella is a beautiful doll. Who forget how to plug into the joy channel, where you can be a knight or a turkey or a kitty or the queen of the world. This passage is about how short a time our children are our master teachers; it's about putting on the shirt and getting up to sit at the table, as turkeys never do.

> *Then, suddenly again, Christopher Robin, who was still looking at the world with his chin in his hands, called out "Pooh!"*
>
> *"Yes?" said Pooh.*
>
> *"When I'm—when—Pooh!"*
>
> *"Yes, Christopher Robin?"*
>
> *"I'm not going to do Nothing any more."*
>
> *"Never again?"*
>
> *"Well, not so much. They don't let you." Pooh waited for him to go on, but he was silent again.*
>
> *"Yes, Christopher Robin?" said Pooh helpfully.*
>
> *"Pooh, when I'm—you know—when I'm not doing Nothing, will you come up here sometimes?"*
>
> *"Just me?"*
>
> *"Yes, Pooh."*
>
> *"Will you be here too?"*

"Yes, Pooh, I will be really. I promise I will be, Pooh."

"That's good," said Pooh.

"Pooh, promise you won't forget about me, ever. Not even when I'm a hundred."

Pooh thought for a little.

"How old shall I be then?"

"Ninety-nine."

Pooh nodded.

"I promise," he said.

Still with his eyes on the world Christopher Robin put out a hand and felt for Pooh's paw.

"Pooh," said Christopher Robin earnestly, "if I—if I'm not quite—" he stopped and tried again—"Pooh, whatever happens, you will understand, won't you?"

"Understand what?"

"Oh, nothing." He laughed and jumped to his feet. "Come on!"

"Where?" said Pooh.

"Anywhere," said Christopher Robin.

So they went off together. But wherever they go, and whatever happens to them on the way, in that enchanted place on the top of the Forest a little boy and his Bear will always be playing.[32]

Children grow up. That's part of what they do. And their relationship to magic and mystery might shift when that happens.

Part of what's beautiful about childhood is the ability to live in the garden, speaking to the fairies. But part of what's heartbreaking about this beauty is that it's impermanent—*mono no aware*. The pathos of things, the excruciating exquisiteness of transience.

We can help to prolong the enchantment, though, to whatever degree we can. Even if we can't keep our babies at the age when they're happily talking to their bear all day—nor, maybe, would we want to—we do have a little power. We can keep the play from being squashed out of their lives. We can make sure they have time to do Nothing. We can guard that jealously for them, and even join them, sometimes, in Pooh Corner, if they'll let us.

CHAPTER EIGHT

It's Not About Me Anymore?

Creating a New Kind of Selfhood

———◆———

One day in the early 1950s, Anne Morrow Lindbergh took herself on vacation.

It was a radical act. She was the mother of five, right in the thick of their chaotic, growing years. She was responsible for their care, for the household, and embedded in a myriad of community relationships that came with their own obligations. It was during a time when the cultural presumption that mothers weren't supposed to leave their children was awfully strong. And yet, she left.

Lindbergh settled down for a brief stay on Florida's Captiva Island. She walked along the shore. She watched the birds. She rode her bike around the island. She baked biscuits and swam and wrote down a series of musings, as they came to her, on love and family and mothering and solitude and contemplation. *Gift from the Sea* was published in 1955, and it became a major bestseller. What she had to say resonated with a lot of people—women, mostly, especially mothers. What I find startling, though, is not that her writing is wise, but that it's still very current on so many levels.

For example, as she muses on her "new awareness, both painful and humorous," about "why the saints were rarely married women," she writes that she is convinced that

> *it has nothing to do with chastity. . . . It has to do primarily with distractions. The bearing, rearing, feeding and educating of children; the running of a house with its thousand details; human relationships with their myriad pulls—women's normal occupations in general run counter to the creative life, or contemplative life, or saintly life. The problem is not merely one of* Woman and Career, Woman and the Home, Woman and Independence. *It is more basically: How to remain whole in the midst of the distractions of life; how to remain balanced . . . ; how to remain strong.*[1]

Every couple of years, *Time* or *The Atlantic* or *The New York Times* runs a major think-piece on the great mystery of whether or not women can "have it all." "It all," of course, is defined as family (even though not every woman wants that) and career (even though not every woman wants that, either). And then, inevitably, someone writes a counter essay to the original essay, and we go around and around on part-time work, on leaning in and opting out. And though the discourse is expanding, little by little, in terms of the kinds of options that are available and socially acceptable for mothers, there still seem to be two very distinct gears: working busily in professional engagements or working busily at home, focusing on kids and their many needs. Many women—and parents of whatever gender these days—do both of these things, in various ratios, at various times in their lives or at certain hours in their day. But sitting on the beach, alone, staring at the birds? Not so much.

The distractions haven't gotten any less distracting. If anything, the balancing act that many of us do between work and home has intensified as working motherhood has become more common; as smartphones pull us to the office or elsewhere even from the park; as it's become the norm for children to be enrolled in a thousand activities a day; in light of the fact that parents are typically much more hands-on now than they have been in previous generations. We have at least as much in front of us as Lindbergh did, if not more.

The German word for what I think a lot of us feel, a lot of the time, is *Zerrissenheit*—a state of being torn into pieces.

This is something that the writer Esther Emery struggled with recently. She describes herself as having a "fundamental craving for silence." But, she writes, attending to this need "felt selfish. *How can I take this time just for me?* I had a baby and a toddler; I was breastfeeding. Surely this call, this deep desire for solitude and internal seeking . . . surely this was meant for someone else?" She'd get up earlier and earlier in the morning to try to squeeze out a few precious minutes in the quiet before everyone else in the house got up, feeling, still, "always and forever the guilt."[2] She'd end her meditation abruptly the moment her husband or children woke up. There were things to be done, people who needed her help and care. Distractions, one could say, details, children to be fed and messes to be cleaned and a cat to be rescued from the cabinet in which the toddler had locked him. Her attention needed to be elsewhere, many elsewheres, pretty much all the time.

The problem of distraction isn't even just about feeling as though there's no time for quiet or contemplation, either. Even when we're focused entirely on caring for our kids, a fundamental part of that work requires us to slice our attention in several different directions.

The philosopher Sara Ruddick talks about vigilance, a sense of being on the lookout for dangers and problems, of constantly scanning one's surroundings as part of parental protection. Is the toddler about to jump off the steep edge of the jungle gym? Who's that person approaching? Do they seem safe? Is that broken glass on the ground? Is it about to start pouring rain?

For most of us, this sense of vigilance doesn't take up our full mental bandwidth—that would be, indeed, anxiety-producing and exhausting, probably. I think for a lot of us it's more like an app running in the background, constantly whirring, and perhaps draining our battery a little faster than it would otherwise as we attempt to engage in the fun or the pleasant or the needs of the moment. We're just hanging out at the park, doing what we do, talking and laughing and playing, but some piece of us is constantly surveying the situation to make sure that nothing is awry. The vigilance is there, a necessary distraction, the antithesis of the relaxed state a person must be in if they wish to turn inward for spiritual or creative contemplation.

Another challenge to turning inward is in the fact that, in order to engage fully with our kids, we need to venture out of our own headspace entirely. That is, as feminist theologian Valerie Saiving articulates, "in order to answer a child's eager questions, the mother must be able to transcend her own habitual patterns of thought; she must meet the child where *he* is at that moment. It is absolutely impossible to communicate with a young child without somehow abandoning one's own perspective and looking at the world through *his* eyes."[3] It gets hard to think through one coherent idea or even to just hear your own quieter, intuitive self (what the Bible calls the still, small voice) if you're working to take on your kid's perspective in order to better understand her. Parenting requires us to go outside our selves, not deep into them.

Of course, there aren't just psychic and psychological challenges in the tension between our own needs and those of our kids—there are a lot of straight-up logistical issues, too. Shir, for example, sometimes still goes ballistic when I try to take a shower in the morning. He also is wont to do everything he can—grabbing my leg, demanding I pick him up, sobbing, running after me—to keep me from leaving for work, for an evening meeting, for the gym.

So then what? Do I never take a shower? Do I give up on a career because he'd rather I never go to a meeting? Do I just never go to the gym? (Well, it's not like I get to that third one so often. But even so!) Do we just stop caring for ourselves entirely so that we can be available at all times, in every respect? Is that even what's best for our kids?

Chanie Blackman, a Hasidic Jew in the Chabad tradition, told me that her paternal grandmother gave Chanie's mother—the new daughter-in-law—some valuable advice early in her mom's marriage: She should always feed herself before serving her children dinner. And if the kids ask why, Chanie recounted, her mother was instructed to tell them, "I'm making a mother for you."

Mothers (and fathers) are made—again and again, through small and large acts of self-care. That's how we become the people who are able to parent our children—filling up our own proverbial tanks of gas. The person that my children get when I don't take care of myself—when I'm hungry, or resentful, or low on solitude or whatever else—isn't the mother that I want to be for them. I make myself into *that* person by being mindful of my own needs. It's a gift for them—they want a happy mom who can really show up for them. As Chanie concluded from her grandmother's lesson, "anything that I do to nurture myself is no longer a selfish thing."[4]

That can look like a lot of things. Sometimes it's about keeping yourself fed and boldly claiming your shower, even if your toddler is bereft and shrieking. Sometimes it might be about taking time for the gym or a two-hour bike ride or to journal or paint or even a few days away at the beach all by yourself. Sometimes it's about being brave enough to just plunge through your prayer or meditation practice even when the kids and their infinite needs are filling up the room.

Esther Emery, for example, finally figured out how to focus on her own spiritual urges in the midst of the demands of family life. One day, she was in the middle of sitting meditation when her two-year-old woke up, but rather than get up to greet him, she decided to just stay put and keep breathing. The world, it turned out, didn't end. "My son wandered over to me," she writes. "I kept breathing. He sat on my lap. I kept breathing. He looked out the window with me. I kept breathing. And then he wandered over to his trucks and started to play." As it turns out, there was space for her own needs to be met, even when the children were around. These days, she no longer regards meditating in front of her kids as selfish. Rather, she says, it not only makes her more relaxed, more patient, and more open, but it's also something precious that she can offer to her children. She writes that, in meditation,

> *I show them that I am capable of being calm. I create a baseline of emotional neutrality. This is not what I look like when we are in traffic and late for a swimming lesson. This is not what I look like when the middle child has just smeared blue paint all over the deck (again). This is not what I look like when I have just ended a difficult phone conversation, the subject of which they neither hear nor grasp. And yet, I am capable of this. My children can expect this of me, and eventually of themselves.*[5]

We need to carve out for ourselves pockets and corners of life without distraction, and regard our own self-care as a legitimate obligation. Our basic well-being, alone, is reason enough. But it's also true that when we do so, we become more capable, available parents to our children, and we model something exquisitely valuable for them—as Emery put it, they learn to expect for themselves what we can provide for ourselves. And one can only imagine that they will grow up in a world with even more noise and competing demands than the one in which we now live. When we make space for focus and self-care, we give them the tools to do that for themselves; they learn so much from just watching us. When we set aside time to prioritize our own needs— even, or especially, the need to watch the birds for an hour a week, or for a week each year—we make of ourselves mothers. We make of ourselves fathers. We make of ourselves human beings. And we show our kids that they can do that, too.

A month or so after Yonatan was born, I finally consented to leave him with Nir and a few bottles of pumped milk for a couple of hours at a stretch. At first I didn't want to go—I had gotten used to always being available with my snack rack[6] in case he got hungry. I obviously trusted Nir to care for his son, but I just didn't want to separate from my baby. My reluctance was most likely partly about the hold that the bonding hormones had on me, partly about the actual emotional intensity (for me, in any case) of this new relationship, and partly just first-time mom anxiety.

Finally I left, for the two to three hours I could manage

without needing to pump. And oh, it was so good to get away! I went to the gym and remembered what it was like to have a body that did things other than nurse and nap. I sat in a coffee shop with my laptop and organized things for our taxes. I combed through the typeset proofs of the anthology I was editing. The work for both projects was excruciatingly mundane (by which I mean: really boring). But man, it just felt so good to leave the cloister of motherhood for a bit and to do things that regular adult humans had to do sometimes. To feel like a person again.

A lot of things get thrown into a blender when we have kids—our logistics, our finances, our priorities, probably our sanity a little bit. And for most of us, our identity—our very sense of selfhood—also gets taken for a spin. You know? Suddenly what you want and what you need gets put on the back burner, and who you are and have been in the world shifts dramatically. The baby's hunger at two a.m. takes priority over your exhaustion. Her seven thirty p.m. bedtime means that you're probably going to say no to that night out with friends (at least most of the time, given what babysitters cost these days). Your love of travel is at odds with the fact that your vacation days now cover the times when day care is closed. Even your most basic needs become deprioritized; after Yonatan was born, I discovered that I could go a *lot* longer without peeing than I ever had before. I was so busy soothing, feeding, changing, and getting him to sleep that answering nature's call was often, well, pretty far down the list. Simply put, when you become a parent, so often, it's not all about you anymore. Or hardly at all.

This is, at least in part, a wonderful thing. Comedian Carol Leifer became a mom at fifty with her partner Lori, and was surprised to discover how it changed how she lived in the world. As she put it, "Motherhood single-handedly rips you out of being self-involved. That thing about stepping in front of a speeding train to save your child becomes a stone-cold fact. And that focus on my son, the selflessness that it brings, I feel has made me a more generous and compassionate person in other areas of my life as well."[7]

But, of course, it's also hard. This extreme shift in focus isn't necessarily easy for every parent, or something that all embrace comfortably. One recent study found that a majority of new mothers described themselves as lost, lonely, and/or bewildered.[8] Another study found that a majority of mothers felt as though they had lost their identity after having a child; many missed going to work, and most found it difficult to adjust to the fact that they couldn't just go out whenever they wanted to anymore.[9]

A lot of spiritual practices talk about the renunciation of the self—the "ego," it's usually called, the impulse to make everything about me, me, meeeeeee. Mastering that impulse is considered one of the great achievements in pretty much every religious tradition. For example, the kabbalists talk about *bittul ha-yesh*, the nullification of one's "somethingness," that which makes us who we are. It's a means of putting God in the center of our thoughts and actions—not ourselves.

As the eighteenth-century kabbalist Issachar Baer of

Zlotshov formulated it, "The essence of serving God . . . is to attain the state of humility, that is, to understand that all your physical and mental powers and your essential being depend on divine elements within. You are simply a channel for the divine attributes. . . . You have no independent self and are contained through the Creator."[10]

Issachar Baer is saying that when we serve as a channel for something else—for God, for love, for giving, for service, for care—that "independent self" falls away. And we do this through various actions that emphasize humility. From a spiritual perspective, this is a good thing, because that need to make it *all about me all the time* interferes with understanding that we are, ultimately, a small part of the great interconnected everythingness.

This should be great news for parents, right? Every day we're given a crash course in quenching our ego and our desires, in extending ourselves in the care of another. As the French feminist philosopher Luce Irigaray once put it, "The path of renunciation described by certain mystics is women's daily lot."[11] Mothering is synonymous with giving over the self, with humility. So we should be in fantastic shape, spiritually, then, right?

Except that it's more complicated than that. As Carol Lee Flinders points out in her masterwork *At the Root of This Longing: Reconciling a Spiritual Hunger and a Feminist Thirst*,

> *Formulated for the most part within monastic contexts, [precepts of spiritual practice] cancel the basic freedoms—to say what one wants, go where one likes,*

enjoy whatever pleasures one can afford and most of all, to be somebody—that have normally defined male privilege. That is, men in any given social class have always possessed these liberties to a far greater degree than women of the same class. To the extent that he embraced these disciplines, therefore, a man entering the religious life would have experienced a dramatic and painful reversal of status: hopefully, an all-out assault on ego. Yet no one around him would have been in any doubt that he had undertaken that reversal voluntarily. Women, on the other hand, have not been in a position to renounce those privileges voluntarily because they never had them in the first place. . . . *If you knew nothing about mystical literature, you might think their precepts had been excerpted from a book of counsel for young brides in just about any ancient and/or traditional culture we know. They sound remarkably like the mandates young girls have always received as they approach womanhood and that, in veiled forms or under tacit threats, they still receive.*[12]

That is, women have historically been—and perhaps are still—raised with the message that they shouldn't have desires in the first place, that they should, well, be self-sacrificing and giving and put their needs second to those of their children, their partners, their employers, their families.

It's an ancient notion, that of the mother working tirelessly for others. Proverbs 31, for example, praises the "woman of valor" who rises early in the morning, "watches over the affairs of her household and does not eat the bread of idleness."[13] But she's not just old news; this valorous woman has been a pretty constant figure in art and literature over the last two thousand years. The old mother in William Butler Yeats's "Song of the Old Mother," for example, says, "I rise in the dawn, and I kneel and blow / Till the seed of the fire flicker and glow / And then I must scrub and bake and sweep / Till stars are beginning to blink and peep."

More recently, an ad[14] went viral that talked about "the world's toughest job." Prospective candidates were told about what was "probably the most important job," and described work that involved standing constantly, with no breaks, no vacations, no sleep, and no pay—and then, the big reveal: This is a job description for moms! Moms work so hard, for free!

It is telling that, even in 2014, the ad felt it necessary to clarify that we were talking about moms—not dads, not parents in general. However much actual parents are dividing labor around the house (and, of course, plenty of families have two moms or two dads or only one parent of whatever gender), our culture continues beeping out the same old messages. I saw something similar on Pinterest recently: "A mother is a person who, seeing there are only four pieces of pie for five people, promptly announces she never did care for pie."[15]

These messages run so deep that we often don't see how we've internalized them. It's not for nothing that a major book on gender and salary negotiation is called *Women Don't Ask*. It turns out that men initiate negotiations about four times more often than women do, and that when women *do* ask, it's for about thirty percent less than men.[16]

Men have been, by and large, raised to feel comfortable—entitled—to ask for more money in negotiations. To sit with legs sprawled wide apart, taking up plenty of room on the subway. To have a certain kind of an agency and, yes, selfhood, as they move through the world. The spiritual practice of annulling the ego is a healthy and productive way to address that sense of entitlement.

But for a woman who was told her whole life that she should diet because she's more attractive when she takes up less space, and who has received a million different cues large and small that her career, her ideas, and her contributions to the world will be taken less seriously than those of a man, this is fraught terrain. When Irigaray said, "The path of renunciation described by certain mystics is women's daily lot,"[17] she was being sarcastic. Male mystics made a fuss about giving up freedoms and serving humbly because, for them, it was a countercultural move that produced radical effects. For women, it was just business as usual.

So where does that leave those of us who parent while female? Where does that leave our ego, our sense of selfhood, our real, actual love for our kids, our perhaps sometimes desperate desire to get out there in the world and, you know, do taxes or something, anything to reclaim our sense of being someone other than Mommy? What does it mean for our ego—and our spiritual potential—when we enter the crucible of self-sacrifice that is motherhood?

There's a version of the story that's not very good for the

mom. If you've been told your whole life that you should not feel entitled to take up space, to be somebody, to ask for whatever it is that you need to ask for—well, becoming a parent might only exacerbate that sense of self-negation and make it even harder to know who you might be in the first place. There's a generation or two of women who only began to ask themselves "Who am *I,* independent of my caring for others?" after their kids grew up; for many of those women, the process was a difficult one that included some regret about the time missed before they figured out how to manifest their own self-satisfaction.

But maybe there's another possibility for how this breaks down, as well. That is, maybe mothers know—have possibly known for a long time, whether or not they were in a position to write about it—something else about selfhood that never made it onto the radar screens of the guys in the monasteries and yeshivas? That is to say: What if our acts of selflessness can actually bolster the self, in a deep, authentic way?

When Tracey was in the sixth grade, she got a horrible case of head lice. In order to spare her long, beautiful hair, her mother, Ella, had to comb it out thoroughly—a time-consuming process—twice a day. It was hardly how Ella fancied spending her time, not with the millions of other things that needed to happen each morning and evening in a family of four with two working parents.

And yet Ella found that this extra time, set aside to help her child with yet another task, had an unexpected consequence. It had been a rough year for Tracey and Ella—as adolescence often is between girls and their mothers. But, Ella reflected, "there, in all the mayhem of making her do her homework, dealing with her hormonal storms, and everything else, there was a twenty-minute span where I just touched her in helpful ways, and she liked being touched in those ways, and we were quiet together." And in this quietness, not only did Tracey and her mom create something of a détente and help themselves find each other amidst the difficulties of the year, but it created a space of calm togetherness that Ella discovered she herself badly needed. "Head lice, those horrid little buggers," she reflected, "became a reminder of our simple human connectedness and the possibility of peace." That possibility infused her days, offering her powerful nourishment.

The work of parenting has the potential to both develop our selfhood in healthy ways and to encourage us to grow in empathy, generosity, caring, and connection. In fact, rather than being an all-or-nothing proposition as far as our ego and self goes, parenting might bolster that ego; it might help us get someplace new entirely.

In contemporary culture, self-sufficient autonomy is so often considered the big marker of maturity—existing as an isolated, independent self (whose ego can then, once it's mature, get broken down in contemplative practices, as the dominant narrative around spiritual development tells it). The psychologist Dana Jack, however, suggests a different model, one of the relational self in which our selfhood and our interpersonal connections actually support one another. In this model, she writes, "intimacy facilitates the developing authentic self and the developing self deepens the possibilities of intimacy."[18] The more we give to others, the more we can be our true selves. The more we are able to live authentically, the more we have to give. In other words, the more we are able to see another's *Thou*, the more our *I* can be present.

And even more than that, philosopher Sara Ruddick suggests that we can't even fully see the *Thou*s in our lives if our *I* is not intact. She argues that we need to be able to let go of our egocentrism in order to make space for a true encounter with another, but, paradoxically, that work has to come from a place of security. For, she writes, "A person who counts herself as nothing lacks the confidence needed to suspend her own being to receive another's. The soul that can empty itself is a soul that already has a known, respected, albeit ever-developing self to return to when the moment of attention has passed."[19] In other words, you need to be in a solid place in order to let go of yourself to fully encounter someone else. Real empathy, she suggests, involves finding another without looking for yourself in there—seeing who they are as themselves, not as a projection of your own stuff. You need to know who you are in order to be able to do that effectively.

I don't know about you, but there are a few people in particular in my life—my partner, some cherished friends, my brother—who I feel really, actually see me. And when I'm with one or more of these people, I feel able to be the best, brightest, shiniest version of myself. And at the same time, these are the people who kick my butt, both explicitly and not, to be better than I am. When I am most seen as a Thou by someone else, I feel more whole, and that enables me to be more giving, because empathy and compassion are in the driver's seat. The kind of giving I'm able to do when I'm full up on love isn't the exhausting, boundaryless, somewhat in-discriminate doing for others that I sometimes get sucked into—you know, the kind that makes you want to tear out your hair and say, "Why didn't I just say *no* to this?!" Giving just feels different when it's offered from a rooted place of selfhood and connection.

And with my kids, well, more than anyone else they force me to really see myself. There's no bigger clarification of my priorities and values than having to communicate to these small human beings in formation. I can decide how Yonatan and I talk about the presidential election, about the home-less man on the street, about the contents of his kiddie Bible. His questions to me—Why doesn't that man have a house? Why would Abraham do that to his son?—push me to better understand my own perspective on the world, and ideally make me more thoughtful about what version of that I want to download into someone else's brain.

But more than that, being with my children is both an uncomfortable mirror and the most rooting thing that I have. If the answer to "Mommy, will you read me a story?" is that Mommy is busy answering a not-actually-urgent work email or engaging in a heated conversation about something that feels very important with strangers on Twitter, well, Mommy might need to check herself. And when I get a little too caught up in what's happening out *there*—the conversations about who's doing what that make me feel jealous or insecure or unspeakably nosy—a tiny little tushy in my lap can bring me back to where I really am, to what really matters. When I'm able to be *actually* present with my kids, it fills up my proverbial batteries with love and connection. It regrounds me in who I am, and from there, it becomes easier to remember what it is I am meant to be doing in my own actual life, and gets me out of the house of mirrors that is others' ideas about (or my perception of their ideas about) who I am and what I'm supposed to be.

In *Gift from the Sea,* Anne Morrow Lindbergh writes, "I believe that what [a] woman resents is not so much giving herself in pieces as giving herself purposelessly. What we fear is not so much that our energy is leaking away through small outlets as that it may be going down the drain."[20] Selflessness in and of itself is not a problem; it's a lack of intentionality that might be.

That intentionality can look like a lot of different things. For example, Ella didn't originally consider the act of combing out her daughter's lice as a purposeful gesture aimed at fostering intimacy; it was just yet another task that she had to perform in her role as mother. But as she entered into it, she found heartfelt quiet at its center. When we go looking for that connection, when we give out of love and the desire to see another—even, or perhaps most especially, our own children—we often find that it helps to nurture our own sense of selfhood on levels that we might not anticipate.

Lindbergh writes, "Purposeful giving is not as apt to deplete one's resources; it belongs to that natural order of giving that seems to renew itself even in the act of depletion. The more one gives, the more one has to give—like milk in the breast."[21] In what ways do we give that deplete our selfhood? That have us feeling, like the women in one of the new mom surveys, lost and bewildered? And in what ways do we give that fill us up, that foster something fundamental to our own selfhood? What does parenting look like when we give purposefully?

Because it's true that "becoming zero," in the manner of the mystics, is one path to the awareness of our interconnectedness with everything. But living through and into that interconnectedness is, I believe, also a means of getting there. We can experience our interdependence with others—most especially with our families, most *especially* with our kids—in ways that also serve to nurture our selves, and that even help us to grow.

In Pirkei Avot, a first-century collection of Jewish wisdom, the great sage Hillel asks three questions that, I think, get to the heart of the paradox of parenting and selfhood: "If I am not for myself, who is for me? And if I am only for myself, what am I? And if not now, when?"[22]

CHAPTER NINE

Seeing Everything with New Eyes

How Parenting Changes Our Vision of the World

———◆———

One day, shortly after Yonatan was born, I was walking down the street when I saw a man approaching me who, well, let's just say that he was unusual-looking. In the past, my gut response—before any intellectual reaction kicked in—might have been to regard him with curiosity, or even perhaps with a flash of revulsion before catching myself.

This time, though, before any other emotional reaction popped up, my first instinct was to wonder how this person's mother saw him. And as soon as I had that thought, I found myself flooded by an overwhelming feeling of love, compassion, and concern for this stranger on the sidewalk. I just wanted him to be okay. I wanted, desperately, for the world to be kind to him, for him to flourish in happiness and peace.

And then, somehow, the feeling extended, and I found myself wishing the same thing for everyone I could see on the street—older women with shopping bags, twentysomething guys blaring music out of their cars, the shopkeeper at the doorway of his store. I just wanted them all to be cared for, protected, and able to shine their gorgeous selves, brightly.

Then it struck me that this is probably how the great, encompassing everythingness—the vast stillness I call God—relates to us. When we are able to enter its flow, the force of the universe carries us to care, to joy, and to the ability to live out the best of ourselves. And that the love pouring through me as I walked down Beacon Street was divine love, manifest in a way that could help me encounter the whole world anew.

I don't think it's a coincidence that this incident happened not very long after I became a mother.

This moment on Beacon didn't cause me to go home and upend my entire life and all my priorities. It was, however, one strong, early indicator of the impact parenthood was having on how I saw the world and other people. My sense of myself, and what that meant about my work, creativity, relationships, interactions with strangers, and even the daily news, was shifting and it would be years before I would be able to articulate how.

Becoming a parent changes you—on levels you don't necessarily anticipate or understand. Although those changes take root in your relationship with your own kid, human beings are rarely fully compartmentalized. We are transformed as parents—through the work of being boo-boo kissers, lullaby singers, and vomit janitors—and this invariably affects other aspects of our lives. As we grow more patience, compassion, and boundary-setting disciplinary skills, we might find that those traits manifest in more places than we perhaps thought that they would. Many of us find that our attitudes about our work, our art, and our activism, our relationships, our exchanges with the people we encounter during the course of our day, our dreams, and our visions for our lives as a whole have changed radically following the arrival of our children into our lives.

Some of those changes are relatively concrete. A lot of working parents, for example, talk about how the new, snuggly demands on their time have forced them to become more efficient and more ruthless about their priorities. Crystal Black Davis, the mom of a toddler who runs a gourmet marketing firm, reflected,

> *I feel like now frivolity is not necessarily what I'm able to engage in anymore. Every moment and every minute has to have a purpose. Because I'm a mom, I want to focus on [my son], so there's not a lot of idle time. I still make time for me, but I want to make sure that I'm balancing my time, and [that I'm] being a good mom to him and being able to devote the time that I have to my business.*[1]

For Black Davis, parenting has shaped how her energies are invested, and pushes her to be thoughtful about her choices. For many of us, the intensity of parenting can be incredibly clarifying. Looking through the lens of working life, for example, some parents decide that their top priority is in getting to experience their children's transient young years as fully as possible, at home with them. Others continue working but decide, rather than leaning in, to lean back[2]—to pursue work that's part-time, flexible, or less demanding in terms of evening or weekend hours. For others, like Black Davis, love for their children helps them to better identify their passions or focuses them in regard to their professional time. Some may feel pushed to excel at work to model for their children what professional satisfaction can look like, and others may double-down with work to best provide for and/or open doors for their kids.

For some parents, the lack of "frivolous" time is a real problem—artists, for example, and other folks who do creative work often rely on the opportunity to stop and engage when inspiration strikes. Their work depends on being able to run an idea or image to the end of its thread. But many artist parents have to choose between responding to the muse and the demands of external reality—a kid at the age that requies near-constant minding, a kid who's hungry *now*, a kid who has decided that it's actually a great idea to try playing baseball in the living room, or the school pickup time that somehow always arrives just as the work has begun to flow. Plenty of creative parents struggle with the fact that, more often than not, the muse winds up getting pushed aside so that they can meet their kids' needs.

Poet Ingrid Wendt wonders if a shift in art-making parents' expectations for their work could be useful, and even fruitful. Rather than finish a whole poem in one sitting, as many poets without kids are used to doing, she wonders,

> What if we could just lower our standards enough to write down, every now and then, that one good line flitting through our consciousness before it floats out of reach . . . ? What if we could be more deliberate in our collection of these little language scraps . . . and when we had a moment or two away from the kids, or the bills, or the job, we could sort through and cluster and group them, just as a quilter puts together the matching pieces of cloth . . . ?[3]

In other words, it's not just that it is still possible, even in a time-strapped life, to capture the art that wants to be made. Rather, Wendt suggests, the demands of parenting can give rise to entirely new types of creative processes, and perhaps new kinds of art, as a result.

For novelist Elisa Albert, too, becoming a parent has given her access to a new sort of creative possibility, a fresh well from which to draw. She muses,

> There can be a new urgency to our work when we are mothers, in part because maybe we're feeling so much so intensely for our children. That's a valuable place to work from. The stakes are so high when you're nurturing new life; it can really awaken in you a new and important urgency, if you let it.[4]

Indeed, making art and engaging in other creative pursuits after kids can be a challenge—but *everything* can be a challenge. We have less time, we're exhausted, money may be tighter, and so forth. But at the same time, the power and intensity of our experiences with our little humans can offer rich, fertile territory to explore.

The growth that we undergo with and through our kids isn't always easy or comfortable or convenient, but it can make space for new and important types of thinking, doing, and being—whether focusing time we used to spend aimlessly, quilting poetry from the scraps of inspiration we collect, creating meaning from new depths of emotion, or something else entirely. The sixteenth-century Italian kabbalist Menahem Azariah of Fano talked about this growth, writing,

> *Just as a seed cannot grow to perfection as long as it maintains its original form—growth coming only through decomposition—so these points could not become perfect configurations as long as they maintained their original form, but only by shattering.*[5]

In order for a seed to become something new—to grow into the tree, shrub, or flower it was meant to be all along—it must change shape, change form. The pit must grow roots and let out sprouts. In order to flourish, it has to be willing to crack open, and to cease existing exactly as it had been. This can be frightening, of course, but sometimes it's exhilarating. Our children help us grow—they crack us open, they push us from our original form. Sometimes it feels like we're sprouting. Other times we might feel shattered as our children smash into every aspect of our lives and identities. But even then, maybe it's that the unnecessary parts of us are just decomposing to make room for who we need to be, and who our children need us to become.

I think this is true in parents' professional, emotional, and creative lives, and it's true in a lot of our adult friendships, as well. Sometimes that's about a shift in how a parent spends his or her time (less of it, probably, out at the bars or clubs than perhaps previously) and sometimes it's about changing priorities and allotting less time for ancillary hobbies. Some friendships are deep enough to weather this change, but they might not all be.

Naomi Shihab Nye's exquisite poem "The Art of Disappearing" talks about how sometimes a need to refocus can impact social relationships: "When they invite you to the party / remember what parties are like / before answering . . . If they say We should get together / say why?"[6] For Nye, these relationships—the nonessential ones, the ones that are about small talk at a party or someone you haven't seen in ten years showing up at your doorstep—are an unnecessary distraction that divert her from where she feels she needs to be. For, she writes, "It's not that you don't love them anymore. / You're trying to remember something / too important to forget. / Trees. The monastery bell at twilight. / Tell them you have a new project. / It will never be finished."[7]

Nye is talking about the solitude necessary to make art, or maybe just to take in, fully, the gloriousness of everyday moments, too precious to squander with people with whom she doesn't feel a real connection. But I think this sensibility also applies to parents—especially those of us who struggle with the short supply of solitude found in our kids' early years. Mixed-media artist Wangechi Mutu articulates the changes in her life after her daughter was born:

> It's made me very clear about my relationships and not in a way that I'm dismissive of my friendships. I'm way clearer about which friendships are truly meaningful and caring of who I am as a whole person. Some people can't deal with the part of [you that's] a mother. You're not the person who stayed up with them until 4 a.m. . . . Your friendships start to rank themselves. Some of them are organic and some of them you end up having quiet divorces.[8]

The friendships that are "truly meaningful and caring of who [Mutu is] as a whole person"? Those are the ones that last. For her, and for me, too. For me, the sense of not having time for frivolity that Crystal Black Davis articulated really manifest powerfully as I've had to make hard choices about my social time. Before kids, I had a lot more patience and bandwidth for a night out or a friendly lunch with people with whom I wasn't that close. But these days, most of my time is spent either working or parenting. Every once in a while, Nir and I get it together to go out, just the two of us. In order to meet friends, though, I need to take time either from my work, my kids, or my precious night's sleep—and if I take time from work, chances are I'll need to make up that time later (meaning, stealing time from my kids or my husband or my sleep). Is what's on offer so good that it's worth the inevitable trade-off?

It's not that I don't meet friends anymore. But, like Mutu, what that means is that I'm very selective about who I see, and how I spend the rare few hours I might have on my own, when I could be doing a thousand other things. My standards for social activity have gotten pretty high—fortunately, living in an observant Jewish community, there's often time for everyone to get together on Shabbat, to hang out at synagogue and to hook up for dinners and leisurely lunches. But beyond that, only a few people, the ones who feed and nourish me on the most fundamental level, make it onto the schedule—and then, honestly, not even that often.

The urgency of being part of my children's lives, of raising them, of kissing their sweet cheeks, has brought to the fore the question Mary Oliver asks in her poem "The Summer Day": "Tell me, what is it you plan to do / With your one wild and precious life?"[9] Both professionally and socially, having kids has been something of a refiner's fire, a burning away of the things that are not essential. If someone's going to compete for my time, there better be something real there.

It's not that I don't miss getting out more often, being more current on what's in the movie theater, being able to say yes to a party invitation without the hassle and expense of a sitter, or having more time for solitude, crafts, and dancing. But during my kids' younger years, I have chosen this other thing, and part of how I can experience raising them as more joyful more of the time is to own that choice fully. They'll be older soon enough; they won't need me as much, they'll be able to be home alone for stretches of time, and then they'll be able to drive themselves wherever it is they need to go. Then they'll probably leave the nest for points uncertain. These years are intense, and they're not without trade-offs—but so is every stage of life, every chapter.

The Talmud says, "What is of secondary importance should not be more weighty than the essence."[10] It's intended as a legal statement about deriving points of law. But for me, as a parent, it's also a powerful statement of priorities. The essence of my life carries, now, a certain weight—my kids, my partner, maybe my work is at the center. Everything else is secondary, and a lot of things just don't weigh as much as they used to. My kids have tipped the scales of my priorities, and, as the Talmud says elsewhere, "My feet take me to the place I love."[11] My own wild and precious life has been shaped and formed by the wild, precious lives I am now tasked to raise. I mostly don't have time for the monastery bell at twilight these days, but there are other things, now, that are "too important to forget," too brief to miss—Shir's giggle, talking to Yonatan about ancient Egypt during bath time, snuggles and songs and stories and, yes, even the discipline and tantrums and putting on of socks and the millions of mundane moments that are the warp and woof of our lives together.

Our lives change as a result of parenting in some concrete ways—how we spend our time, who we choose to meet for lunch or dinner. But some of the biggest impacts are less tangible—we regard the world with a different set of eyes. Our new vision can have implications both immediate and far-reaching, both in regards to the people in our daily lives and across the globe.

The lightning bolt memo that I got walking down Beacon Street, for example, is one that's familiar to a lot of parents—suddenly seeing others through the lens of our feelings for our kids. For one doctor, having a child had an indelible impact on her interactions with her patients. She reflected,

> Whenever people would say, "Having a child will really change you . . ." or "You'll see this differently as a parent," I thought, well, intellectually I can understand how much a person can love a child, but that must be an exaggeration. It really hit me the most when I returned to my pediatric surgery rotation. I had been on pediatric surgery as a junior resident before we had Mary Elizabeth. I cared a lot about the patients. I was very sensitive to the families, the babies, the children. But after I had Mary Elizabeth, the first time I had to operate on a child, I remember looking down and thinking, "This is someone's child."[12]

In other words, she cared about her patients before becoming a mom, but the love and tenderness that this surgeon felt for her own daughter changed how she regarded and interacted with other people's kids as well. The doors of her heart were broken open, and the love that spilled out, spilled out everywhere.

For choreographer Makeda Thomas, this awareness made her more sensitive, less tolerant of real or even fictional scenes of brutality. As she put it, "I used to be able to watch certain violent scenes in films or television, but I can't anymore. I'm always thinking, 'That could be somebody's child.'"[13] Even a violent movie—in which an action scene is staged—draws her in, empathetically, to experience a character's hurt from the vantage of someone who loves him. Other people's suffering, for Thomas, stopped being theoretical; their pain is refracted through her maternal heart and she experiences it as something that's real, something that matters.

For some parents, this empathetic caring generates a sense of responsibility. For Carrington, a yoga teacher, motherhood helped her to understand the spiritual principles she had long espoused from a totally different perspective.

As a yoga teacher, we are always talking about oneness and connection, which sounds really great in a yoga class, but not everyone can take that off of their mat. When you have a child, you say, "ok, I am gonna take care of my child, and my child has these friends, and if they were in trouble, I would take care of them, too, and I know about that family that's connected to him, and so I would take care of that kid, too." It shows you how connected we are, and how much bigger and broader your web is. Without kids, I think it's easier to stay in your small bubble.[14]

As much as Carrington might have understood concepts like "interconnection" in theory, before kids, they took on a different meaning—a different sort of heft—when she faced down the responsibility she had for her own kid. She began to see herself as part of a web of relationships that carried this sense of obligation outside the confines of her own little family unit. She began to understand, in effect, what Martin Luther King Jr. tried to articulate when he said that all people "are caught in an inescapable network of mutuality, tied in a single garment of destiny. Whatever affects one directly affects all indirectly."[15]

If Carrington was responsible for her child's friends, and the friends of her child's friends, perhaps those implications spread wider and wider, inviting her to consider for whom she's really responsible. Does she have a sense of obligation to all the families in her community? In her city? Beyond the city limits? It can be hard to think through the practical implications of leaving the "small bubble" of our own individual lives, but a lot of folks begin asking a new set of questions when they become obligated to protect and nurture their children. If someone else loves this other kid as desperately as I love my own, shouldn't I make sure that he, too, is safe and cared for? Shouldn't I do unto this child as I would wish others to do unto mine?

Some mystically minded folks, in the kabbalistic tradition and elsewhere, argue that everything is interconnected as part of one great underlying spiritual unity—that even if we all seem to be separate, we're actually akin to the seemingly differentiated waves in the sea, or like ice in a glass—appearing separate, but, really, just water. If we're part of this great everythingness, so is our kid. And the other kid down the street, and the one halfway across the world. And everybody else, whether they're nine or ninety. We're all interlinked on a deep level, and thus need to care for one another.

Or maybe we're not connected on that level, maybe our responsibility for others doesn't have a theological basis, just an ethical one—though I'm not sure that "just" is the right word for that, if it's true. The Torah commands us to pursue justice,[16] to love our neighbor as we love ourselves,[17] and to not stand idly by the blood of our neighbor.[18] We are obligated to be involved in what happens to other people—to keep them safe, to keep them from harm. Obviously, there are nonparents who have asked and powerfully lived these questions about interconnectedness and responsibility. For a lot of parents, though, even those like Carrington who espoused these values in theory, something about bringing home a child—and doing the exhausting, profound, daily work of raising her—changes how we embody them.

Of course, this isn't how all people react to parenthood. There is certainly a NIMBY mentality (Not In My Back Yard, that is) to be found in various corners of the world, most especially in an American culture of individualism and self-reliance. The acronym generally refers to residents who oppose a proposal for some new development in their area—whether fracking, homeless shelters, power plants, military bases, prisons, or something else—because it may impact their own lives negatively, even if they believe that such a development could exist *somewhere*. It's fine to have these things, in other words, but they should just be someone else's problem. They might oppose a fracking proposal not because of its environmental impact, but rather because having such activity locally may negatively influence real estate values or cause an unpleasant disturbance. Stories run the gamut from communities in suburban Chicago rallying against the development of housing units for African Americans in 1959[19] to the small town in Nova Scotia fighting the development of a recycling plant that would bring jobs to the area in 2013.[20] In both of these situations, and many others, parents were very much involved—their interest in taking care of their own particular children and homes trumped other possible concerns.

This mentality certainly also plays out in battles that have a real impact on kids' lives. Sometimes the question is about the zoning of school districts to keep out low-income students or students of color.[21] Other times parents who send their children to private school lobby to slash public school budgets in order to lower their own taxes.[22] Of course, when extracurriculars, arts classes, social workers, and enrichment classes are cut, the people who suffer most are the public school kids.

The philosopher Erich Fromm once noted, "If a person loves only one other person and is indifferent to all others, his love is not love but a symbiotic attachment, or an enlarged egotism."[23]

Of course, it can be hard to get outside our specific concern for our own families. It is certainly true that I love my own children more desperately than I love anyone else's children, and I feel a larger sense of obligation to care for them than I do for others. That's pretty natural, and understandable—I think most of us feel this way. The Talmud even makes clear that, if forced to choose between helping members of your family or those outside your family, you should help your own family first.[24]

But it's so rarely a question of either/or. And perhaps it's our love for our children, these tiny little beings for whom we would do anything, that shows us how to best love others. Why should something harmful only be not in my own backyard? Shouldn't we worry about everyone else's backyard—the backyards where other people's children live? And more to the point, when is it actually important to compromise my own comfort levels because there is a need more pressing than my own personal ease? And is it possible that, sometimes, when we venture our concerns beyond our own backyard, that's when real impact is possible for everybody? That's when we can form coalitions to halt an environmentally destructive practice that might cause health concerns for those in its vicinity. That's when we can work to transform school districts for the betterment of everybody's kid. That's when we can create diverse communites rooted in tolerance and trust, in connection and understanding. It can be done. It has been.

There's a story in the biblical Book of Kings[25] that muses on this question. When it opens, the prophet Elijah has found himself in a frightening famine. God commands him to go visit a widow who, he is told, will feed him. Elijah goes to her and asks her for something to eat. She replies that she only has a tiny amount of flour and oil, and she was planning to use it to make cakes for herself and her son—she knows they're going to die of famine, but she wants them to have at least this one last meal. And Elijah says, if you make these cakes for me instead, I promise, you'll have plenty of food to last out this famine—but if you don't, you won't, and this one last meal won't make a difference in the long run.

She's a widow, a mother. This woman's responsibility is to care for her son first, and everyone else after that. But, paradoxically, how she ensures her own survival is by looking outside her own small circle—by engaging with the needs of the collective. Of course, the literary mechanism here is one of divine intervention—Elijah, with help from the character of God, ensured that the barrel of meal and jar of oil remained full, no matter how much was taken from it, and the family "ate for many days."[26] Shortly afterward, the son falls ill, but Elijah—whose prophetic powers include that of healing—is able to revive him. Of course, if Elijah had been turned away or starved to death, he wouldn't have been around to heal her child. The mother's act of giving saved them all, by generating a sort of karmic return in bounty and by deepening her relationship with this healer, who was then on hand at the moment he was most urgently needed.

One can absolutely understand how this woman might initially be wary and not trusting of this stranger. She's protective of her son during a frightening, dire time. But this story underscores the fact that we're not islands—our survival often depends, quite concretely, on our capacities for empathy and generosity.[27]

There's a popular cultural narrative that talks about mothers as naturally peacemaking. Mothers are often depicted as the loving, relational figure, forcing a truce between warring brothers, or holding down the hearth while the men go off to fight. Sometimes mothers are depicted as Mater Dolorosa, the mother of sorrows who nurses war survivors or weeps over the bodies of the dead. But, of course, this image, like so many other images of women, is complicated.

Maternal protectiveness of children has manifested plenty of times in a racist or xenophobic antipathy to outsiders, or in happy support of a country's war against enemies perceived or actual. Mothers in Nazi Germany were just as complicit, and sometimes just as murderous, in regards to the Final Solution as other categories of citizens,[28] and white mothers in the Antebellum South certainly exploited the men and women who were enslaved on their plantations.[29] Mothers physically, emotionally, and sexually abuse, and even murder, their children; they encourage their children to risk their lives committing acts of terrorism, they sell them into the sex trade. There's nothing magical about or inherent to mothers that makes them naturally averse to the horrors that humans have perpetrated on one another for millennia.

But Sara Ruddick suggests that, although a tendency toward creating peace might not be *inherent* in mothers, the work of raising children can lay the important groundwork for far-reaching peacemaking. Ruddick argues that the more parents work to engage an "imaginative grasp of what other children mean to other mothers"[30] (and parents in general, I'd suggest), the more they may move into sympathetic identification with nonviolent political techniques. In other words, the surgeon who sees his patients in a new light, the yoga teacher who gets a new insight about her responsibility to others, the artist who is suddenly averse to violence in movies—they're all, in working the muscle of empathy, sowing the seeds for a robust nonviolent practice. In addition, Ruddick argues, nonabusive parenting values nonviolence as process—for example, a parent may want her kid to go (the eff) to sleep or to get to school, but might not consider it reasonable or appropriate to drug him or drag him forcibly into the classroom in order to achieve these goals.[31]

In fact, Ruddick suggests, the everyday work of creating and maintaining spheres in which children can thrive—spheres of peace and safety, of nurturance and protection—offers unique tools for creating peace or engaging in nonviolent resistance in the world at large. For, she writes,

> *The practice of mothering taken as a whole gives rise to ways of thinking and acting that are useful to peace politics. . . . Nonviolent action, like maternal practice at its best, requires a resilient cheerfulness, a grasping of truth that is caring, and a tolerance of ambiguity and ambivalence. For mothers, issues of proper trust, permissible force, and the possibility and value of control are alive and complex in daily work as they are in nonviolent action.[32]*

In other words, even though there's nothing inborn in the people who happen to raise babies that makes them great activists, the work of parenting is a powerful and unique space in which to practice some of the most important dimensions of nonviolent work, every day, through every tantrum and refusal to do homework, through every trip to the ER and every negotiation about exactly how much dinner needs to be eaten in order to get dessert. And once the decision is made to cross the bridge and work for change beyond one's own family, the tools developed at home become indispensable.

For a lot of parents, crossing that bridge doesn't happen intentionally; many become "accidental activists"[33] in the wake of a tragedy that breaks them out of the comfort of their usual lives. Trayvon Martin's[34] and Jordan Davis's[35] mothers, after their sons' murders, began fighting to repeal "Stand Your Ground" laws; Candy Lightner's thirteen-year-old daughter's death in a hit-and-run accident prompted her to start MADD, Mothers Against Drunk Driving;[36] the 2012 Sandy Hook massacre caused terrified and empathetic parents to organize for stronger gun control laws.[37]

In Argentina and Chile, mothers impacted by military dictatorship in the late seventies and early eighties—specifically, policies of kidnapping, imprisonment, torture, and murder—organized powerful acts of nonviolent resistance in the process of trying to find their children. They demonstrated and marched weekly in public during a time when opposing the government was dangerous indeed, demanding accountability in regards to their own children and others who had been "disappeared." In Chile, one woman said, "I do not ask for justice for my child alone, or the other women just for their children. We are asking for justice for all. . . . If we find one disappeared one I will rejoice as much as if they had found mine."[38]

These *madres* did not transcend their particular love and loss—they grieved as hard as ever for their own missing children. However, their love for their particular children gave them the emotional push to do difficult, painful, often dangerous work in the face of a repressive regime, and in that work, they extended their love to others, and expanded the circle of care and concern to encompass all those who had disappeared. The empathy that they began to practice when mothering their own children helped to fuel their work in seeking justice for the children of others as well.

Similarly, it's perhaps not a coincidence that one of the most powerful groups fostering dialogue between Israelis and Palestinians in the Middle East is the Parents' Circle Families Forum[39]—formerly the Bereaved Parents' Circle. The organization is comprised of Israelis and Palestinians who have lost a family member in the ongoing violence that's plagued the region; they come together to engage in dialogue, to foster mutual respect, and to generate understanding in the hopes of helping to end the conflict. They work with Palestinian and Israeli political leaders to educate them on the importance of the reconciliation process in crafting agreements, and have a number of ongoing projects, such as engaging 25,000 Israelis and Palestinians a year in dialogue.

The ethos of the Parents' Circle, as with the *madres*, is one of caring for everyone's kids. Certainly, there are parents in the Middle East and elsewhere on local, national, and international stages whose personal losses propel them to seek vengeance. But members of the Parents' Circle and others working toward peace have decided that their own loss is already one too many, and that their work should be in preventing other parents from having to suffer similarly—in doing what they can to foster reconciliation, in the hopes of ending the conflict altogether. This work of dialogue and understanding can certainly be understood as an extension of the work we do as parents.

As noted in the last chapter, feminist theologian Valerie Saiving writes: "in order to answer a child's eager questions, the mother must be able to transcend her own habitual patterns of thought; she must meet the child where *he* is at that moment. It is absolutely impossible to communicate with a young child without somehow abandoning one's own perspective and looking at the world through *his* eyes."[40] It may be impossible for Israelis and Palestinians to communicate effectively without being willing, to some degree, to abandon their own perspectives and to endeavor to look at the world through one another's eyes. Of course, one need not be a parent to do this, but parents have a lot of practice, and that practice may be indispensable when engaging in the difficult work of facing violence and suffering. "When you have this huge pain," Siham Abu Awwad, whose brother Yusuf was killed in the conflict, says in a video produced by the Parents' Circle, "and you have a way to use it as a power . . ."[41] Her pain is so profound because of the depth of her love for her brother; she chooses to use both as a force to propel her forward, to push her into challenging dialogue —to forge a solution rather than allow others to hurt as her family has.

In 2011, the Parents' Circle created the Blood Relations Project, which involved Israelis and Palestinians donating to a mutual blood bank, with the slogan "Could you hurt someone who has your blood running through their veins?"[42] This project's impact comes from the bond that we experience in intimate physical connection, and the sense of empathy that it generates. It, too, takes aspects of a relationship well known to parents and deploys them in order to foster connection not only within a family, or even a community, but among groups of people who have long been antagonistic. The tools of parenting are used for peacemaking.

Some people struggle with whether or not to use the "mommy activist" label in their work. Bettina Elias Siegel worked for years as a lawyer in the food industry, and eventually became a school food advocate and a writer on the impact of food policy on children. For her, the movement into activism came when she saw her children "uncritically absorb" the marketing messages in unhealthy, highly processed food, and when she realized how ubiquitous this food—with its harmful, untested chemical additives—was in their lives.[43] She reflects, "Motherhood doesn't lend me any special moral authority in addressing those issues, but it has driven them home in a uniquely profound way."

Elias Siegel has found that playing the "mother card" in her activism can cause people on several sides to take her work less seriously. On the one hand, she is often presented as a "mommy blogger" by those who wish to delegitimize her opinions and elide her years of experience in the industry; on the other, she sometimes gets flack from feminist peers for identifying publicly as a mother, since her personal stake in the fight can be seen as reducing her credibility.

But Elias Siegel maintains that it's important for her to own her relationship to this work, and the personal place from which it comes.

"There are many paths to activism," she muses, and "the childless advocate may even be operating on a higher moral plane than those of us who started out selfishly trying to protect our own children." But, she notes, as a parent, she has particular insights to bring to the table—in her case, an insider's understanding of the challenges around getting kids to eat vegetables or working with a school principal. Sure, she muses, "historically, putting mothers on a pedestal was a backhanded way of keeping women down. But should throwing away the pedestal mean ignoring the unique perspective motherhood brings?"[44] Her own work has been shaped and informed by her love and care for her kids; this is, rather than something to downplay, Elias Siegel argues, something that should be worn proudly.

Of course, plenty of folks have engaged in acts of repairing the world before having children, or without having kids at all. Poet Staceyann Chin, for example, was so accustomed to the model of the child-free activist that she was afraid that becoming a mother would stifle her own activism. In an interview with the website Mater Mea she says that, before she had her daughter, she worried a lot that becoming a mother would impact parts of her that she didn't want to change. For, she says, "I felt like I would be sitting around writing poop poems. . . . I thought that she would make me less able to talk about the unpleasant things in life or be loud or want to go out there and march."

In the end, though, that's not what happened. For Chin, the power of the change is almost uncomfortable to name because her previous feminist outlook didn't allow for the possibility that having a child could have such a positive impact on her worldview. But, she says,

> Motherhood—has made me more centered, more steeped in my politics. I worried that [my daughter] would soften me in ways that would make me less effective as a human rights activist, but I think she's underscored the need for that kind of work and has connected me with other women. . . . Before Zuri I used to think about "Oh, saving little girls," these arbitrary little girls. When I put pen to paper now, the ink spread begins with her and then it radiates to the other people in the world who I might want to save as well. But now there's this sort of tangible, focused person for whom I would like to make the world better.[45]

Chin found herself surprised by the power that the particularity of her love, and feelings of responsibility and protectiveness for this one child, had on her engagement with the wider world. She was involved in activist work before, but *how* she thinks about that work, and what it means to her, was unalterably different after becoming a mother.

Indeed, this metamorphosis is a blessing, and a powerful one. When our love helps us to become brave and invested in one another, we may find that our parental transformation becomes a whole-self transformation, something that can help us to expand our vision outside our backyard, into the world as a whole. There's a Buddhist Metta Sutta, a loving kindness meditation, that echoes this idea:

> *Even as a mother at the risk of her life*
> *Watches over and protects her only child,*
> *So with a boundless mind should one cherish all living*
> *   things.*
> *Suffusing love over the entire world,*
> *Above, below, and all around, without limit,*
> *So let one cultivate an infinite good will toward the*
> *   whole world.*[46]

The selflessness and concern that this teaching identifies as the hallmark of maternal love is considered, here, to be a model for how all people—parents or not—should engage with the world as a whole.

The incredible work that some folks do doesn't mean, though, that we all have to be activists in the traditional sense to be able to have a meaningful impact on the world, or to let this game-changing love change who we are and how we live. As parents, we wield an immense power every single day as we engage in the deep and daily labor shaping someone else's psyche. Do we teach our children complacency, how to live off the pain and work of others? Do we teach them compassion, empathy, engagement with the world around us and a sense of their own connection with those they encounter? What do they learn from us when we encounter strangers in the street? What do they learn from us when members of our community are in crisis? What words do we use when we talk about war or other kinds of suffering we read about in the newspaper? What do they learn from us when we're frustrated with the customer service we've received? Having kids doesn't have to turn us all into Nelson Mandela or Dolores Huerta. But maybe we can try to show our kids how we love them by acting out that love in the wider world. We can try to be the kind of people who feel responsible for leaving the world a little better than how we found it. Maybe we can model that sense of responsibility, and help our children understand that that's part of their job, too.

Rabbi Tarfon, the ancient sage, once said, "You are not required to complete the task, but neither are you free to give up on it, either."[47] This—the work of caring for our children, of going deep with them and into ourselves, of allowing raising them to transform us, our lives, and our engagement with the whole world—this is our new project. It may never be finished. We may never reach an endpoint in our relationship with our children, and in the energy and labor and effort and love and passion and sleepless nights and worry and hope and triumph and concern and care that we pour into the task of raising them, day after day after day. But nor are we free to give up on it, either.

This is our sacrifice, our *korbon* of love. Every bumped head that we kiss, every lullabye we sing, every late night and early morning and sticky, messy "craft" project and tantrum navigated and every little moment of quiet, when we can actually take in the fullness of our child, however briefly— every ounce of our parenting is an offering that, like the ancient sacrifices in the Temple, sizzles on the altar of love. Its smoke rises high, to the heavens, and each time, we are palpably changed, created anew.

CHAPTER TEN

What Gives Us Goose Bumps

Parenting as a Mystical Encounter

———◆———

When I was in high school and college, I was a vocal—and smug—atheist who delighted in telling anyone who'd listen (and a few who wouldn't) that history and archaeology *really* don't back up a literal read of the Bible. Religion was a crutch for the insecure, a way of helping people feel better about the bad things that happened in life and a means of finding hope in some future reward that was probably never going to come.

I'm sure I was a real treat to be around.

But when I was twenty-one, a series of experiences that I couldn't quite categorize began kicking me upside the head. I'd be walking alone around my college campus at night and suddenly everything seemed to take on a softness, an illumination of some sort. My mind would go still. I would feel like I was dissolving, like the hard edges that defined me would get fuzzy, and the place where I stopped and everything else began wasn't so clear.

I tried to ignore these moments, but they kept recurring, and I eventually—somewhat reluctantly—went searching for some sort of framework in which to make sense of them. It was only then that I discovered that most religious thinkers throughout history had a much more complex take on God than anything I'd previously considered.

I learned that mystics of pretty much every world religion described the divine as something of the Great Everythingness and the Great Nothingness, the transcendent force that was—in a nutshell—the whole of the created universe plus maybe something more. God was not something separate from me, but rather the reality into which I could melt, in moments of awareness of my own small self as not distinct from, but rather a part of, this great whole. It was this melting—the sense of my particular, small self falling away into something larger, enveloping—that caused me to take pause in the first place.

I began to embrace this groove, and for a long time I framed my spiritual life in terms of transcendence and immolation—bringing myself into a place where, as Kabbalah scholar Daniel Matt puts it, "word, mind and self dissolve momentarily. . . ."[1] It would happen in moments of intense prayer or meditation, or even just out on a walk—anytime I could allow myself to let go of the proverbial controls. I'd find the edge of the sense of largeness of everything, and, however briefly, my selfhood would fall away and

I'd feel part of the rippling dance of Creation before popping back into my usual experience of consciousness.

I understood that most of the time I was meant to live in my body, in my usual ways of being, but I tried to dissolve, and to dissolve again, into God, though my contemplative disciplines. I tried to follow the kind of advice suggested by a sixteenth-century kabbalist named Hayyim Vital, who instructed:

> Strip your body from your soul, as if you do not feel that you are clothed in matter at all—you are entirely soul. The more you strip yourself of material being, the more powerful your comprehension. If you sense any sound or movement that breaks your meditation, or if any material imagining arises within you, then your soul's contemplation will be severed from the upper worlds. You will attain nothing, since supernal holiness does not abide with anyone attached by even a hair to the material realm.[2]

This notion echoes a lot of Western religious thinking. In Christianity, Saint Augustine, who lived in the late fourth/ early fifth century C.E., was a particularly notable champion of the idea that the soul and the body are separate—and that the soul was where our focus should be—and his ideas influenced a lot of Church doctrine and later European philosophers.

When I was just getting into spirituality, as far as I could tell, the whole point was to chase, and sometimes to capture, these experiences that seemed to expand me beyond the normal limits of my body, experiences that brought my consciousness into communion with what philosopher Paul Tillich called the "ground of being."[3] Eventually, though, I developed a more sophisticated view of religion and religious practice. I came to see that the goal of spiritual practice was perhaps more truly about service to others, becoming a better person, and responsibility to the whole, not just chasing the next moment of feeling twinkly and high. But still, when I thought about "being connected to God," this solitary, out-of-body feeling of transcendence was, more or less, what I considered the gold standard.

So imagine my surprise when Yonatan was born. I had been ordained as a rabbi the previous year, and I assumed that I had already sorted out my relationship with the divine. Sure, there might be ebb and flow in the strength of my connection, but I figured I had a pretty good handle on what it was going to be like, more or less for the duration of my life. How could having a kid really change anything?

Ha.

In hindsight, the fallacy is visible from a million miles away. At the time, though, I'd been operating with the same set of assumptions for more than ten years, and I had no reason to think that my experiences of the transcendent were, if not revealing objective truth about the nature of God, than at least as close as I was going to get from down here in my little Earth suit.

And that's just the thing. Mothering turned out to be *all*

about the Earth suit—both the kid's and mine. It started with pregnancy, whether I was feeling him wriggle and kick inside me or lying on the couch with nausea, heartburn, or fatigue; it was harder to feel transcend-y when I was brought into my body, again and again and again. Pregnancy felt like the opposite of what Hayyim Vital advised. And then, all these other things happened—childbirth, meeting my son, nursing him. Being with him, being blown wide open by the very fact of him in the world, especially in those early days, which were mostly deeply, relentlessly embodied.

In the first stages of Yonatan's life, the most important connection I had with him was physical—his sleep, his poop. The transfer of sustenance from my body to his, breast to mouth. Even as we got to know him on a less physical level—through his smiles, his reactions to things, his disposition—it was all mediated through the physical realm. Teething. Illness. Learning to crawl, to stand, to walk.

It seems glaringly obvious when I write this. Of course every experience in the world is not only mediated through our physicality, but *is* our physicality. Of course the acts of creating and caring for another human being would drive that home. But my religious thinking didn't take these things for granted, and so when I couldn't melt my consciousness into the Great Whole of Everything during prayer because my heartburn was particularly bad, or because I was toting around a slightly fussy baby or chasing after a toddler, it was frustrating. Was I just going to be "clothed in matter" now forever, unable to get the good, groovy God juice? Was having a kid going to keep me from accessing the holy? That just didn't seem right. But most of the mystics whose practices I admired and tried to emulate were men, or women operating out of the Christian monastic tradition—that is to say, people who were not, for a whole host of socioeconomic and historical reasons, engaged in the intimate care of small people. Was access to the divine really limited to those who had a room of one's own?

As I was able to step out of the fog of fatigue, I began to think and write about this question, and to talk to likeminded mama friends. Slowly I came to the understanding that the answer was, actually: "No." When I was able to hear and trust my own intuition, I found that it countered my long-standing beliefs. When I was able to let go of my assumption that "connection with God" was synonymous with one kind of experience—the melting thing—I discovered that I'd been having a different kind of experience for some time, and though that experience wasn't what I had believed brought me into connection with God, in truth, I was connected.

When I was pregnant, even from the very beginning, I would find that I'd pray with my hands around my belly, as though it were both the place from which my prayers originated and to which I was trying to direct some measure of divine flow. After Yonatan was born, I'd pray with him in the sling and find myself kissing his head and whispering the words of the liturgy into his ear, as though he was a secret conduit to the transcendent, a portal to infinity. I began to understand that, in a sense, he was. And that if he was, we all were. Even from down here, even when we were most decidedly attached to the material realm.

The sixteenth-century kabbalist Moshe Cordovero wrote,

> *The essence of divinity is found in every single thing—nothing but It exists. Since It causes every thing to be, no thing can live by anything else. It enlivens them.* Ein Sof *[infinity] exists in each existent. Do not say, 'This is a stone and not God.' God forbid! Rather, all existence is God, and the stone is a thing pervaded by divinity.*[4]

That is, our Earth suits are part of this great transcendent wow. Even if I don't have a certain kind of an affective mystical *feeling* when I pray with a kid strapped into a sling (or pulling at me from behind, or snuggled up in my lap), it's all part of the exquisite, holy beyond.

I understand that my story is pretty unusual. Most people don't get degrees in theology and spend years trying to work out the theory in their own lives before having kids. A lot of folks have kids and are startled by the hugeness of the experience, and they don't necessarily have language to describe what's happening. It's like they've found themselves suddenly in this big room full of light, with no real idea how they got there.

My mom, for example, as I've mentioned, didn't believe in God until she had kids. She was culturally Jewish, sure, but of the secular-intellectual sort, skeptical at best about any sort of supernatural claim. When my brother was born, though—well, I'm guessing she got hit upside the head with a big dose of awe and wonder. She told me a number of times when I was growing up that becoming a mom changed everything for her in her thinking about God, but, unfortunately, she died before I thought to ask her more about what she meant, what she felt, what she experienced. I'll never really know. But it's clear that *something* profound happened when my brother and I showed up. Something worldview-altering.

And the twentieth-century social activist Dorothy Day—eventually known for her devout Catholicism—hadn't been particularly religious in her youth; she struggled with her desires and despair, as so many of us do. The birth of her daughter, however, was an unexpected revelation. "No human creature could receive or contain so vast a flood of love and joy as I often felt after the birth of my child," she reflected. "With this came the need to worship, to adore. . . . Through a whole love, both physical and spiritual, I came to know God."[5] Both physical and spiritual—not an abrogation of the body and its experiences, but using and embracing these things as part of the on-ramp to the holy.

Another woman who never considered herself spiritual and would exclaim emphatically, "I hate organized religion!" told Rabbi Nancy Fuchs-Kreimer that, the night she brought her new daughter home from the hospital, "I walked around the house for hours and hours, just sensing her presence. I kept thinking, This is like being in a temple! I am dwelling in sacred precincts! It was not that my daughter was God but just that the divine was somehow in our midst."[6] Here, too, a new mom found herself, unexpectedly, in a new, strange space, one she never expected to enter. Birth, and its twin, death, are, for so many people, two of the greatest keys into this room—flush up against the holy, surrounded by life, by ultimate meaning, interfacing with reality in a new way.

Not everybody has these kinds of experiences, of course. And even of those who do, not everyone frames them in religious language—whether or not the feelings themselves correlate to what early twentieth-century theologian Rudolf Otto described as the *numinous,*[7] this raw sense of sacredness—a nonrational experience with something that feels outside the usual sense of self.

And even the fact that lots of people describe that type of feeling in different language doesn't mean that there's some objective, singular spiritual experience or encounter with the divine to be had. Given that everything else in our lives is filtered through the specificity of who we are—the particulars of our story, our cultural background, our historical moment, and so forth—there's no reason to think that *this* isn't as well. The context in which we find ourselves matters, and impacts not only how we make sense of what happens to us, but our spiritual experiences too.

Does a teenage boy who emigrated from Mexico and was raised strongly in the Catholic tradition experience the *numinous* in the exactly the same way as a secular, third-generation, Chinese-American stay-at-home mom living in the suburbs? Maybe not. I mean, heck, my own encounters, and vocabulary, changed pretty tremendously just by virtue of having a kid. I thought I already had the master set of keys to the door opening my awesome ancient tradition, but then I discovered it was more complicated than that. I'm not saying anyone changed the locks; I suspect that the main door still works fine for a lot of people. But the keys in my own hands changed—what I need, what I want, and how I see the world were transformed as I became a mother. And when I want to get up close to the big, big light, I now go looking for a different entry point.

It's possible that our kids can be important teachers who help us better find the doorways to the transcendent. That is, perhaps the work we do to care for our kids trains us to attune more closely to the still small voice that is so often hidden in our day-to-day—the voice of deepest insight that some of us call God. Rabbi Emma Kippley-Ogman mused on this when her son Otto was still a small baby. For, she says,

> I've been in awe of the way that communication happens without words. The way [Otto] makes it totally clear what he wants without having words to say, and this dance of learning how to understand him. How much more so is the divine in the world. We're both human, Otto and I have ways of understanding through our humanity. But with God—what is communicated if I'm listening right? How am I attuned to understand what's coming? Parenting a newborn and infant feels like training in that art. What am I listening for? What do I make of it? How do I hold that and honor that and respond to that?[8]

And that art—of attunement, of hearing the murmurs beyond what's spoken—changes and shifts as our children grow. When is the kindergartner feeling frustrated and expressing it by acting out? When is the sixth-grader insecure and desperate for reassurance but embarrassed to ask for it? As we learn a particular kind of discernment from tuning in to our children, it could make us better able to hear what else might be offered to us from the deep—from our inmost selves, from the transcendence beyond that. If we're willing to try to listen. If we let our children show us how to get in.

In a discussion of how parenting impacts our experiences of the divine, I would be remiss to not address the language we use to talk about God. After all, so many of us have specific connotations of the G-word in our heads or hearts—images instilled by our religious education, the scripture or liturgy we grew up with, or even just what we've absorbed from contemporary popular culture. For many of us, these metaphors and ideas about God can actually impede a more direct experience of the transcendent, and carefully unpacking the language we use to talk about the divine might allow something different to happen. But not only that: The metaphors themselves, if we can open them up, have a power that can be useful to us as parents (and as humans) and can illuminate our encounters with our kids from surprising and potent angles. Our experiences matter. So do the words we find to describe them. And those two things can shape each other, even if we don't always see how.

Ask people to imagine God and, consciously or unconsciously, most people will go straight for the dude in the sky. The one with the thunderbolt. The menacing glare. Who sees you when you're sleeping and knows when you're awake, and who might zap you at any moment because how long *has* it been since you've been to services, anyway?

This is, for better or worse, the metaphor that reigns in our culture. The bearded God who looks like Zeus on the ceiling of the Sistine Chapel might have come from Renaissance-era Christians' infatuation with Greek iconography, but there's also plenty of anthropomorphism in traditional Jewish texts. The Torah talks about a God who took the Israelites out of Egypt with a mighty hand and a strong arm, whose nostrils flare in anger. God is referred to as a king all over the Bible, all over Jewish liturgy, in the standard formula for benedictions. Sometimes we hear about God as shepherd, as father, as master. Sometimes God is named in more abstract terms—Jews talk about God as rock, as place, as redeemer—but even so, that guy with the beard has a pretty strong hold on our collective imagination.

Many, many Jewish commentators take pains to note that all that anthropomorphic—and, frequently, male—language is, really, just metaphor. "The Torah speaks in the language of human beings,"[9] the ancient rabbis said, meaning that we use familiar language to help us access something that's beyond our comprehension. The medieval philosopher Maimonides is adamant that anyone who takes literally any of God's physical descriptions—of having a body, of having a gender, even having "emotions" like humans do—is committing idolatry.[10] And still, the metaphors that dominate Jewish texts for God are of the king, the shepherd, the master, the father.

For Christians, the image is similarly entrenched; despite almost every denomination's repeated insistence that God "transcends the human distinction between the sexes,"[11] the image of the earthly, embodied, male Jesus and his Heavenly Father—after all, Jesus had a human mother—dominates much Christian thinking and writing. And these representations impact how parents think of themselves, their children, and the work of raising them.

As entrenched as the image of God-as-father is, there are places in traditional texts where pregancy, birth, and nursing are used as metaphors for the divine, and they can help us understand the power of these human acts.

For example, in the beginning of the Book of Exodus,[12] we meet a woman who is eventually identified as Yocheved, Moses' mother. The text tells us that she conceived and gave birth to a son, and saw *ki tov*; she saw that he was good.

There are a lot of linguistic echoes in the Torah—places where words are repeated in new contexts to add another layer of meaning. They're literary hyperlinks, if you will— they refer back to a whole other story or situation or law and infuse our reading of the text in front of us. For example, using a word for defiling the ancient Jerusalem Temple when talking about adultery tells us a lot about how the Bible understood what marriage was, and what was at stake when those vows were broken.

When Yocheved sees her son *ki tov*, there is a major

resonance. That is, the same language appears at a crucial moment earlier in the Torah—during the creation of the world. God, in the first chapter of Genesis, creates the heavens, the Earth, the seas, the light—and then, it says, "And God saw the light, that it was good."[13] God saw the light *ki tov*. And over the course of the next week, as God creates trees and grass and sun and moon and fish and creepy-crawlies and cows and the whole thing—after almost every day of creation, God saw *ki tov*. That it was good.[14]

When Yocheved creates life, she is, the text implies, like God. She has brought something into being, and when she looks at her creation, she regards him with a divine eye. While babymaking isn't *creatio ex nilhio* in the strictest sense, there's an awe and reverence for the mere fact of this new child's existence.

The Bible returns again and again to birth and nursing as potent metaphors. When Moses is frustrated with the people Israel's constant disobedience in the wilderness, he complains to God, "Did I conceive all these people? Did I birth them, that you should say to me, 'Carry them in your bosom, as a guardian carries a nursing child. . . .'?"[15] The implication is that Moses isn't the mother of these people, God is—and so they should be God's problem. In other biblical texts, Zion is sometimes described as a mother who loves her children or one who suffers labor pangs.[16]

The ancient rabbis writing in the first five centuries C.E. went even further with this whole set of metaphors. They describe Moses and Aaron as being like a nursing woman's two breasts.[17] Manna is described as breastmilk,[18] as is the divine voice of revelation itself.[19] It's suggested that Mount Sinai itself served as a gigantic breast that nursed the Israelites, infant nation that they were,[20] and God is elsewhere described as the Israelites' wet nurse.[21]

Before I had kids, I found the female metaphors for God as limiting as the male ones—mere semantic distractions that kept me from accessing the Great Eternal Wow Beyond Language. But after kids, down here in the Earth suit, I've found that they resonate more deeply. Sometimes, when I was nursing Yonatan or Shir, I'd see my baby gaze at me with a look of awe that all of his needs were met; in his helplessness, he was shown loving compassion, and was cared for as he needed it most. Nurtured. Sustained. I'd think, This is how I can understand the story of manna nourishing the Israelites in the desert. God as nursing mother. Suddenly it made sense.

In fact, I occasionally experience the transcendent in a way that's not so dissimilar from what I saw in my babies' eyes or what I read about having happened to the Israelites in the desert. This sense of being fed something essential at a time when I feel most vulnerable. Those moments when I've called out, "Help me" in prayer—whether in formal prayer or in more spontaneous moments, and felt, suddenly, like I had help, somehow. Like, at the very least, I wasn't alone.

There are other places where Jewish traditional literature talks about God in female terms and makes use of mothering language. Some commentators make the connection between the language of God as *HaRachaman*, the Compassionate One, and *rechem*, the womb.[22] The immanent aspect of the divine, referred to in rabbinic and kabbalistic literature as the *Shekhina*, is generally described in female-gendered terms, and often likened to a mother—and vice versa. For example, the Talmud tells us that "whenever Rav Yosef would hear the footsteps of his mother, he would say: 'I shall stand before the *Shekhina*, who is approaching.'"[23] The *Shekhina* is sometimes described as the mother who, since the destruction of the Second Temple, suffers along with her children in exile. Some texts go as far as to suggest that the *Shekhina* menstruates, as reflected in the waxing and waning of the moon that determines the Jewish calendar.[24]

Once I became a parent, and experienced the exhausting, wonderful, difficult work of raising my children, I began to see all of these metaphors in a different light—in a way that, perhaps, might have been there in the liturgy all along.

When I was younger, I'd think of "Our Father" as, you know, the God that gets mad at you when you don't do your homework. But now, when I think about the divine in the metaphoric clothing of a parent—of whatever gender—I think about the desperate desire of a parent who wants to watch kids grow and flourish and become the best possible version of themselves. I think about how a parent regards his or her child with a tender eye, with compassion and concern.

One mom, named Katherine, reflected on how she was changed in becoming a mother.

> *I think I'm more understanding of the humanity of everyone, you know? We are all in our own stages of development. When someone is saying something silly or stupid*

or self-centered then I just think, "Oh well, that's where
you are." You kind of approach it in the same way as you
do if your kid is trying to swim and can't swim and you
have to figure out whether that's his fault or whether
that's just where he is right now.[25]

When I encounter God-as-parent language in the liturgy,
I think of this sometimes. Perhaps, during the High Holy
Days, when we exclaim, *"Avinu Malkeinu!"*—"Our Father,
our King—we have sinned before you!"[26] it's less about
begging God not to ground us for breaking the proverbial
window with our baseball and a little more about asking to
be seen for who we are right now—as the kids who are learning to swim the best we can, but who can't get better any
faster than our abilities will allow. And that maybe it's OK
to be just where we are. There are days when that possibility
offers me a great deal of solace.

But this God-as-parent language is complicated and slip-
pery, precisely because there are deep spiritual lessons we're
learning from both sides. Are we, as parents, always the ones
in power offering unconditional love and compassion to
someone powerless who may constantly be making mistakes?
Might we be able to learn and understand that we, too, are
loved with such fiery fierceness, and forgiven for our inevitable limits? Or are we, as my friend Laura puts it, "at the
mercy of an incomprehensible and absolute power that wakes
us up in the wee hours with strange demands and that we
promise to serve and adore all our days (in which case we're
maybe learning that loving God is a devastating disruption

of everything I thought was my life)," and that that's actually a perfectly wonderful thing? She sums up the problem succinctly: "Who is it that has the absolute power in the mother/infant dyad? Who's at whose mercy? Some days it changes like every ten seconds."

For my friend Eliana, living in that reality was a gamechanger. A few years ago, when her son Barzilai was an infant, she was home with him and serving as his primary daytime caregiver. "Naturally," she told me, "the dynamic with this seven-month-old was that I was bigger than he and I was in charge of taking care of both of us." One morning, during the month before the High Holy Days, she was wearing him in a sling while praying. When she got to the *Avinu Malkeinu*—the "our father, our king," part of the liturgy of the season—she had something of a revelation that changed their relationship. "Compared to the *Avinu* in the song, Barzilai and I are actually exactly the same size. I just happen to be a barely older model." In other words, as large and powerful as she generally felt in relation to this small, relatively helpless and entirely needy little guy, the prayer helped her see her own smallness, and how her own humanity and Barzilai's were really leveled out—and, perhaps, how she was needy and Barzilai was powerful. The difference between her, as a grown woman, and this tiny baby suddenly didn't seem so significant at all.

Perhaps the language we've developed for God has stuck precisely because it's useful in helping us to access some important means of connecting. But I wonder if finding new metaphors—not of God as Daddy, not of God as Mommy, necessarily, but working in those general realms—might open up other kinds of experiences for us as well.

For example, picture a woman who's pregnant. She and the fetus are, in some respects, separate, and in some respects, they're one being. They eat as one. They breathe as one. It's not always strictly clear where the mother ends and the fetus begins; there are parts of a fetus's DNA in the mother's own bloodstream at as early as eight weeks.

This is how the mystics in the Jewish tradition and elsewhere talk about God—not with this metaphor, per se, but with this general set of ideas. We are all, mystics would tell us, part of one great interconnected being. We are all interlinked, and this connection binds us, sustains us, and nourishes us in ways that we may never fully comprehend. Remember Cordovero? "Since [the essence of divinity] causes every thing to be, no thing can live by anything else. It enlivens them."[27] The fetus is in some sense separate from the mother, in some sense dependent on her, and at the same time, interlinked, interdependent with her. How might thinking of ourselves as gestating, embedded in something larger, impact our sense of spirituality?

That's just one image for how we might relate to divinity. What other kinds of possibilities can those of us who have been engaged in the work of parenting offer to the larger conversation? What wisdom about the workings of the universe and the nature of the transcendent have we learned by managing tantrums and waking up in the middle of the night, nursing babies and helping bigger kids face their fears? If Torah speaks in the language of human beings, it's also true that the human beings expand our sense of Torah—of the holy, of the possible. And the images that infuse our lives can give us new ways to describe our encounters with eternity, new possibilities for understanding them. Theology has been dominated, for many hundreds of years, by people who have not been their children's primary caregivers. I wonder how things might look if more of us with this complex, cuddly, messy, exhausted reality began to insert our voices into the mix.

But expanding or opening up how we envision and describe God can only get us so far. On the one hand, all these metaphors—God the judge, God the shepherd, God the father, God the nursing mother, the God that gestates the world and all of us, or God the redeemer—have the potential to influence our prayer or other kinds of spiritual experiences. The images can offer an on-ramp, of sorts. But these metaphors rein in something that transcends language and keeps us from tapping into the great everythingness. Thinking of God in human terms as a "someone" who has experiences that are like my own profound experiences of parenting can be useful when I'm looking for a means of expressing the sacred from my little reference point down here. But at a certain point, perhaps it's also OK to break out past those metaphors, to go beyond the horizon, to break out into the unboundedness of infinity.

———

Maybe we are all separate beings. (I mean, none of us knows, really, for sure, how this all works.) But even if we are, even if the feelings of interconnection are just feelings, that sense of mystical communion can be deep and powerful. And perhaps this theological language can give us a way to articulate some of the spine-tingling feelings we have when we're with our kids—feelings that are hard to name, feelings for which contemporary secular culture doesn't offer easy descriptors.

Cognitive science tells us that young infants don't necessarily know where they end and their caregiver begins;[28] whatever the reality might be, those babies feel a sense of oneness with the big monkeys holding them, feeding them, snuggling them.

Truth be told, I sometimes feel that sense of oneness with my kids, as well. Of course, it was easier when they were tiny—when they were nursing, when they fell asleep on me, when they were content to snuggle for hours with their head on my shoulder. But even now, it happens, in brief flashes—during that moment when the laughter and tickling turn ecstatic and all conscious thought falls away, during sleepy moments in the middle of the night when one of them crawls into bed, and neither of us are fully asleep or fully awake, during the rare moment when one of them looks deep into my eyes for a minute, and the love that flows through me enfolds us both. Just as quickly as it comes, it's gone. But it was there. It happened.

This is one of those places where I could get in trouble for romanticizing parenting—giving the highly misleading and unhelpful impression that my relationship with my kids floats on a cloud of magical bliss most of the time, which of course it doesn't. There are plenty of times when I feel bewildered by the short strangers with bad table manners who live in my home, times when I want them to just . . . stop . . . touching . . . me . . . for . . . a . . . minute, times when their lives were probably saved by the evolutionary trick of making kids cute.

And there are plenty of other times when the best parts of being with them are really about the fact that we are totally independent entities. Yonatan's thrill when we got to the part where Charlie finds the last Golden Ticket was about his awesome little beginner's mind, the fact that he's not jaded enough to have assumed that it was definitely going to happen. When Shir enlists me to assist in his elaborate taking-care-of-Teddy rituals, I get to learn more about who he is, how he makes sense of his life. So much of both the headaches and the joy is in the fact that they're entirely separate people, growing and seeing the world from their own vantages.

But even in the reality of that separateness, there can be these powerful moments of, well, union. I think it's possible to have that experience with anyone, if you're able to go deep enough into the now with them. It can happen in laughter, in tears, in an embrace, in a moment of deep shared understanding and revelation. These experiences are rare—at least for me—but when they happen, they take us, even for a second, outside our usual ways of being.

Christian theology talks about *kenosis*, the sense of opening the self to allow the divine to flow in. Jewish mystics talk about *deveikut*, the process of clinging, cleaving, or attaching oneself to God.

And it's not for nothing that this cleaving, this opening, this union is often framed in the language of love. The Sufi poet Rumi writes to God, "The minute I heard my first love story / I started looking for You, not knowing / how blind that was. / Lovers don't finally meet somewhere, / they're in each other all along."[29] The Jewish liturgical poem "Yedid Nefesh," sung at the beginning of every Shabbat evening service, is full of visceral yearning: "Let Your affection be sweeter than a honeycomb or any other taste. Splendorous one, most beautiful radiance of the world, my soul is sick with love for You. . . ." The most famous love poem in the Jewish canon, the Song of Songs—the tale of two lovers seeking, and perhaps finding, one another—is often interpreted to be the story of human/divine mystical connection. It's the story of the union Hayyim Vital describes that I explored at the beginning of this chapter—though I no longer agree with him that we have to leave our bodies in order to get there.

This union is usually framed in the language of adult lovers seeking and sometimes finding one another, but I think that the love that parents experience is at least as powerful a framework. After all, what the Sufis and kabbalists are talking about is not just everyday love—it's the transcendent love that pours through you, from someplace else. It's the love that's larger than you, that you happen to inhabit and offer out. It's about grace and effulgence and the overflow of compassion and goodness. I don't know about you, but that's a lot of how I experience my love for my kids—a *kenosis,* a longing for *deveikut*—which manages to be sometimes both overpowering and full of a delicate tenderness all at once.

I wonder if our experience of intimate connection with our children can't be thought of as a sort of mystical encounter in its own right, if it can't be understood as an engagement with the infinite, a moment of transcending the smallness of our usual everyday selves and experiencing the Big Bigness. These ridiculous, vulnerable, sweet, irrational, surprising little humans are a mystery in and of themselves, and when we let ourselves go into that mystery with them, they can take us out into Mystery itself.

I don't believe, anymore, that I can only get into the good transcendent stuff when I'm alone. Sometimes, when we take one another's hands, we can go there together.

There's a photograph of Yonatan and me together one summer night, when he was about a year and a half old. Nir, Yonatan, and I were traveling, out late, and had wandered into an empty courtyard lit by street lamps as we made our way back to our hotel. It was one of those enchanted little moments; my son was toddling around on cobblestones, laughing, delighted by the freedom we afforded him. In the photo, I'm sitting on the ground, my arms outstretched, trying to convince Yonatan to run into them for a hug. But he's laughing and dashing away, a half-blur as far as the camera-phone was concerned.

I feel like my parenting looks a lot like that a lot of days. Sure, sometimes (OK, a lot of the time) my kids want more of me than I feel like I have available to give. But there are plenty of other times when I'm calling to them, arms wide open, trying to coax them to me for even just a moment. I just want to bring them back to me, to return to that place—if only for the briefest second—of connection. Come over here for that hug, that kiss, that cuddle! Please?!!

We do this almost from the moment they're out of the womb and in our arms—I mean, maybe we nibble on babies' toes because, on some level, we want to consume them. Obviously, this desire is in part a biological reaction, nature's way of ensuring that we feel attached to and excited by our children,[30] but oxytocin's allure isn't mutually exclusive with other kinds of power in the parent-child bond. That is, I wonder if the longing that we feel sometimes for our children, the longing to bring them back into our arms, isn't of a piece with the longing of the Rumi poem, of the "Yedid Nefesh," of the ardent searching in the Song of Songs. The desperate calling to return to a place of connection, of cleaving: "My soul is sick with love for you."

And when I think about my own longing for my child as being of a piece with my longing for the divine, and that my craving for my little love can help me into the boundlessness of Love itself, it opens up space for both.

———

The mysticsm I've been talking about here sometimes happens to people during prayer, meditation, and contemplation. But the experience isn't limited to those searching for the divine, using traditional (or less traditional) God language. Even the sensations that precipitated my own spiritual searching weren't totally unique in my life—I'd had that sense of melting, of losing myself many times before. When I was a teenager, I'd immolate myself in the sea of guitars and the mosh pit at punk shows, and I'd go to dance clubs and feel my self blurred by the thumping beat and rhythm. Musicians, athletes, and artists often talk about this sense of losing themselves when deep in their work, and it's not for nothing that entire branches of the religious family tree have developed around the power of sexual intimacy. People can have encounters with something beyond themselves, whether or not they consider themselves believers of any sort. And here, as much as anywhere, the profound internal shifts that parenting so often causes can have major implications.

Kristina Jordan Cobarrubia experienced this through her love of flamenco dancing. There's a notion in flamenco known as *duende*—a "magical, elusive moment, when everything, the dancer, the guitarist, and the singer are all moved by each other and moving as one." Cobarrubia says that "it's fleeting, but when it happens, everyone can feel it, including the audience." But for her, even after ten years of studying flamenco, she had never had *duende*. She was good, sure, and she'd seen other dancers experience it, but, though she had feelings, deep moments, there was no *duende* in sight.

And then she became a mother. She'd danced many

times since giving birth, but one day, she was slated to perform at a family-friendly matinee, so her daughter got to see
her on stage for the first time. Cobarrubia's first song began,
and then she looked out into the audience and spied her
two-year-old looking up at her.

"And suddenly it flooded me," she recounted.

> *My love for her overwhelmed everything else. My arms
> took on a new life, a new force. Though dancing slowly,
> every fiber of my being was awake with energy, and
> passion filled my heart. I heard cries of "Ole!" from the
> other artists and I realized that this was it! This was
> duende! The catapult of feeling that projects you solely
> into the now, the very moment, all your concentration
> changing into the essence of pure presence. The song filled
> my body with a fire of spirit, and I felt so intensely I
> thought my heart might burst.*[31]

I don't know if Cobarrubia herself would label this as an
experience of the divine, but, as Daniel Matt put it, "There
are moments when the self uncovers its vast ground of
being, its interface with all that exists. Mystics have no monopoly on such moments."[32] In *duende*, Cobarrubia tapped
in. Her love for her daughter had opened her, changed her,
made her, for the first time, able to access this deep experience of unity.

Sometimes our children themselves offer us the way in.
And sometimes how they change us *is* the way in.

My children have transformed me. They have given me

entirely new means of experiencing the divine, and under-standing what God is or can be. They have offered me fresh possibilities for living, loving, and serving that have upended entirely my notion of what spiritual practice is all about. They have expanded my capacity for joy, for sorrow, for feeling in general. They've made me more sensitive in some respects, and less self-conscious in others. Maybe the ongoing, impossible work of learning when to stop trying to control the situation, control who they are, control what they want, is also teaching me to let go more fully at other times. Or maybe they've just split my heart open in a way that makes it possible for me to let everything else in. I don't know, maybe I'll never know. This, too, is part of the mystery.

Afterword

It's almost never the big moments, is it?

It's Shir, whimpering in his room when he's supposed to be asleep, and then calling, "Can you help me?" and emerging into the living room a moment later, his pajama shirt on inside out, except for how his arm's stuck, because of the one sleeve that he couldn't quite pull out.

It's Yonatan, singing some song he learned in kindergarten to the mirror, bopping his hips in a gleeful, dorky, gorgeously unselfconscious way that I know he'll probably lose in a few years.

It's Yonatan, getting paradoxically whiny and entitled at the end of a day that already had an unusual number of experiential and gastronomical treats in it—and how he finally turns back into a reasonable child after he's told no, firmly, a few times.

It's Shir, crying because he just bashed his face somehow

into my leg and it hurts, and how he's finally soothed and calmed to a few rounds of "The Lion Sleeps Tonight," which hasn't been part of our repertoire for over a year.

I still can't believe my dumb luck, with all of this. That these beautiful, exquisite children are mine to love—to clean up, to be pushed to the limits by, to get woken up by, the whole package. Somehow they've been left in my care, clueless and unwitting as I usually am about all of this, not to mention so often feeling grumpy and taking them for granted. When I'm able to really contemplate the responsibility of caring for them, it's pretty darn humbling. I hope I live up to it, at least some of the time.

Our growth in this spiritual practice of loving and caring for our children isn't always linear. It's most certainly a "practice" in the true sense of the word—something we try, again and again and again, sometimes hitting the right notes and sometimes not quite getting there. We all have days when we're off, sometimes a lot of them. As with every practice, though, we return, and return again, and try to do better this next time, to put more of ourselves into the work, to be more present, more plugged in.

And the more we practice—the more we work the muscles of empathy, of I-Thou, of radical amazement and *teshuvah*, the more we're able to find the wonder and awe in the everyday, excruciatingly mundane moments with our kids—the stronger those muscles get. There'll always be the times that we're exhausted, anxious, impatient, and frustrated. But regarding our parental labor as a practice might make those times fewer. And maybe it'll be just a little bit easier to get out of that place, to recover from the exasperation and find, once again, the sponteneity and joy that these beautiful, ever-changing creatures can offer us.

The more I return, with intentionality, to the spirituality inherent in the work of parenting, the more I find that my cisterns stay fuller, longer. I still have lots of days with plenty of struggle, and I still mess up all the time. But through the process of writing this book, of trying to remember to take my own advice, I've found that I have a greater sense of possibility, too. I've found more doors ajar that open to places I can be besides that same sad space of unconscious reaction. Most of those doors lead to being able to actually experience the moment that is now, or to the eternal moment that is always. There, I'm able to have better conversations with my thoughtful, sweet big boy, to be more free when I play with my giggly munchkin. There, I'm less likely to try to hustle my kids from place to place, and I'm more cognizant of the fact that there's a lot of great scenery along the way. I'm more apt to glimpse the divine hiding behind their eyes, and to feel the holy between us when a moment turns unexpectedly tender and I am exploded with love for them.

In Pirkei Avot, the second-century collection of Jewish wisdom, the sage Ben Bag Bag is quoted as saying, in regards to Torah: "Turn it and turn it, for everything is in it. Look into it, grow old and worn over it, and never move away from it, for you can not find any better measure than this."[1]

I think parenting is like this—turn it and turn it, every which way you look at it, the whole universe is there. Joy and pain and love and suffering and hope and frustration and

exasperation and redemption and the ever-growing possibility of becoming, each day, a little bit more who we were
meant to be. We grow old—and, yes, OK, worn—by the
work of caring for and nurturing our children. We remain
embedded in it as long as we live, long after our kids grow
up, sprout wings, do whatever happens after this chapter of
our lives together. We are permanently marked by it. And
this work, and this transformation, is Torah. It's real Torah—
truth-teaching, wisdom, a path to the sacred. The work is
fully woven into our lives—when we lie down, when we rise
up, when we sit at home, and when we're walking by the way.
When we choose to live it fully, that's when we begin to understand: We may never find any measure better than this.

Acknowledgments

◆

First of all, so many kinds of gratitude to my incredible editor, Whitney Frick, and the whole great team at Flatiron Books. And to the incomparable Jill Grinberg—thank you, thank you, thank you.

Laura Jackson has been my first reader, *hevruta*, handholder, and drill sergeant for almost twenty years. I am so grateful for her friendship. The wonderful Judy Greenberg also went painstakingly over everything, offering just the right insights.

Thanks to the vast village it took to raise this book and care for me and my family while it happened, including Kirsten Cowan, Karissa Sellman, Diane Bernbaum, S. Bear Bergman, Hanne Blank, Leigh Ann Craig, Jen Taylor, Wendy Love Anderson, Eddie Dinel, Sarah-Bess Dworin, Sam Feinsmith, Shoshana Waskow, and Michael, Kalman, and Yonit Slater. A special thanks to my colleagues at Ask Big Questions and Hillel for their support and friendship through this process, most especially Josh Feigelson and Sheila Katz.

Cheers to the independent coffee shops of Evanston, especially Coffee Lab, Unicorn, Hoosier Mama, The Other Brother, and The Brothers K.

Gratitude to my brother Ben for love and support, always.

Special love to my littlest and greatest teachers, Yonatan, Shir, and Nomi. The Torah you teach is the best Torah.

Most of all, thank you to Nir—my rock, my love, cleaner of vomit and giver of care. I'm so grateful that you put up with my *mishegas*, make me better, and even consent to letting me write about you a little bit in these pages. *Neshikot*.

Notes

———◆———

Introduction

1. Merle Feld, *A Spiritual Life: Exploring the Heart and Jewish Tradition* (Albany, NY: SUNY Press, 2007), 70.
2. *Yom tov sheini shel galuyot,* the second festival day in the Diaspora. Babylonian Talmud, Beitzah 4b–5a. You can eat it.
3. Babylonian Talmud, Avodah Zara 30a. The answer is that you have to dilute the wine with water, because a snake might risk his life for pure wine, but not the watered-down stuff. (You think I'm kidding? Look it up yourself.)
4. Babylonian Talmud, Pesachim 110a. They recommend drinking an odd number of drinks, so if you decide to have a second round, you're better off committing to that third.
5. Thanks to the great Parker Palmer for this anecdote, shared at his home in Madison, Wisconsin, on November 6, 2014. Parker was in the audience at this lecture when this exchange happened.
6. Yes, we have a few records of women's spiritual lives at various points—*tekhines,* for example, are prayers from the seventeenth to twentieth centuries written in the Yiddish vernacular, for women, often by women, that consecrate various moments in their lives and days. But even they tell us relatively little about how mothers

themselves actually *experienced* their children, what they felt, how those interactions really went. That's where I'm really most full of questions.

1. So Much Is Different Now: Parental Love as a Portal to Infinity

1. Private correspondence with Baruch Stone, researcher at Harvard Medical School, May 2, 2014.
2. Virginia Woolf, "Professions for Women," in *Collected Essays* (London: Hogarth Press, 1966), 2, 285.
3. Needless to say, most poor women and women of color didn't get to be seen as saintly, delicate flowers. Also, interestingly, the "angel in the house" notion came as a response to eighteenth-century urbanization and anxieties about the ways that city living would foster women's independence—so it was a way of keeping her in her place. For more on this, see Linda Colley, *Britons: Forging the Nation 1707–1837* (New Haven: Yale University Press, 1992), 241–44. For example, from p. 241: "Who in the future would bear the children, worried Lord Kames, now that so many women were intent on enjoying themselves outside the home?"
4. All quotes are from cards found on http://www.bluemountain.com/ (replete with illustrations of butterflies, flowers, and cartoon bears), accessed May 13, 2014.
5. bell hooks, *All About Love: New Visions* (New York: William Morrow, 2000), 4.
6. Fred Rogers, *The World According to Mister Rogers: Important Things to Remember* (New York: Hyperion, 2003), 53.
7. Becky Bailey, *Easy to Love, Difficult to Discipline* (New York: William Morrow, 2001), 129.
8. Sara Ruddick, *Maternal Thinking: Toward a Politics of Peace* (Boston: Beacon Press, 1989), 121.
9. Ibid., 119.
10. "Elul Reflections: When Pesach Falls in August," *D'yo Ilu Yamey*. Accessed May 14, 2014: http://ktiva.blogspot.com/2013/08/elul-reflections-when-pesach-falls-in.html.
11. Carol Lee Flinders, *At the Root of This Longing: Reconciling a Spiri-*

tual Hunger and a Feminist Thirst (San Francisco: HarperSanFrancisco, 1998), 265.

12. Thanks, Dr. Aryeh Cohen, for getting it and for being smart.

13. Midrash Sifra, Kedoshim 45 (discussing Leviticus 19:18).

14. Deuteronomy 6:5.

15. Personal correspondence, April 17, 2015.

16. Ibid.

17. Maimonedes, Mishnah Torah, Hilchot Yesodei HaTorah, 2:2.

2. Sweeping Cheerios from the Floor: Finding Inspiration in the Mundane

1. Aaron Traister, "Is My Kids Making Me Not Smart?" Salon.com, December 4, 2009. Accessed March 6, 2015: http://www.salon.com /2009/12/05/traister_parenting_makes_me_dumb/.

2. Betty Friedan, *The Feminine Mystique* (New York: W. W. Norton, 1963), 15.

3. Max Kadushin, *The Rabbinic Mind* (Binghamton, NY: Global Publishing, 2001), 194–212.

4. See, e.g., Shunryu Suzuki, *Zen Mind, Beginner's Mind* (Boston: Shambhala, 2011).

5. Ethan Nichtern, "Buddhist Quote of the Day: Thich Nhat Hanh Says Do Your Dishes Before You Change the World," Beliefnet .com. Accessed on March 13, 2013: http://blog.beliefnet.com /onecity/2009/11/buddhist-quote-of-the-day-thich-nhat-hanh-says -do-your-dishes-before-you-change-the-world.html#sthash .aBTKDqFD.dpuf.

6. Kathleen Norris, *The Quotidian Mysteries: Laundry, Liturgy and "Women's Work"* (Mahwah, NJ: Paulist Press, 1998), 87.

7. See, for example, Abraham Joshua Heschel, *God in Search of Man: A Philosophy of Judaism* (New York: Macmillan, 1976), 43–52.

8. Terry Tempest Williams, *When Women Were Birds: Fifty-Four Variations on Voice* (New York: Picador, 2013), 85.

9. Natalie Goldberg, *Writing Down the Bones: Freeing the Writer Within* (Boston: Shambhala, 2005), 3.

10. Moses De León, *Sefer HaRimmon*, ed. Elliot R. Wolfson (Atlanta: Scholars Press, 1988), 181–82.

11. Avraham Isaac Kook, Orot HaKodesh, 3:184.
12. Norris, *The Quotidian Mysteries*, 10.

3. Frustration! Anger! Desperation! Transforming Hard Feelings

1. Adrienne Rich, *Of Woman Born: Motherhood as Experience and Institution* (New York: W. W. Norton, 1986), 21.
2. Jane Lazarre, *The Mother Knot* (Boston: Beacon Press, 1985), 85.
3. Peggy O'Mara, "A Lantern for Lori," *Mothering* 128 (January-February 2005): 8.
4. Personal correspondence, April 22, 2015.
5. Rumi, "The Guest House," in *The Essential Rumi*, trans. Coleman Barks (San Francisco: HarperSanFrancisco, 1995), 109.
6. Donna Rockwell, "True Stories About Sitting Meditation," *Shambhala Sun*, March 2003.
7. Rabbi Kalonymus Kalman Shapira. Derekh Hamelekh, Derushim LePesach, s.v. Bekhol Dor Vador Chayav Adam Lir'ot Et Atzmo Keilu Hu Yatza Mimitzrayim. Translated by Rabbi Sam Feinsmith, to whom I am grateful for alerting me to this source.
8. Rabbi Alan Lew, may his memory be a blessing and a light.
9. Deuteronomy 6:5–9.
10. This is an oft-quoted but acknowledged to be liberal interpretation of the original teaching.
11. Tamar Fox, "Saying Goodbye to My Foster Child," Kveller, April 16, 2015. Accessed April 22, 2015: http://www.kveller.com/saying-goodbye-to-my-foster-child/.
12. Personal correspondence, April 22, 2015.
13. Ibid.
14. Anne Neville, "Twenty Years and One Little Boy Later," Hip Mama, May 4, 2009. Accessed November 11, 2014: http://www.hipmama.com/features/twenty-years-and-one-little-boy-later-anne-neville.
15. Personal conversation, March 18, 2015.
16. Babylonian Talmud, Bava Kamma 92b.
17. ADD Health: The National Longitudinal Study of Adolescent to Adult Health; a joint project of the National Institute of Health and the University of North Carolina Population Center.

Accessed November 19, 2014: http://www.cpc.unc.edu/projects/addhealth.

18. Marguerite Lamb, "7 Secrets to Raising a Happy Child," *American Baby*, May 2008. Accessed November 19, 2014: http://www.parents.com/toddlers-preschoolers/development/fear/raising-happy-children/.

19. Thomas Merton, *Seven Storey Mountain* (New York: Harcourt Brace and Co., 1948), 83.

20. Arthur Green, "Eco Kabbalah Spirituality," in *Best Contemporary Jewish Writing*, ed. Michael Lerner (San Francisco: Jossey Bass, 2001), 123.

4. I Have So Much Control Over Someone's Life, But Ultimately I Have No Control: Rethinking Power and Powerlessness

1. Allison Gopnik, *The Philosophical Baby: What Children's Minds Tell Us About Truth, Love, and the Meaning of Life* (New York: Picador, 2010), 139.

2. William Makepiece Thackeray, *Vanity Fair*, vol. II, chapt. 2. The 1994 film *The Crow* quoted it, and is sometimes cited as its source.

3. Genesis 21:22–24, 26:26–30, Deuteronomy 29:9–12, and elsewhere.

4. Genesis 31:54, Psalms 50:5, and elsewhere.

5. And elsewhere in the Bible, such as in the covenant between God and humanity after the flood in Genesis 9:8–17, or with Abraham in Genesis 15:18.

6. Exodus 19:5

7. F. Brown, S. Driver, and C. Briggs, *The Brown-Driver-Briggs Hebrew-English Lexicon* (Peabody, MA: Hendrickson Publishers, 2001), 136.

8. Exodus 32.

9. Numbers 11:2–6

10. Numbers 14. A land flowing with milk and honey, that is.

11. Rebecca Goldstein, *Properties of Light* (New York: Mariner Books, 2001), 200.

12. Ibid.

13. Ibid.

14. Exodus 24:7.
15. Kathleen Norris, *The Quotidian Mysteries: Laundry, Liturgy, and "Women's Work"* (Mahwah, NJ: Paulist Press, 1998), 53.
16. Jeffrey Salkin, "How to Be a Truly Spiritual Jew," published by the Union of Reform Judaism. Accessed April 9, 2015: http://urj.org /worship/worshipwithjoy/letuslearn/s16howtobe/.
17. Rabbi Abraham ibn Ezra, commentary on Leviticus 26:44.
18. Yehonatan Gefen and others, "Laila Tov" from *HaKeves HaShisha-Asar* (Netanya, Israel: NMC United Entertainment, 1991). In English, *The Sixteenth Sheep*. It's potentially the best children's album ever made, but it's better if you understand the lyrics. Sorry.
19. Jeremy Kalmanofsky, "Parent at Prayer," *Tikkun* 8, no. 4 (July–August 2003).
20. Ibid.
21. Abraham Joshua Heschel, *The Prophets* (New York: Harper Perennial Modern Classics, 2001), 29.
22. Kalmanofsky, "Parent at Prayer."
23. Heschel, *The Prophets*, 276.
24. Job 38:4–7, 31, 33. The entirety of Job 38–39 is a smackdown in this vein.
25. Michael Sommer, "Loss of Fear," *Superman Sam* blog about Sam's illness, December 12, 2013. Accessed December 3, 2014: http://supermansamuel.blogspot.com/2013/12/loss-of-fear.html.
26. Ibid.
27. Kalmanofsky, "Parent at Prayer."
28. Rainer Maria Rilke, "Requiem for a Friend," in *The Selected Poetry of Rainer Maria Rilke*, ed. and trans. Stephen Mitchell (New York: Vintage International, 1982), 73.

5. Speaking on Your Heart: Prayer as Lullabye, Lullabye as Prayer

1. Lydia Maria Child, *The Mother's Book* (Boston, 1831), 5, found in Adrienne Rich, *Of Woman Born: Motherhood as Experience and Institution* (New York: W. W. Norton, 1986), 45–46.
2. I Samuel 1:10.
3. I Samuel 1:12–13.

4. Babylonian Talmud, Taanit 2a.

5. Abraham Joshua Heschel, "Prayer," in *Moral Grandeur and Spiritual Audacity: Essays*, ed. Susannah Heschel (New York: Farrar, Straus and Giroux, 1996), 341.

6. Genesis 1:27.

7. Mishnah Brachot 5:1.

8. Ibid.

9. Interview with Jane Kanarek, July 9, 2012.

10. Birkei Yosef (no. 1).

11. The Rema on the Shulchan Aruch, Orech Hyim, 98:1.

12. Mishna Brurua Orech Hyim 104:1, also found in Shaarei Tshuvah, Orech Hyim, 104:1–4.

13. Sefer Hasidim 432.

14. Personal correspondence with Rev. Micah Jackson, March 23, 2013.

15. Thank you to Dr. Aryeh Cohen for alerting me to this story, told by Rav Yehuda Amital.

16. Lawrence Hoffman, "Women's Prayers and Women Praying," from an unpublished address to the "Illuminating the Unwritten Scroll: Women's Spirituality and Jewish Tradition" conference, Los Angeles, November 1984.

17. Aliza Lavie, *A Jewish Woman's Prayer Book* (New York: Spiegel and Grau, 2008), 100.

18. Ibid., 146. Translation adapted by Ruttenberg, from Lavie's.

19. Hava Pinchas Cohen, "A Mother's Early Morning Prayer," in *A Jewish Women's Prayer Book,* ed. Aliza Lavie (New York: Random House, 2008), 12–15.

20. Numbers 6:24–26.

21. Thanks to the good Dr. Shabana Mir for fielding my query on this. Personal correspondence, March 26, 2015.

22. Unfortunately, I haven't been able to track down a source for this, and the person who told me about this tradition is no longer alive. So it might be true, or it might be the result of an elaborate game of White People Telephone. But it's a beautiful notion, so I'm including it as a theoretical or actual example of parental blessing.

23. Thanks to Rabbi Dorothy Richman for this story, many years ago. Needless to say, the Kotzker probably didn't mean this story the way that I do—his understanding of the obligatory nature of formal

prayer, at least for men, gives it a very different cast. But that doesn't mean there aren't other sparks of light to pull from it.

6. Exhaustion and Poop: Finding Meaning in the Body Stuff

1. Personal correspondence, May 10, 2015.
2. Personal conversation, May 13, 2015.
3. "How Motherhood Changes Us: Jenny." Accessed November 19, 2014: http://www.howmotherhoodchangesus.com/jenny/.
4. Mary Martin Wiens, "These are the lines of a story," published March 6, 2013, at http://www.stevewiens.com/2013/03/06/these -are-the-lines-of-a-story/. Accessed September 18, 2014.
5. Babylonian Talmud, Kiddushin 30b.
6. Thank you to the wonderful Hanne Blank for pointing me to this. Hanne Blank, "Real Women," HanneBlank.com, June 23, 2011. Accessed March 13, 2015: http://www.hanneblank.com/blog/2011/06 /23/real-women/.
7. Robert Martone, "Scientists Discover Children's Cells Living in Mothers' Brains," *Scientific American*, December 4, 2012. Accessed September 22, 2014: http://www.scientificamerican.com/article /scientists-discover-childrens-cells-living-in-mothers-brain/.
8. Walt Whitman, "I Sing the Body Electric." Accessed July 26, 2015. http://www.poets.org/poetsorg/poem/i-sing-body-electric. Yes, he was probably talking about sex in this verse, but I think it applies to nonsexual physical connection as well.
9. Saint Benedict, for example, said that "the ancient monks feared that this supplementary rest made the soul lose the spiritual vigor that the sacred vigils had inspired and furnished an occasion for illusions of the devil." Bernard Bachrach and Jerome Kroll, *The Mystic Mind: The Psychology of Medieval Mystics and Ascetics* (New York: Routledge, 2005), 92.
10. Joanna Cook, *Meditation in Modern Buddhism: Renunciation and Change in Thai Monastic Life* (New York: Cambridge University Press, 2014), 89–92.
11. Thanks to Dr. Jay Michaelson for this particular detail.
12. Morris M. Faierstein, "Tikkun Leil Shavuot," *Conservative Judaism* 61, no. 3 (Spring 2010): 76–79.

13. Thomas Merton, ed., "Fire Watch, July 4, 1952," in *A Thomas Merton Reader*, ed. Thomas P. McDonnell (New York: Bantam Doubleday Dell, 1996), 213.

14. Ibid.

15. Ibid., 214.

16. Ibid.

17. Brother Roger of Taizé, *The Rule of Taizé* (Brewster, MA: Paraclete Press, 2013), 22.

18. Merton, "Fire Watch, July 4, 1952," 221.

7. Pecking Under the Table: How the Magic of Child's Play Can Infuse Our Lives

1. Peter Gray, "Freedom to Learn," *Psychology Today*, September 6, 2014. Accessed January 21, 2015: http://www.psychologytoday.com/blog/freedom-learn/201409/playing-children-should-you-and-if-so-how.

2. Tuesday, January 13, 2015, if you must know.

3. Shannon Meyerkort, "I Hate Playing With My Children!" Scary Mommy. Accessed January 1, 2015: http://www.scarymommy.com/i-hate-playing-with-my-children/.

4. Sarah Vine, "Play With My Children? No Thanks, It's Far Too Boring," *Daily Mail*, August 14, 2014. Accessed January 13, 2015: http://www.dailymail.co.uk/femail/article-2725508/Play-children-No-thanks-far-boring-says-SARAH-VINE-expert-warns-parents-play-offspring-risk-stifling-development.html.

5. Mary McCoy, "Confession: I Hate Playing With My Kid," She Knows.com, September 8, 2014. Accessed Januaray 13, 2015:http://www.sheknows.com/parenting/articles/1046677/confession-i-hate-playing-with-my-kid.

6. Lucy Sweet, "Why Playing With Your Kid Can Be (Whisper It) A Little Bit Boring," Parent Dish. Accessed January 13, 2015: http://www.parentdish.co.uk/kids/why-playing-with-your-children-can-be-boring-parents/.

7. "Wait, I'm Supposed to Play With These Kids?" RenegadeMothering.com, Accessed January 13, 2015: http://www.renegademothering.com/2011/05/15/wait-i%E2%80%99m-supposed-to-play-with-my-kids/

8. Ibid.

9. Tim Brown, "Tales of Creativity and Play," TED Talk filmed May 2008. Accessed December 17, 2014: http://www.ted.com/talks/tim_brown_on_creativity_and_play?language=en#t-389255.

10. Ibid.

11. Antoine De Saint-Exupery, *The Little Prince,* trans. Katherine Woods (New York: Harcourt Brace Jovanovich, 1943), 7–8.

12. Arthur Green, *Tormented Master: The Life of Rabbi Nahman of Bratslav* (Tuscaloosa, AL: University of Alabama Press, 1979), 172–73.

13. Mihaly Csikszentmihalyi, *Flow: The Psychology of Optimal Experience* (New York: Harper Perennial, 1991), 3.

14. Ibid., 53.

15. When Mothers With Pacifist Tendencies Need to Let Go and Remember That Their Kids Will Probably Not Become Violent Warmongers Because of Cardboard Swords They Had When They Were Five.

16. Sara Ruddick, *Maternal Thinking: Toward a Politics of Peace* (Boston: Beacon Press, 1989), 90.

17. Csikszentmihalyi, *Flow: The Psychology of Optimal Experience*, 74.

18. "Stuart Brown: Play, Spirit, and Character," interview with Krista Tippett. *On Being*, June 19, 2014. Accessed December 28, 2014: http://www.onbeing.org/program/stuart-brown-play-spirit-and-character/transcript/6359.

19. In order to deal with the complexities of this interaction, the brain actually builds new circuits in the prefrontal cortex—actually grows as a result of play. It also, researchers have found, activates the brain's entire neocortex, and of 1,200 genes that one study measured, about a third of them were "significantly changed" by just a half-hour of play. For more on this, see Jon Hamilton, "Scientists Say Child's Play Helps Build a Better Brain," *NPR Morning Edition*, August 6, 2014. Accessed January 13, 2015: http://www.npr.org/blogs/ed/2014/08/06/336361277/scientists-say-childs-play-helps-build-a-better-brain.

20. Debra Leong and Elena Bodrova, "Why Children Need Play," *Scholastic Early Childhood Today,* accessed January 13, 2015: http://www.scholastic.com/teachers/article/why-children-need-play-0.

21. Gwen Dewar, "The Pressure to Play With Your Kids." From the blog of *BabyCenter.com*, posted February 22, 2011. This claim is based on

the research of the anthropologist David Lancy. Accessed January 13, 2015: http://blogs.babycenter.com/mom_stories/the-pressure-to-play-with-your-kids/.

22. "Stuart Brown: Play, Spirit and Character," interview with Krista Tippet. *On Being*, June 28, 2014. Accessed January 13, 2015: http://www.onbeing.org/program/stuart-brown-play-spirit-and-character/transcript/6359.

23. Leslie Jamison, "The Empathy Exams," in *The Empathy Exams: Essays* (Minneapolis, MN: Graywolf Press, 2014), 5–6.

24. Babylonian Talmud Shabbat 31a.

25. Mark 12:31, Romans 12:15, 1 Peter 3:8.

26. For example, Hadith 13, Surat Al-Ma'idah 5:32 (which interestingly parallels the Mishnah, Tractate Sanhedrin 4:5).

27. Dhammapada 129, 130, 133, as well as the practice of reading the *Tibetian Book of the Dead* to the dying, and "A Prince Gives His Life to a Tiger" in the Jataka Tales. Thanks to Mia Jacobs for these citations.

28. Exodus 22:21, 23:9, Leviticus 19:33–34, and so on.

29. Kirk Byron Jones, *Holy Play: The Joyful Adventure of Unleashing Your Divine Purpose* (San Francisco: Jossey-Bass, 2007), 166.

30. Nachman of Breslov, *The Empty Chair: Finding Hope and Joy—Timeless Wisdom from a Hasidic Master*, adapted by Moshe Mykoff (Woodstock, VT: Jewish Lights, 1994), 101.

31. Madeleine L'Engle, with Carole F. Chase, *Glimpses of Grace: Daily Thoughts and Reflections* (New York: HarperOne, 1997),147.

32. A. A. Milne, *The Complete Tales of Winnie-the-Pooh* (New York: Dutton Children's Books, 1994), 342–44.

8. It's Not About Me Anymore? Creating a New Kind of Selfhood

1. Anne Morrow Lindbergh, *Gift from the Sea* (New York: Random House, 1975), 23.

2. Esther Emery, "Why I Think You Should Sometimes Ignore Your Children," on Deeperstory.com. Accessed August 12, 2014: http://deeperstory.com/why-i-think-you-should-sometimes-ignore-your-children/.

3. Valerie Saiving, "The Human Situation: A Feminine View," *Woman-Spirit Rising—A Feminist Reader in Religion*, eds. Carol Christ and Judith Plaskow (New York: HarperCollins Books, 1992), 43.

4. Conversation with Chanie Blackman, Medford, Massachusetts, February 15, 2012.

5. Esther Emery, "Why I Think You Should Sometimes Ignore Your Children," on Deeperstory.com. Accessed August 12, 2014: http://deeperstory.com/why-i-think-you-should-sometimes-ignore-your-children/.

6. Thanks to j wallace skelton for this phrase.

7. Interview on "Motherhood Later . . . Than Sooner" website. Accessed September 11, 2014: http://www.motherhoodlater.com/features/CarolLeifer.html.

8. Bianca London, "First-time mothers don't fully enjoy motherhood until baby is six months old as they struggle to come to terms with life-changing event," *Daily Mail,* November 5, 2013. Accessed September 11, 2014: http://www.dailymail.co.uk/femail/article-2539854/First-time-mothers-dont-fully-enjoy-motherhood-baby-six-months-old-struggles-come-terms-life-changing-event.html.

9. Deni Kirkova, "First-time mothers are 'lost, lonely and bewildered' for a year after baby's birth—but don't despair! It gets DOES get better," *Daily Mail*, January 15, 2014. Accessed September 11, 2014: http://www.dailymail.co.uk/femail/article-2487702/First-time-mothers-lost-lonely-bewildered-year-babys-birth—dont-despair-It-gets-DOES-better.html.

10. Issachar Baer of Zlotshov, Mevasser Tzedek, 9a-b.

11. Carol Lee Flinders, *At the Root of This Longing: Reconciling a Spiritual Hunger and a Feminist Thirst* (San Francisco: HarperSanFrancisco, 1998), 68.

12. Ibid., 84–85.

13. Proverbs 31:27.

14. "The World's Toughest Job," produced by Cardstore.com. Accessed November 11, 2014: http://www.youtube.com/watch?v=HB3xM93rXbY.

15. The quote is attributed to Tenneva Jordan, and was accessed on September 22, 2014 at http://media-cache-ak0.pinimg.com/736x/12/57/a7/1257a716051bdfad09b0d7c87d612c8d.jpg.

16. Alexis Coe, "'Don't Ask, Don't Get': How to Fix the Gender Gap in Salary Negotiations," *The Atlantic*, January 10, 2013. Accessed November 11, 2014: http://www.theatlantic.com/sexes/archive/2013/01/dont-ask-dont-get-how-to-fix-the-gender-gap-in-salary-negotiations/267024/.

17. Flinders, *At the Root of This Longing*, 68.

18. Ibid., 296.

19. Sara Ruddick, *Maternal Thinking: Toward a Politics of Peace* (Boston: Beacon Press, 1989), 122.

20. Lindbergh, *Gift from the Sea*, 40.

21. Ibid., 41.

22. Mishnah Tractate Avot 1:14.

9. Seeing Everything with New Eyes: How Parenting Changes Our Vision for the World

1. "Interview with Crystal Black-Davis," *Mater Mea*. Accessed February 25, 2015: http://www.matermea.com/crystal/5e5qyv0limzszvogph00y17vqm5kzx.

2. For example, W. Bradford Wilcox. "Moms Who Cut Back at Work Are Happier," *The Atlantic*, December 18, 2013. Accessed February 20, 2015: http://www.theatlantic.com/business/archive/2013/12/moms-who-cut-back-at-work-are-happier/282460/.

3. Ingrid Wendt, "Noodles and Sauce," in *Mamaphonic: Balancing Motherhood and Other Creative Acts* (New York: Soft Skull Press, 2004), 10.

4. Personal correspondence, February 19, 2015.

5. Menahem Azariah of Fano, "On the Tehiru," from *Yonat Elem*. He's discussing a complex theological principle, but I maintain that the emotional truth I extrapolate from it is in there as well.

6. Naomi Shihab Nye, "The Art of Disappearing," from *Words Under the Words: Selected Poems* (Portland, OR: The Eighth Mountain Press, 1995).

7. Ibid.

8. "Interview with Wangechi Mutu," *Mater Mea*. Accessed February 25, 2015: http://www.matermea.com/wangechi/azudp5i9ykuphvp5mt7wo0x7qkunok.

9. Mary Oliver, "The Summer Day," in *New and Selected Poems* (Boston: Beacon Press, 1992).

10. Babylonian Talmud, Bechorot 14b.

11. Babylonian Talmud, Sukkah 53a.

12. From the introduction to the "How Motherhood Changes Us" website. Accessed January 30, 2015: http://www.howmotherhoodchangesus .com/about-project/.

13. Interview wtih Makeda Thomas, *Mater Mea*. Accessed February 18, 2015: http://www.matermea.com/makeda/lzaqbev3f8ptsakidrxigje7 7y2ya6.

14. "How Motherhood Changes Us": Carrington. Accessed January 30, 2015: http://www.howmotherhoodchangesus.com/carrington/.

15. Martin Luther King, "Letter from Birmingham City Jail," in *The World Treasury of Modern Religious Thought*, ed. Jaroslav Pelikan (Boston: Little, Brown, 1990), 607.

16. Deuteronomy 16:20.

17. Leviticus 19:18.

18. Leviticus 19:16.

19. Harry Rosen and David Rosen, *But Not Next Door* (New York: Astor-Honor, 1963).

20. "Negative feedback towards new development in N.S. community," by CTV Atlantic, *CTV Atlantic News*, March 11, 2013. Accessed February 19, 2015: http://atlantic.ctvnews.ca/negative-feedback -towards-new-development-in-n-s-community-1.1191335.

21. Daniel Hertz, "You've probably never heard of one of the worst Supreme Court decisions," *Washington Post*, July 24, 2014. Accessed April 9, 2015: http://www.washingtonpost.com/posteverything/wp /2014/07/24/youve-probably-never-heard-of-one-of-the-worst -supreme-court-decisions/?hc_location=ufi.

22. "A Not-So-Simple Majority," *This American Life*, September 12, 2014. Accessed April 9, 2015: http://m.thisamericanlife.org/radio -archives/episode/534/transcript.

23. Erich Fromm, *The Art of Loving* (New York: Harper Perennial Modern Classsics, 2006), 42.

24. Babylonian Talmud Baba Metzia 71a.

25. I Kings 17:7–24.

26. I Kings 17:15.

27. Thank you once again to the amazing Laura Jackson for both re-

minding me of this story and for this reading of it, which is really hers.

28. See, for example, Wendy Lower, *Hitler's Furies: German Women in the Nazi Killing Fields* (New York: Houghton Mifflin Harcourt, 2013).

29. See, for example, Thavolia Glymph, *Out of the House of Bondage: The Transformation of the Plantation Household* (Cambridge: Cambridge University Press, 2008).

30. Sara Ruddick, *Maternal Thinking: Toward a Politics of Peace* (Boston: Beacon Press, 1989), 177.

31. Paraphrased from ibid., 170.

32. Ibid., 220. One study indicated that including women in peacebuilding efforts increases the probability of ending violence by 24 percent because they "bring a more comprehensive peace plan to the negotiating table by addressing societal needs rather than solely focusing on what will make the warring parties happy." Of course, the study looked at "women," and not "mothers," but given the cultures and communities investigated and the age of the women involved, it's likely that most if not all of the women in these stories were mothers. See Laurel Stone, "Can women make the world more peaceful?" *The Guardian*, August 11, 2014. Accessed February 25, 2015: http://www.theguardian.com/global-development-professionals-network/2014/aug/11/women-conflict-peace-society?CMP=twt_gu.

33. Shannon Watts, "American Moms One Year After Newtown: No More Silence About Gun Violence," *Huffington Post*, December 9, 2013. Accessed February 25, 2015: http://www.huffingtonpost.com/shannon-watts/american-moms-one-year-af_b_4405280.html.

34. Joy-Ann Reid, "Trayvon Martin's parents still fighting 'Stand Your Ground' 2 years after son's death," *The Grio*, February 26, 2014. Accessed February 25, 2015: http://thegrio.com/2014/02/26/trayvon-martins-parents-still-fighting-stand-your-ground-2-years-after-sons-death/.

35. Lucia McBath, "'Stand Your Ground' Killed My Son," *USA Today*, February 20, 2014. Accessed February 25, 2015: http://www.usatoday.com/story/opinion/2014/02/20/stand-your-ground-michael-dunn-jordan-davis-column/5655819/.

36. From the MADD website, accessed February 25, 2015: http://www.madd.org/about-us/history/cari-lightner-and-laura-lamb-story.pdf.

37. For example, https://momsdemandaction.org/, accessed February 25, 2015.

38. Ruddick, *Maternal Thinking*, 231.

39. For more information, go to http://www.theparentscircle.com/, accessed February 19, 2015.

40. Valerie Saiving, "The Human Situation: A Feminine View," in *WomanSpirit Rising—A Feminist Reader in Religion*, eds. Carol Christ and Judith Plaskow (New York: HarperCollins, 1992), 43.

41. "Blood Relations—The Israeli Palestinian Blood Donation Project. Accessed February 20, 2015: https://www.youtube.com/watch?v=3GZxLcGSCow#t=133.

42. "Israelis, Palestinians Forge Relations in Blood Donations," *The Nobel Women's Initiative*, September 25, 2011. Accessed February 19, 2015: http://nobelwomensinitiative.org/2011/09/israelis-palestinians-forge-relations-in-blood-donations/.

43. Bettina Elias Siegel, "Why I Play the Mom Card," *New York Times*, May 12, 2014. Accessed May 5, 2015: http://parenting.blogs.nytimes.com/2014/05/12/why-i-play-the-mom-card/?_php=true&_type=blogs&emc=edit_tnt_20140519&nlid=42356437&tntemail0=y&_r=0.

44. Ibid.

45. Interview with Staceyann Chin, *Mater Mea*. Accessed Febuary 19, 2015: http://www.matermea.com/staceyann/232u0ntw9tg44ct3fhfn3f97disnyr.

46. Ji Hyang Padma, *Living the Season: Zen Practice for Transformative Times* (Wheaton, IL: Quest Books, 2013), 54. Thanks to Karissa Sellman for alerting me to this text.

47. Mishnah Avot 2:21.

10. What Gives Us Goose Bumps: Parenting as a Mystical Encounter

1. Daniel C. Matt, *God and the Big Bang: Discovering Harmony Between Science and Spirituality* (Woodstock, VT: Jewish Lights Publishing, 1996), 78.

2. Hayyim Vital, *Shaarei Kedusha*, Part 4, in *Ketavim Hadashim me-Rabbeinu Hayyim Vital* (Jerusalem: Ahavat Shalom, 1988), 5, 10–11.

From Daniel Matt, *The Essential Kabbalah: The Heart of Jewish Mysticism* (San Francisco: HarperSanFrancisco, 1996), 122.

3. Paul Tillich, "The God Above God," in *The World Treasury of Modern Religious Thought*, ed. Jaroslav Pelikan (New York: Little, Brown, 1990), 304.

4. Matt, *God and the Big Bang*, 39.

5. Dorothy Day, *The Long Lonliness* (San Francisco: HarperSanFrancisco, 1997), 131–58.

6. Nancy Fuchs-Kriemer, *Parenting as a Spiritual Journey: Deepening Ordinary and Extraordinary Events into Sacred Occasions* (Woodstock, VT: Jewish Lights Books, 1998), xix.

7. Rudolf Otto, *The Idea of the Holy*, trans. John W. Harvey (London: Oxford University Press, 1973), 8–11.

8. Interview with Rabbi Emma Kippley-Ogman, June 11, 2012.

9. Sifrei Bamidbar, Parshat Shelach, Piska 6, and elsewhere in rabbinic texts.

10. Maimonides, *Mishneh Torah, Hilchot Yesodei HaTorah*, chapt.1 and the first third of *Guide for the Perplexed*, ad nauseam.

11. From the Catechism of the Catholic Church, #239, approved by Pope John Paul II in 1992.

12. Exodus 2:1–2.

13. Genesis 1:4.

14. Ilana Pardes argues convincingly in *Countertraditions in the Hebrew Bible* (Cambridge, MA: Harvard University Press, 1993) that Eve, too, asserts herself as a co-creator, with God, or a creator of the caliber of God, when she gives birth to her first child. See Genesis 4:1— God is the *koneh* of heaven and earth, its creator, and Eve says, *kaniti*—I created a child with God, or like God.

15. Numbers 11:12.

16. Isaiah 66:6–11, Psalm 87:5, and so forth.

17. Midrash Song of Songs Rabbah 4.

18. P'sikta Zutarta Bamidbar Behalot'kha, Sifrei Zuta 11.

19. Exodus Rabbah 5:9.

20. Song of Songs Rabbah 8:2.

21. Deuteronomy Rabbah 7:12.

22. Some people also make the connection between and references to God as *El Shaddai* and the fact that in Hebrew "breast" is *shad*. But it's less

clear that that's the meaning; *El Shaddai* could be a reference to breasts, a translation of the phrase, "the deity that is enough" (*El Sh'Dai*, like the song, "Dayienu") or something else.

23. Babylonian Talmud, Kiddushin 31a.

24. Sharon Koren, "Mystical Rationales for the Laws of *Niddah*," in *Women and Water: Menstruation in Jewish Life and Law*, ed. Rahel R. Wasserfall (Waltham, MA: Brandeis University Press, 1999), 103.

25. "How Motherhood Changes Us." Accessed October 21, 2014: http://www.howmotherhoodchangesus.com/katherine/.

26. Rosh Hashana and Yom Kippur traditional liturgy.

27. Matt, *God and the Big Bang*, 39.

28. Douglas Heaven, "Emerging Consciousness Glimpsed in Babies," *New Scientist,* April 18, 2013. Referencing research published in *Science* DOI: 10.1126. Accessed October 21, 2014: http://www.new scientist.com/article/dn23401-emerging-consciousness-glimpsed-in -babies.html#.VEauTdR4qJo. See also Christof Koch, "When Does Consciousness Arise in Human Babies?" *Scientific American*, August 1, 2009. Accessed October 21, 2014: http://www.scientificamerican .com/article/when-does-consciousness-arise/.

29. Jalal al-Din Rumi, *The Essential Rumi*, trans. Coleman Barks (San Francisco: HarperSanFrancisco, 1995), 106.

30. Johan N. Lundström, Annegret Mathe, Benoist Schaal, et al., "Maternal status regulates cortical responses to the body odor of newborns," *Frontiers in Psychology*, September 5, 2013.

31. Kristina Jordan Cobarrubia, "Madre De Baile," in *Mamaphonic: Balancing Motherhood and Other Creative Acts*, eds. Bee Lavender and Maia Rossini (Brooklyn, NY: Soft Skull Press, 2004).

32. Matt, *God and the Big Bang*, 71.

Afterword

1. Mishnah Avot 5:22.